PAUL WELLER

SOUNDS
FROM
THE
STUDIO

IAN SNOWBALL

RED PLANET

Contents

Foreword

For as long as I've taken an interest in the sights, sounds and smells of rock'n'roll, the music of Paul Weller has been there. From pre-teen sightings of controlled aggression in monochrome, bouncing out of the TV in the front room singing about 'The Modern World', to the textured high art modernism of a 'White Sky' falling down on me, his music fills the senses of this fan, now in his Fifties.

And I am a fan, there's no two ways about it. I've always gone with, and at times obsessed over, what Paul's done from 1978 onwards – apart from a wobble around the later years of the Style Council when I was immersed in shit haircuts and guitars and more interested in Creation and Factory Records' output than Paul's (and Mick's) music. Between *The Cost of Loving* and the scrapped album *Modernism – A New Decade*, he crossed more genres in two years than most bands could muster in 20 (I now declare *Confessions of a Pop Group* as one of the greatest works in his canon). He was right, I was wrong.

Take away the parameters of the two bands he formed and subsequently stopped and Paul's body of work, from *In The City* to *Saturns Pattern*, shows a similar line all the way through – an unquenchable thirst for moving forward and a sense of "let's try it this way." The musicians may change; the producers may change; the studios may change; the style of songs and melody will of course change; the lyrics, from biting social observations to love lost and found, will change. But at the centre of each recording session will be a true belief that this is the greatest record he'll ever made – "hope you dig it and, if you don't, well it's your fucking loss".

The release of a Paul Weller album is one of life's true excitements for me. I still have fond memories of jibbing off work and queuing at HMV in Oxford Street to buy *Stanley Road* in the summer of 1995 or getting the 140 bus to Harrow to buy *Our Favourite Shop* on the day of release from Our Price in the summer of 1985. Then the mad rush home to play the vinyl or CD on the music system of the time at full whack and drive my poor old Mum and Dad, Nan and Grandad, girlfriend, flatmate – whoever – mad for the next few days.

And as the days became weeks, you got to know every lyric, every cymbal crash or jagged guitar. And it stays with you. Those moments in life where you're in a certain frame of mind, either having a shit day at work or after a ruck with the missus, the melody of 'Cold Moments' or a lyric from 'Mermaids' can suddenly picks you up and put you in a place where everything else becomes insignificant. Or the glorious opposite: being at a wedding or a club night when the DJ drops 'A Town Called Malice' and the dancefloor erupts into pure joy as dancers from seven through to 70 throw caution to the wind and we all pull moves with smiley faces.

A few years ago, I was working in the beautiful setting of the Oxfordshire countryside driving from pillar to post cleaning office water coolers, as was my job then. It was early September and the English weather was at its very best. Not too humid to be uncomfortable but certainly warm enough to have both windows down, arm out and feeling the breeze whilst hammering round leafy lanes in my white van.

I had a copy of Paul's first solo album and put the CD in the system. From the opening bars of 'Uh Huh, Oh Yeh' through to the last fade of 'Kosmos' (before it came back in ten minutes later), I felt that sense of being at one with the world – when the music runs through your soul and "graciously gives you that lift." I'm no hippy or space cadet by any stretch, but that moment lives with me. That's the beauty of a Weller album.

Every release takes me back to a different time and place. But above all else, the timeless music is a constant connection to how Paul Weller has influenced my life through his music and words. God bless him for that. Long Live PW!

Stuart Deabill, April 2017

Introduction

May 2015 welcomed the arrival of Paul Weller's latest album *Saturns Pattern*. Including The Jam, Style Council and his solo work, it meant that by 2016 he had recorded a staggering 23 studio albums over a period of forty years. An impressive output of musical graft, and graft is what Paul Weller does. At the time of finishing this book, Paul was in the final days of completing album 24, *A Kind Revolution*.

The same year that *Saturns Pattern* was released, the spirit of The Jam was as strong as ever. An exhibition about the band was held in London's Somerset House; there was a book collaboration between Nicky Weller (Paul's sister), Russell Reader, Gary Crowley and Den Davis called *Growing Up With The Jam*; an official documentary on The Jam directed by Bob Smeaton was premiered on Sky Arts, and The Jam's drummer, Rick Buckler, was the first member of the band to have his autobiography published.

In October, a six CD box set called *Fire And Skill was* released containing 20 live Jam concerts which included a Nashville gig in 1977, Rainbow in 1979, Bingley Hall, Birmingham from 1982 and one of the last Wembley Arena concerts in December 1982.

After nearly five years of planning and then months of hard work filling up ten rooms in Somerset House, Nicky Weller, Den Davis, Russell Reader and Gary Crowley opened the *About The Young Idea* exhibition. It ran for three months and was bursting with Jam related memorabilia that included clothes, posters, personal possessions and even a mock-up stage with Rick's 'great white' drum kit with guitars once owned by Paul and Bruce placed lovingly upon it. Punters could only dream of seeing all three members walk onto that stage, grab their instruments and play just one more time.

It didn't happen of course. Life's not like that. On Thursday, June 25, there was a private viewing at Somerset House. Invites were sent out to family members and friends as well as fans of The Jam.

The following night Paul performed at Hyde Park supporting The Who. Two nights later he was again playing on the same bill as The Who, only this time the audience was much bigger. On Sunday, June 28, Paul played on the Pyramid Stage at Glastonbury. Included in the set was 'That's Entertainment', 'Start' and 'Town Called Malice'. For Paul, it had certainly been a few nostalgic days and it was all about the band that had launched his career and had meant, and continued to mean, so much to so many people.

But any attempt at trying to elicit from Paul a slither of hope that the band might reform on some golden day in the future was met with his usual uncompromising reaction. "Don't ask me about bands reforming because I'm just not fuckin' interested!", he told one journalist who dared to mention it. He's made it clear time and again that no amount of money would get him back on stage again with Bruce and Rick under The Jam aegis.

Paul has always been a man with his sights firmly fixed on tomorrow and his fans shouldn't really expect anything else from him. His modernist way of thinking is something to be admired, not judged or criticised just because *we* want to hear songs that take us back to being kids again. Just as we have our desires, so does Paul. When he writes a new song, we still benefit, we still enjoy it, we still continue to buy it. It's a win win situation and long may it continue.

Making music is all that Paul ever wanted to do. A&R man Chris Parry, who was responsible for signing the band to Polydor, pointed out to the authors of the book *Thick As Thieves*, "Paul was in no doubt that he was going to be very famous in the UK," a sentiment also shared by Paul's younger sister Nicky. "I think Paul made his mind up quite early on that music was the thing that he wanted to do," she said. "When he was 14 he was already practising his autograph."

Where did all begin for Paul? The Beatles were amongst the bands that contributed to his first musical awareness and education. Growing up in the 1960s it would have been impossible not to have been touched by the Fabs and for Paul their influence proved to be life changing.

Paul was actually born John William Weller on 25th May 1958 but his parents changed his name to Paul within days. And the connection to the name of The Beatles bass player wouldn't go unnoticed on the young Weller.

Paul was barely a teenager when he decided he wanted to play the bass (he'd already had an acoustic guitar that had been gathering dust under his bed). He eventually acquired a Hofner, just like the one that McCartney played.

Soon Paul was learning Beatles songs from a Beatles songbook and playing along with his best friend, Steve Brookes on guitar. Once The Jam were formed they also played songs that The Beatles covered like 'Twist and Shout' and 'Roll Over Beethoven'. Paul later recorded his own versions of The Beatles' 'Sexy Sadie' and a fabulously soulful version of 'Don't Let Me Down', both songs included in Paul's *B Sides & Rarities* collection box set.

There was also the Smokin' Mojo Filters project that must have been a thrill for Paul. The Smokin' Mojo Filters were formed in 1995 to record a version of The Beatles' 'Come Together' for a War Child fundraising record called *The Help Album*. The group's line-up included Paul McCartney, Paul Weller, Steve White, Noel Gallagher and Steve Cradock.

The Beatles were probably the most significant band during Paul's formative years but there were other influences too. Once Paul discovered The Who, things started to change again. The Jam would go on to record Who songs like 'So Sad About Us' and 'Disguises' and Paul would adopt the Rickenbacker as his guitar of choice – just like The Who's songwriter and guitarist Pete Townshend had done.

Steve Brookes remembers how he and Paul used to swap records that they owned. Steve was into Free but Paul wasn't much of a fan (only later did he embrace them). Paul bought a copy of *Exile On Main Street* by The Rolling Stones but not thinking very much of it, he gave it to Brookes. But they sat around, like teenagers did back then, listening to Led Zeppelin, the Groundhogs, Elvis, Chuck Berry and of course

The Beatles. Brookes also recalls how Paul especially liked the *Smokin'* album by Humble Pie. For Paul it was one long voyage of discovery.

Humble Pie had Steve Marriott in the line-up and he had played in another band from the Sixties that Paul particularly admired, the Small Faces. During Paul's years in The Jam, he would find himself doing his own versions of Small Faces songs such as 'Get Yourself Together'. In an interview Paul said of the Small Faces, "They had everything; the look, the music and Marriott's voice. They were so unique, so fantastic." Over the years, he has performed other Small Faces songs like 'Tin Soldier' and 'Here Comes The Nice'.

Another major band from that wonderful stable of Sixties artists that caught Paul's imagination (possibly via his Mum Ann because she was a huge fan) were The Kinks. Such was the influence they had on Paul, The Jam released one of their songs, 'David Watts', as a single and it was a top 40 hit in August1978.

But it wouldn't just be all about the bands from the Sixties for Paul. Far from it. Growing up he discovered more forms of music that he would embrace – soul, jazz, funk, house, reggae, folk, basically anything that moved him. Without doubt, his own song writing across the past four decades has reflected these various styles of music, much to the pleasure and enjoyment of his family, friends and fans.

Music is obviously important to Paul, that cannot be denied. But so are books. *Absolute Beginners* by Colin MacInnes is one of his favourites. "A book of inspiration," he said of it. One astute publisher picked up on that and added it to the front cover of a new edition of the book three decades after its initial publication in 1959.

Absolute Beginners was set in London in 1958, the year that Paul was born. It's a story of kids frequenting coffee-bars and jazz dens and witnessing the birth of rock and roll. The story also references the racial tensions that were reaching a boiling point around that time.

The book's story certainly wasn't lost on Paul and neither was the title, as evidenced when The Jam released 'Absolute Beginners' in 1981. And in the film adaptation of *Absolute Beginners*, the Style

Council's 'Have You Ever Had It Blue' was included in the soundtrack. That association made the film cool and helped to introduce a new generation of young people, old Jam fans and new Style Council fans to the book. And let's be honest, Bowie's own 'Absolute Beginners' is pretty damn fine too.

When Paul appeared on BBC Radio 4's *Desert Island Discs* he mentioned the book. In the same programme he said 'Tin Soldier' by the Small Faces was one of his all-time faves. Incidentally, a settee was his object of luxury…

Another film that caught Paul's interest was *Bronco Bullfrog*. He and writer Paolo Hewitt were once spotted in the early Nineties waiting in the queue outside the National Film Theatre in London to attend a rare showing of the film. They were almost certainly already aware of the film that was set in 1970 and featured East End kids with their suedehead apparel and swagger.

It's no surprise that Paul's music has also found its way onto soundtracks. The aforementioned 'Have You Ever Had It Blue' was the first, but since then The Jam's 'Town Called Malice' has appeared in both *Billy Elliot* and *Football Factory*, the latter written by big Jam fan John King. Paul also penned a song called 'No Need To Be Alone' that was featured in *Outside Bet*, a film that starred Bob Hoskins, Jenny Agutter and Phil Davis. The film was based on a novel called *The Mumper* written by his friends Mark 'Bax' Baxter and Paolo Hewitt (although at that time Paul and Paolo's friendship had soured and they were not talking to each other).

In November 2015, it was announced that Paul had scored the music for a boxing film called *Jawbone* starring Ray Winstone and Jonny Harris (Harris also wrote the screenplay). Paul wrote the music after reading the script, he hadn't seen anything or been guided in any way. Again, this was Paul discovering what else he could turn his talents to.

Absolute Beginners is also about young people with a keen sense of style and an interest in fashion and having disposable readies to realise their ambitions. Fashion and style are of the utmost importance to Paul and his own sense of it has contributed to him being dubbed the 'Modfather'.

But there's fashion and there's Mod. And Mod has been a constant for Paul. An interviewer once asked him. "Does Mod still exist?" to which Paul replied, "Well it does in my house."

In the book, *Tribe: Made In Britain* (Snowball/McKenna), Irish Jack Lyons recounted the first time he met Paul. Paul was playing a gig in Cork and Steve Cradock introduced them to each other. A well-prepared Jack had taken along some items to show Paul, including a handwritten letter from 1969 addressed to him from Pete Townshend and his old Goldhawk Club membership card from 1965. Naturally, the items were of great interest to Paul. Before they parted company, Paul grabbed Jack's hand and said, "Jack, I've been reading about you since I was 16. You know they call me the Modfather... well, you're the fucking Godfather. Yeah man!"

Mod as a way of life has always been a serious matter for Paul. As the years have passed and the state of society, politics and the music industry have changed, many people have looked to Paul for guidance about what being a Mod is all about. Paul has responded by simply being himself and, in true modernist fashion, moved on to the next thing that grabbed his interest. There has always been something else to do, to learn, discover, listen to, wear.

Paul's Mum Ann said his interest in clothes started when he was very young. "I used to knit Paul and Nicky's clothes, jumpers and cardigans. When Paul was about eight he said to me, 'any chance I can have a real jumper... you know, like from a shop?'"

Regarding Mod fashion, Paul certainly hasn't allowed himself to get bogged down in only a few, predictable styles. Yes, he has always liked a nice pair of shoes, a button-down shirt, a coat and suit that all have echoes of the Sixties, but it's not a suit, shirt or pair of shoes that makes someone cool; it's the person wearing them. Take the Harrington. Many people wear them and look good, but when Paul Weller wears something as simple and classic as a Harrington he looks *really* good.

Also, when it comes to fashion, with Paul there is often an unexpected element of surprise. When Steve White was drumming in the Style Council in 1983, the football casuals were growing in popularity. Countless young men were splashing their hard-earned cash on Lyle and Scott or Pringle jumpers, Fila tracksuits, Adidas trainers or Lois jeans. Being a keen football fan and of a certain age, Steve was fully aware of the Casuals' interest in designer sportswear. He'd been recording in Solid Bond Studios, which was near Marble Arch, and one Thursday, which was his pay day, he walked to the nearby Pringle store and treated himself to a new jumper. Steve returned to the studio and showed Paul. Paul must have been impressed because later that day he disappeared for an hour and when he returned he was laden down with bags stuffed with Pringle jumpers!

The above examples of music, books, film and fashion all offer an insight into Paul Weller as a man and his desire to share the things that push him along his own life's pathways. Paul has been a source of inspiration for many years and continues to be. What's more, his music, lyrics and unique sense of style continues to attract the attention of a new generation and they become fans too. You only have to attend one of Paul's gigs to see the evidence, and the legacy.

What is for sure, the yellow bricks on Paul's incredible road are still being laid. Despite fast approaching 60, being happily married and watching his children grow up, he is still making incredible, relevant music.

Talking to *The Irish Times* in May 2015, Paul confidently pointed out, "Of course I'm going to write more songs and make an album, because that's what I do in life."

Sounds From The Studio is a book about Paul Weller's 23 studio albums across 40-years. It's a book about Paul Weller's 23 dreams. Weller, Weller, Weller!

An interview with Paul, August 2016

After having recorded 23 studio albums, what would you say is the one all important thing about studio work that you've learned?

Not to have too many pre-conceived ideas and just see what happens because sometimes they are the little magic moments you never expected. But what I've learnt over the years would be no use to me as a youth! I had very strict ideas on what I wanted it to sound like, sometimes for the better, sometimes not. Now I like to see what unfolds.

In my interviews for this book, several people told me that when they've worked with you in the studio they've always found you as being open-minded and willing to experiment. How important is this to you – that you approach studio work this way?

Again, that has changed over time because I'm just glad to let the musicians in question fly and see where they take it. Most of the time they do something wonderful that adds and can even transform a track. I might give them an idea or reference but that's all. I'm lucky I play with great musicians with wonderful artistic minds.

Something else that interviewees told me was that they have always found you to be encouraging and have belief in them when they maybe didn't share that belief in themselves. Even Mick Talbot told me that. Is this a conscious thing in you because you see or hear something in the bigger picture?

I guess so, despite my public image of being grizzly and miserable, I'm really a positive person, especially around music. Our old producer Vic Copper Smith-Heaven was always encouraging me in my writing and guitar playing. Musicians are insecure people. I think generally we need a bit of encouragement.

You've worked with a lot of musicians in the studio over the years. What is it that you look for in the people that you invite in to work with you?

They are people I like, as well as liking their playing and vibe. Graham Coxon will play something beautiful and melodic or maybe something more abstract. Andy Crofts will add beautiful harmonies. Guy Barker will play a stunning solo – one take – thanks. Steve White will change the beat around and fuck your head up. Steve Cradock could come and play anything from brilliant guitar to maybe a harp or piano or maybe great drums in a style only he'll think of. And I'm lucky that the list could go on!

I interviewed people like Brendan Lynch for the book. How important have the studio hands, producers and engineers been to your output and direction that an album takes?

Absolute and total – if you're lucky, you'll find a good team, producer and engineer, and a method will happen amongst you. However, that chemistry will only last for a period of time and the clever thing is to know when to all move on. But when it's in sync then great things can happen.

After so many years recording, what keeps you going? What's the drive, the buzz for you to want to keep on making music?

I fucking love making music. Really that's the bottom line. I still believe in music's healing and uniting properties but really, I think music defines me and has helped me through loads of bad times and helped me celebrate the good times. What else would I do? I've only ever wanted to do this.

And what about your internal processes?

Well, it runs through many thoughts and feelings really. Sometimes we'll demo a new tune and straightaway I'll feel it's got something going on. Other times we may go through many changes before we find it. Some songs I'll never find "it." But generally, I wanna be either excited by a tune or really moved by a tune's beauty or feel I captured what I wanted to say in the lyrics. If I don't feel any of those things then I start to question what I'm doing. My bar's set pretty high so I'm aware of trying to top the last album. That's difficult, but a challenge. I wanna make music that moves people or makes people move, whatever – I would hope some of it will touch people.

Acknowledgements

This book is dedicated to Barry Pearson.

A big thank you to Loz whom with wings of speed we fly spirited into our tomorrows. I would also like to thank Nicky Weller, Russell Reader and Den Davis for sharing with me the vision at the start, my good pal Stuart Deabill for continued support (without *Thick As Thieves* this book wouldn't have happened), my beautiful daughter Josie, Neil Cossar, Barry Cain, Mark Neeter and all at Red Planet, and Mark and Maxine Boxhall – COW album four is going to be fab!

And thanks to: Jan Stan Kybert; Aziz Ibrahim; Eliza Carthy; Ben Gordelier; Lewis Wharton; Brendan Lynch; Mark Boxhall; Hilary Robertson; Noel Gallagher; Steve Cradock; Peter Blake; Matt Deighton; Steve Sidelnyk; Bill Smith; Andy Crofts; John Hellier; Martin Gainsford; Steve Brookes; Rick Buckler; Bruce Foxton; Mick Talbot; Tracey Young; Chris Bostock; Tom Van Heel; and Ann Weller. This book would not have been brought to life if it hadn't have been for your stories and memories.

Thanks, of course, to Paul Weller, without whom this book would not have even been possible. And thank you snappers for offering your support and photos: Tony Briggs, Martin Gainsford, Derek D'Souza and Lawrence Watson.

The Solo Years

"I still look forward to going into Black Barn with Paul. It's like our Mecca. It's an amazing place. It's a place that's given Paul a freedom to do his music and in a way that he hasn't had before. And it's been like that since 22 Dreams. In Black Barn, Paul is free to be a writer, a musician, an arranger, a composer."

Steve Cradock

Saturns Pattern

"I'm where I should be"

One May morning in 2015, Paul showed up to do some filming for a documentary being made on The Jam. He arrived wearing a jacket with a pink Chelsea Football Club button badge on it, full of support for the project and more than happy to talk about the band that brought him to the attention of the masses many years earlier.

The venue where the filming was to be done was a rehearsal studio in Woking. On the same day, Paul and the film crew also spent some of the time visiting various locations that were of particular significance to him when he was growing up in the area and in the early days of The Jam.

The day before Paul's filming, Rick Buckler sat in the same room with the same team being filmed for his contribution to the same project. And, like Paul, he had visited places in Woking from his own childhood and early Jam days. Bob Smeaton had been specifically asked by Paul to direct the documentary. Paul was a fan of Bob's filmmaking and especially praised his magnificent work on The

Beatles *Anthology* film. Grammy Award winner and Jam fan, Bob had also made films on The Who, Jimi Hendrix and Bob Dylan. Paul knew The Jam documentary would be safe in Bob's hands.

The documentary, *The Jam: About The Young Idea*, was premiered on Monday August 24 at the Ham Yard Hotel in Ham Yard, London, the site where the legendary Scene Club once entertained pill popping Mods in the mid-Sixties.

The exclusive screening was attended by many of the people featured in the documentary including actor Martin Freeman, Acid Jazz founder Eddie Piller, music journalist Barry Cain, writer Mark 'Bax' Baxter, Japanese Jam fan Keiko Egawa and founder Jam member Steve Brookes. Out of the members of The Jam, only Bruce Foxton attended the event. *The Jam: About The Young Idea* was aired on Sky Arts on September 5 and met with mass approval from Jam fans.

2015 was turning out to be an exciting year, not just for Paul's more recently acquired fans but for fans of The Jam too. Den Davis, a Jam superfan and memorabilia collector, was the driving force behind the idea of a Jam exhibition, investing both time and money into making it happen. Along the way, Den teamed up with Nicky Weller, her partner Russell Reader and radio presenter and Jam champion Gary Crowley.

"The Jam exhibition came about after a conversation I'd had with Den Davis a couple of years earlier," says Nicky Weller. "I liked the idea and decided that it was worth giving it a go. But it was only after having a look at what we had as a family that I thought an exhibition could really work. My Mum, Paul and myself had found loads of stuff in garages, sheds and lofts that we'd forgotten about. I went through Paul's sheds and found some gems. We had all of our stuff which was much more personal to the family and Den had all of his collection and combining the two meant we had a mountain of Jam memorabilia. What finally ended up in the exhibition only just touched on what we had unearthed.

"Den and I then spent about nine months looking at various venues. We looked in Manchester first then via a connection that Russell had, we went to look at Somerset House. I honestly didn't think we'd have a hope in hell's chance of being allowed to have our exhibition there.

"Russell, Den and myself had to go into Somerset House and present our idea formally. It was quite scary doing a presentation because it wasn't something that any of us were familiar with. But whatever we did worked and the exhibition went ahead in June. Most exhibitions of this kind take anywhere between eighteen months and two years to put together, but we managed to put ours together in just six months."

The Jam exhibition would run for almost three months (Paul would visit several times). As a companion to the exhibition, a CD called *About The Young Idea* and a limited edition book, *Growing Up With The Jam*, were also produced. The book included the likes of Ray Davies, Clem Burke and Sharleen Spiteri talking about what The Jam meant to them.

In May, a second book credited to Paul was also published. *Into Tomorrow* was limited to just 2000 copies, each signed by Paul and Lawrence Watson. Watson had been photographing Paul for more than 25 years and had supplied the photography for another book also published by Genesis Publications in 2008 called *A Thousand Things*. The book was a keepsake, a veritable work of art printed on high quality paper that reflected the price.

On June 26, Paul was billed to play alongside The Who at Hyde Park with Johnny Marr and the Kaiser Chiefs as special guests. The Who were celebrating fifty years in the music business and having Paul Weller present to share in the celebrations was perfect – The Who had been such an important influence on Paul's own song writing throughout his career.

On Thursday, September 17, a few days before setting off on his autumn tour, that also took in America, Paul and designer John

Varvatos spent an evening discussing music and style in front of a small audience at Varvatos' store in Conduit Street, Mayfair. The 'intimate discussion' took the style-conscious musician and fashion designer on a journey that explored the links between style and music. Naturally, Paul had plenty to say and told a journalist from the London *Evening Standard*, "I wouldn't want to name names but for me a lot of them (musicians) look the same, like they've just come out of the woods and have been bear-trapping or hunting." And who can disagree with that?

Paul also gave vent to his thoughts on the current trend of men and beards which possibly made one or two members of the audience sink into their chairs!

The promotion for Paul's new album, *Saturns Pattern*, included a tour of the States and Europe. For the first time in his career, Paul used two drummers live. Both Steve Pilgrim and Ben Gordelier sat beside each other behind their respective drum kits.

The new songs were eagerly lapped up by the audiences. Paul's last gig of the year was held at the Eventide Apollo in Hammersmith on Saturday, December 5. That night, Nicky Weller told the audience The Jam logo wall from the Somerset House exhibition was being auctioned off for a Women's Cancer Detection charity and then introduced her brother and his band onto the stage with the very befitting, "Put your hands together for the best fucking band in the world!"

Paul and his band blew the roof off that night. He later said it was the best show he'd ever done.

At the time of touring to promote *Saturns Pattern*, Paul turned 57. For more than 40 years he's been giving his all on countless stages at venues around the world and he still continues to put everything into what he loves doing and has often voiced his gratitude for being able to do that. Talking to *The Irish Times* in May that year, Paul reminded people that, "Writing songs is what I'm alive for – that and looking after my wife and my family."

The reviews of Paul's live shows around the time of the release of *Saturns Pattern* were universal in their praise. "Weller indulges in nostalgia when he wants to, not because he has to," said Graham Thompson reviewing Paul's gig at the Playhouse in Edinburgh. That night, Paul included 'Town Called Malice', 'Into Tomorrow' and 'Above The Clouds' in the set.

Saturns Pattern was released on May 25 – Paul's birthday – on Parlophone Records. The *NME* wrote, "The Modfather shifts his sound again, moving into acid-spiked psychedelia." Paul Moody in *Classic Rock* said, "Long term fans will breathe a sigh of relief that The Modfather is finally back on familiar turf... Weller has spoken recently about his desire to restore some 'soul' to his music and *Saturns Pattern* signals a reconnection to both his own (and his audiences') core musical values."

Responding to a question about Mod culture in an interview on French television station Telerama, Paul said, "It's got a timeless look. It's also ever expanding. It's a way of looking at things and adapting to your environment."

The topic of Mod is never far from Paul's life and 40 years after *In The City*, people are still curious to hear what he has to say, a testament to his passion on the subject of one of Britain's enduring youth sub-cultures. In the same interview Paul was further able to relate the question of Mod to *Saturns Pattern* – "Those Modernist principles still stand for me. I'm now trying to make 21st Century music."

In another interview, talking about the production of the album Paul said, "I wanted the drums to be bigger sounding." He was clearly game for trying new things, as always, and enjoying the sense of freedom to experiment. Paul threw further light on the process that went into making the album by saying that he had to "dig away" while he searched for the sounds that he was looking for. He said he eventually "hit that seam" and the album was able to move forward.

In that same French interview, Paul was also quizzed about The

Jam. "What's left of The Jam? Well, all three members are still alive." He stood his ground with his belief that The Jam "stopped at the right time." After 35 years of being asked similar questions, Paul replied with all the courtesy and respect that would be expected from a man of his years and position. Paul is fully aware that fans, even after so many years, still want to hear what he has to say about the band that set him on his outstanding career. He *knows* what The Jam means to his fans.

Saturns Pattern was recorded at Black Barn Studios and produced by Paul and Jan 'Stan' Kybert. Paul had first met Jan when he'd been working as the house engineer at Noel Gallagher's studio in High Wycombe. "He's a great fellow – we get on," said Paul. Jan also acknowledged Paul's contribution to his own career saying that Paul encouraged him to, "Get off the desk and into the hot seat."

Saturns Pattern was Paul and Jan's latest collaboration. "I first met Paul when I was an engineer at Wheelers End Studios," says Jan. "I was working with Oasis at the time and one day Noel asked me what I was doing the following week because Paul Weller wanted to do some recording in the studio. I remember it was in the summer because when Paul walked into the studio he was topless with a Martin guitar sticking out of a black carrier bag and the first thing he said was, 'Alright mate, where's the toilet I need a piss.' Paul then laid down a few demos. One of the tracks was called 'One X One', the other 'Going Places' and the third was 'All Good Books'. There were others recorded but only those three made it onto *Illumination*.'

In *Saturns Pattern's* sleeve notes, Paul wrote a lengthy (possibly the most for any of his albums) list of thank yous and acknowledgements. All the musicians who played on the album and the production team naturally got a mention along with his PA Claire Moon, Kenny Wheeler and his son Bill for the ever steady tour management. Paul also gave a nod to his "Dear friends in Woking," his "Beautiful and smart and crazy wife Hannah," his "Lovely Mum Ann and sister Nicky and his brother-in-law Russell Reader." He also gave

"Thanks and blessings to my dear Dad, John Weller – gone but never forgotten." Paul also included this from Frederick Knobfler's *Alternative Prayers*, 1912 - "Thank you universe for being alive and showing me the way. I seek to improve myself along this great path." And to end his lengthy acknowledgements, Paul also thanked the Royal Surrey County Hospital, "For saving my sister" and mentioned the passing of his friend Dean Powell, who had died tragically in September 2013 and house music legend Frankie Knuckles who died in March 2014.

But Paul's list wasn't finished yet. 'This record is dedicated to our dear friend, inspiration, and wonderful man, Ian McLagan.' Ian died in December 2014 after suffering a stroke.

As with any of Paul's sleeve notes, they provide a glimpse into what's going on with him at any particular time and the ones on *Saturns Pattern* speak volumes.

The musicians that played on the album included Steve Cradock, Steve Pilgrim, Andy Crofts, Ben Gordelier, Syd Arthur, Steve Brookes, Tom Van Heel, Hannah Weller, Raven Bush and Josh McClorey.

According to *Classic Rock*'s Paul Moody, the track 'White Sky' is a "palette cleanser for what follows'. The song was a leftover from some demos that Paul had recorded back in 2013 with Garry Cobain and Brian Dougan of the Amorphous Androgynous, an outfit that evolved out of the Nineties' ambient music dance act, the Future Sound Of London.

Paul said the original demos were mostly forgotten until they came to the attention of Jan 'Stan' Kybert. Jan liked what he heard and saw the potential. He took 'White Sky' and "re-jigged it, refined and re-arranged it" and Paul liked the result.

"Right at the end of mixing *Sonik Kicks* in 2012, we were putting together a bunch of B-sides and there were some really good tunes in there," recalls Jan. "'The Piper' slipped out and another great, great song called 'Devotion'. Paul was looking for between six and eight tracks that hadn't appeared on the album. One of those songs was

'White Sky' but for whatever reason, although we dubbed on it, it just wasn't happening and ended up sitting around for the best part of three years. And then when we were doing 'Brand New Toy' and 'Landslide' for the *More Modern Classics* album, I grabbed the files from some previous sessions and took them back to my studio."

Paul had just started working on new songs that would make it onto *Saturns Pattern*. "I was working with that material plus what was on the file I'd taken home that had 'White Sky' on it," says Jan. "I then rearranged the song, added some beats, tightened it up a bit and took it back to Paul and that version pretty much ended up on the record, but only after Ben Gordelier had recorded his drums."

Ben Gordelier remembers how he started working with Paul. "The Moons recorded most of our first album at the barn in 2009/10 so I had met Paul quite a lot already. I also went down there with Crofty when they were recording *Sonik Kicks* and he asked me to play drums on the track 'The Attic'.

"I got involved with the live show in 2012 when Paul played five nights at the Roundhouse in London and needed someone to trigger live samples and sound effects. As I'm a drummer I could play all the percussion parts and any second drum parts. My main instrument is the drums and I really enjoy working in the recording studio, especially editing and equalisation, so drumming and creating samples/sound effects is the perfect job for me. Paul asked me to record drums and percussion on some demos he had recorded with Stan and Charles and I ended up playing on so many of his demos that I'm on every song on *Saturns Pattern* except the track 'Long Time'."

Jan: "The other thing that I heard when listening to the original demo was the distorted vocal part that Paul sings. Traditionally Paul doesn't do distorted vocals. He's not a blues man. But I thought it would really work over the original psychedelic backing track, which was a bit 'Tame Impala', which we all love."

Paul admitted that even for reasons unbeknown to himself, when he wrote the song, and he wrote it quickly, he was thinking about the legendary folk bluesman Robert Johnson. Paul said there are some references about Johnson in the lyrics, albeit in an oblique way.

'White Sky' is a good choice to ignite *Saturns Pattern* and it was released as a download single. The atmospheric sounds that rise up set the scene. It's easy to draw comparisons to the Sgt Pepper build up on 'A Day In The Life'. Paul's 'big sounding' drums work wonderfully with his rock guitar and distorted vocals. The song is weighty and solid and strong and his wife Hannah pitches in on the backing vocals. And yes, "We can all be these Kings for a day!"

"I was just making stuff up and seeing where it went to," says Paul about the song 'Saturns Pattern'. He'd also stumbled across a website of the same title and learned that there was some wind on the planet Saturn that creates an hexagonal shape. Paul liked that imagery enough to include it on the album's sleeve cover.

Considering the song's title further, Paul says he found some connection between it and T. Rex and was able to link 'Telegram Sam' to 'Saturns Pattern'. However, when asked what the song is about he says, "I haven't got a clue really." The track begins with Paul's piano part and then the vocals step in. His current drummer Steve Pilgrim helps with some backing vocals – "Get up in a mind to get up" – and it's a catchy lick. Andy Crofts is also around to deliver some Moog work. 'Saturns Pattern/Sun Goes' was released in both seven and twelve-inch formats.

Paul continued to make comparisons with other great and inspiring songs when he linked 'Going My Way' to The Beach Boys' *Pet Sounds*. He was referring to the process of recording rather than the sound of the song. The song was recorded in bits, "An interesting way of working," says Paul, with sections woven together in the studio under the observant eye of Kybert. It would have certainly been an altogether different process to how, say, *In The City* had been recorded 30 years earlier.

'Going My Way' also begins with Paul on piano. It's a beautiful part that soon steps aside to allow the rest of the band to join in and work through the various sections that Paul had spoken about. Listen carefully and you can hear Paul's finger snaps and hand claps too.

There's some fine drum work from Ben Gordelier. "The drums on 'Going My Way' were a group effort between Paul, Stan, Crofty and myself," says Ben. "Paul or Crofty came up with an idea for the beat in the choruses and they had recorded a rough version of it, so I worked on that and re-recorded it. We all agreed that the outro beat should be simple yet groovy, so I played a simple 4/4 with some very subtle extras and halved the hi-hat pattern. The outro was the easy part so once I had perfected the choruses we let the track run through and I recorded the outro. I seem to remember the outro being a lot longer than what you hear on the album."

Jan: "Another thing about Black Barn is that nothing ever stands still, especially with the new technology that's now getting used. An example of its use was on a track like 'Going My Way' which was done in sections. There's the piano and voice part which was tracked and which Paul wanted to do on his own, there's the bridges that happen after the choruses which help make the song sound really interesting and then there's the band on the two choruses.

"Then there's what we call a coda, which is the band playing the chorus but using a different melody and that takes the song out. So to get the final song there was a lot of cutting and splicing to make it all fit together. In the old days when we were using tape it just couldn't have happened, someone would have died with all the frustration. But working like that is a pleasurable process for me and 'Going My Way' is one of my favourite tracks on the album."

The Moons' Andy Croft was also present throughout much of the recording of *Saturns Pattern*. "I first met Paul back in 2006 when my band at the time, The On Offs, supported him," says Andy. "We swapped numbers and that was it really. In 2008 I got the call to see if I'd be interested in joining the band and here I am all these years later.

"*Saturns Pattern* was where Paul gave me more freedom, not that he doesn't normally, and asked me to arrange backing vocals. This time it was a Moons' rhythm section with Ben Gordelier on drums for most of the album so I felt at home. My main things were adding backing vocal harmonies but I did do other things such as playing bass on 'Going My Way'. That song just came together perfectly and felt right from the word go. Paul had written another classic and I was proud to be on it! I played keys and guitar on other tracks too, but I'd say vocals were my main feature on this. After the previous two albums, I think I may have proved myself enough for Paul to let me kinda run free. My general rule is play for the song however much or little that is. He could do it without us but he digs different ideas and different musicians as they bring a different angle."

A few days after *Saturns Pattern* was released, Paul performed 'Going My Way' on the BBC's *One Show*. Piano playing Paul and his band delivered a beautiful song to a nationwide audience. 'Going My Way/I Spy' was the second single from *Saturns Pattern* and released on July 24. It got to No 1 on the vinyl charts.

'Long Time' has obvious nods to the Velvet Underground and the Stooges, says Paul, referencing also the New York punk scene of the Seventies in the same breath. Paul had, of course, experienced the US Seventies' punk scene first hand. The Jam had played at the infamous CBGBs Club in 1978 and met members of the Ramones in the club's dressing room. Whether Paul had liked or appreciated the Velvets or Stooges' music back then is questionable, but there's no doubt that at some point those bands did make an impression on Paul and they influenced 'Long Time'.

Paul wrote the song in America and it's simply based around two chords. The version that made the album was recorded in one take. This meant it captured all the rawness and pureness. "It had the right feel, was kept loose," says Paul and it totally works as track four on the album.

Jan: "The concept of a demo with Paul is an interesting one now

– I'm not sure it really exists. They are early versions and perhaps should be called that. 'Long Time' was just a version that got mixed after a couple of overdubs. It has that feel of something that was done late at night, banged out, and was never going to capture that same feel again.'

Josh McClorey of The Strypes plays some slide-guitar and Black Barn's house engineer Charles Rees provides the bass part. Drums are supplied by Tom Van Heel, who is also a band member of The Moons.

"I got to know Paul because I basically went and knocked on his door asking if I could be the tea boy," says Tom. "I was looking for some work experience. On my first day in Black Barn I was doing stuff like pulling up cables and making tea and this went on for a week. Then Paul invited me to go with him to a Peter Blake art exhibition in Woking. After that, he invited me back to Black Barn and The Moons were in there and that's how I got to meet Andy and the boys and ended up joining them.

"All the time I kept friendly with Paul and would pop into the barn. On one of those occasions, Paul asked me what I was doing the next week because if I wanted to, I could help him out with some demos. So I stuck around and we ended up laying down 'Long Time'.

"On the day of recording it, none of us (Bill Wheeler on guitar and Charles Rees on bass) had heard the song; it was just a matter of getting behind the studio's house kit, the Union Jack Premier one, and going for it. There was no rehearsing, it was just bang and lay it down. And what we did in that single take became the version that ended up on the album. What got captured was really cool and really raw. It was sort of tight but loose. The song was also a tip of the hat for bands like the Stooges, although we didn't know that at the time. I don't even know if Paul had that in mind at the time either.

"When I started to play the drums on the track what I had in mind was a similar feel to Paul's track 'Green' from *Sonik Kicks*. I sort of wanted to capture that feel but what happened instead was something much rawer and not electronic sounding at all.

"During that week I also played on a few other demos. Paul had a Dictaphone and he would play us some of the ideas that he recorded on it. It was stuff that he'd probably just done at home on an acoustic. It was only 'Long Time' that ended up on *Saturns Pattern* though.

"It was fantastic working with Paul that week. It was just me, Paul and Charles. I loved watching Paul trying different instruments. It felt really creative. It was so exciting. The thing about Paul is he is really open-minded and encouraging and he allowed me to do my thing. I think it's a trust thing with Paul. He has also heard some of the stuff that my band Monroze have done and he likes it and has encouraged me with it. That's what Paul's like."

'Pick It Up' is based around a drum loop that Kybert had knocking around. Paul liked it and added a funky guitar lick on top. This is one of the few tracks on the album that Paul's old faithful Steve Cradock plays on. Syd Arthur also lends a hand and Hannah Weller reappears too.

The actual recording process utilised techniques supplied by Pro-tools, something that Paul discovered to be incredibly helpful and economical. What might have taken weeks to do in the past could now be done in minutes because of Pro-tools. It was an eye opener for Paul and certainly something he might find himself using again for future recordings.

Revealing the meaning embedded in the lyrics, Paul explains that it was a, "Simple message really – whatever's broken you can fix and put back together.

"Whatever shatters – pick it up, whatever happens – pick it up, whatever matters – pick it up."

Jan: "Pick It Up came from a demo Paul did called 'Let Me In'. It got used as a B-side in the end. I was with Paul on the night he was recording the demo of it. I walked into Black Barn and the song hit me and I instantly thought it was brilliant. Paul already had the song pretty much formed from top to bottom.

"I then took the demo back to my place and was working on it. I kept the piano bit, sped up the chorus and dropped a beat in, worked on the arrangement and then I took it back to Paul. But in the meantime Paul had bumped into Olly Murs and it had been agreed they'd do the 'Let Me In' track together. By the time I saw Paul and played him what I'd done with the demo, all he could say was that he liked what I'd done but had already given the track to Olly Murs. I was really disappointed. But what Paul did say was, 'Don't lose that beat.' And then when we were doing *Saturns Pattern* I took a small funky guitar part that Paul played and put it over the drum beat I'd held on to and after Ben Gordelier played the drum part that turned into 'Pick It Up'."

'Pick It Up' was issued as a single in December. The accompanying video featured actor and friend Martin Freeman.

Paul says he wrote *Saturns Pattern* whilst being in a happy positive place. 'I'm Where I Should Be' truly demonstrates this. Paul explains that the song is about him declaring he's happy with his place in the world. He says he has all that he needs and doesn't crave for anything more. "It's a nice feeling to have," he reflects.

For this song, Paul is joined by Andy Crofts, Ben Gordelier and Jan 'Stan' Kybert and they produce a song that can only be described as quality in every way. It's packed full of guitars, keyboards and vocals and the overall production is immense. "I really don't get anxious I leave it all to fate, our lives are all so random, it really don't make sense."

Ben: "Paul's song writing varies from one song to the next so it's hard to describe his typical writing process. The songs can start out as an idea he recorded on his own with just a guitar or piano and a vocal part, there may be a guitar/bass riff that gets worked on or Stan might take ideas home and turn them into demos. Some songs come from a spur of the moment jam at 2am and sometimes Paul has a whole song in his head and knows exactly what he wants. There's no set writing process and I think that's how Paul likes it, it keeps things fresh and exciting for him."

Jan: "Black Barn is wonderful and when I work there with Paul I feel like I have absolute flexibility. The pressure of time constraints just isn't there. There's a sort of attitude that nothing is ever done until it's done. I've gone back to a song like' I Am Where I Should Be', which had been mastered and signed off, but then I've changed eight bars of the outro because something about the bass drum had been bugging me for just four beats. But Paul was just, 'Yeah, just do it.' So having Black Barn offers great opportunities and there's always that option to experiment that one further stage. Paul is always very open to other people's ideas when working in the studio. As a producer it's a good thing, but I can be working on something for four days and I'm nearly at a point to get a mix down and, because there are always visitors coming in and out of Black Barn, someone hears something different and a suggestion is made and something new gets added so then I have to change everything. But these situations are rare. My priority is to make Paul happy, I'm always artist-led in my productions. If I'm happy then that's just a bonus."

Noel Gallagher on working with Paul in the studio: "Every time I work with Paul the process is different. But above all else it's always really interesting and enjoyable. And sometimes it doesn't even work. We've got a few songs that are just hanging in the air, for whatever reason they've never been finished off. But it's always a good laugh and it's easier now than it used to be, when he was drinking. Being in the studio then could be pretty fucking mental. You'd have Paul and Cradock speaking in catchphrases and you just wouldn't know what the fuck they were talking about. You'd have to be pissed yourself to get it.

"Paul has an open mind. He likes to throw a lot of stuff at the wall and seeing what sticks. In contrast, I never go into the studio without a song that is fully finished. I never go into the studio to just see what happens. But Paul is the opposite. Even though you think his songs are well structured and already written in the comfort of his home in front of the fire, they're not. Maybe in The Jam and Style Council days they were, but nowadays I think they're pretty much all written in the studio."

The great House artist, Frankie Knuckles, was on Paul's mind when he wrote the next track on the album, 'Phoenix'. Knuckles had been one of the original pioneers in House music and had delighted many an Eighties' raver with songs like 'Tears' and 'Your Love'. His "deep House style" didn't go unnoticed by Paul.

'Phoenix' is Paul utilising ambient sounds that reminded him of Knuckles' works. He also says there were hints of jazz, funk and disco contained in the track. It's another song that Paul admits was born out of "trial and error." Steve Cradock re-joins Paul on this track as does Hannah Weller. There's some moving Fender Rhodes work from Paul too that helps to whip up a pretty cool atmosphere.

For 'In The Car', Paul's oldest and trusted friend Steve Brookes joins in with some slide-guitar. "I was down Black Barn one day and it was quite straight forward really,' says Steve. "Paul just asked if I wanted to have a go on the track. It was all very informal and I knew that if I'd done something on the song and he didn't like it he just wouldn't use it.

"I actually recorded my slide guitar part in the control room. There was me, Paul and Stan (Kybert) in there. I'd been just sitting in there playing around on a Gibson SG, I think, that was lying around the studio and they said 'Play that again' and then we put some ideas together and recorded it. Paul and Stan recorded quite a bit of what I played but then chopped it up and used what they wanted for the track. There's also some finger style guitar that I played too, I was literally just plucking the chords, but it's very faint.'

The song is Paul's tongue-in-cheek attempt at some 'Surrey Blues'. The guitar intro lasts for over a minute before the other instruments and Paul's second use of distorted vocals join in. The song's title was taken from a 1963 Roy Lichtenstein painting.

'In The Car' is another track created by joining together a collection of creative and experimental sections that helped produce a song with different flavours running through it. "In the car I live my life" sounds like a familiar story to many of us.

Jan: "'In The Car' started off as just an acoustic guitar that had been included on the outro of a different demo song. When I started working on that particular demo I just snipped that guitar part out and started laying it up with some drums and different ideas and reprocessed the guitar part and it became something else. I then took it back to Paul and he said, 'Yeah, let's try a few things with it'. So we developed it further and it became 'In The Car'."

'These City Streets' is a love song. "All this love must add up to something bigger'," says Paul. It's also about Paul's current reflections on his long-standing love affair with London. Since the mid-Seventies Paul has been captivated by the magic of the city and almost 40 years on he's still under its spell. 'These City Streets' is possibly the most atmospheric song on *Saturns Pattern*. You're in the backseat of a car taking in the sights as it slides through the screaming streets…

Liam Magill from the Syd Arthur band contributes backing vocals on the track and Raven Bush (also of the Syd Arthur outfit) plays violin. Steve Brookes returns to play some more guitar and as does Steve Cradock.

Steve Brookes: "For 'These City Streets' Paul actually phoned me and asked me to play on it. Before that I'd played on a demo that included just Paul and Ben. During that demo we'd gotten a bit of a vibe going and Paul liked it and that's why he asked me back into the studio to record the song again. There was me, Paul and 'Chopper' Cradock all playing together at the same time and we got that vibe and feel that you can hear on the record.

"The thing with Paul is that he likes the people he's working with in the studio to put their own spin on what's being done. He doesn't really give direction. If he likes something you're doing he'll say, 'Do it again, do that again' and it sort of builds from there and you get a feel for what needs to be done. I also played on '(I'm A) Roadrunner', which was on the deluxe version of *Saturns Pattern*. That only came about because there was me, Paul, Ben, Andy Crofts and Bill Wheeler in the studio. Bill played some grungy guitar over the track and Paul liked it and wanted to jam it out, so we went through it a couple of times before recording it and putting it on the album.

"I think *Saturns Pattern* is great, a real achievement. It's always good fun playing with Paul. There's no pressure on either of us. To think it's been over 40 years since we were learning to play our guitars together in Paul's bedroom in Stanley Road while listening to Beatles records. And we idolised The Beatles – they were the biggest influence on us. And once we were ready, we played our very first public performance in the music room at Sheerwater School. We then progressed to the Woking Working Men's Club and little guest slots at places like the Albion pub in Woking."

'These City Streets' was accompanied by a video and band member Andy Crofts got the job to make it. "A while back I made a short silent film called *A Girl In Paris* which featured Tara Griffin as well," says Andy. "I showed it to Paul and he was really impressed and mentioned making a music video for him in the same style. The song is about the millions of lovers that have walked, embraced and kissed over the centuries and I thought that was a lovely concept.

"My idea for the video was to simply film a girl lost in a daydream making her way across the city streets of Paris to meet her lover. I didn't want anything complicated, just nice shots and a kinda *film noir* feel. Paul wanted Tara to be in it after seeing the original video so that was good as she looks great on film. It was Paul's idea to have me meet her on the bridge and embrace at the end of the video. It's a new wave video with a beautiful girl and a killer song."

On Boxing Day, Andy also revealed another film project he'd been working on, simply titled *ONE*. "It was something I'd thought about for a while but kinda chickened out of as it's such a big job. Since joining the band I always took a video camera with me and started making little videos in 2008 but in hindsight I guess I was just practicing.

"I just wanted to make something that I would want to see as a fan, something a little different with an artistic edge. I've always done photography, so filming felt pretty natural and maybe some of the more *film noir* or arty shots come from the photographic side of the brain.

"I didn't start until March 2015 but I just filmed everything I could and got others to put me in it now and again. It's haunting looking back at the Bataclan footage in Paris. We know that venue so well so I think it all felt a little close to home for us when we heard the tragic news on the TV. I didn't want the film to have a storyline as such, I wanted it to just fall together with Paul's interviews and music leading the way. It's a fly on the wall film at the end of the day not a Hollywood blockbuster, thank God!

"I'm certainly not a professional. I don't know any of the technical stuff. I teach myself as I go along. In fact, I'm glad I'm not because what I wanted to make wouldn't have worked if it was all smooth and professional. I leave in all the shaky cameras and other imperfections. I like all that stuff as it feels real. I'm so sick of rules about how you should make things properly. I probably broke every rule in the film bible but who cares. It was filmed with love and inspiration and I believe people feel that. Maybe I'll make another 'one' or two... we'll have to see."

"It's one of the best things I've done," Paul told the *NME* about his forthcoming album *Saturns Pattern* and the proof *was* in the pudding. It was a fantastic achievement.

TRACKLISTING

1. White Sky
2. Saturns Pattern
3. Going My Way
4. Long Time
5. Pick It Up
6. I'm Where I Should Be
7. Phoenix
8. In The Car
9. These City Streets

Sonik Kicks

"That Dangerous Age"

I n August 2011. Paul, released 'Starlite'. "Here's a brand new track called 'Starlite' in time for the summer," said Paul. "It's not from the forthcoming album, it's just for now. Its part Balearic beat, poetry and psychedelic music. I hope you like it." The single was limited to just 3000 copies.

Paul spent much of 2011 in the studio writing and recording new material for his next album. In November, he announced that the new album would be out in 2012 and would be called *Sonik Kicks*.

Sonik Kicks was released on March 19, 2012. In May, Paul flew out to the States and on the May 17 he played an intimate show at New York's CBGBs Club, or rather the site that had once been the home to the club. The event was linked to fashion designer John Varvatos who was running a campaign for a new Mod related line he'd designed. Miles Kane was also at CBGBs that night. The venue was nothing like how Paul remembered, telling *Rolling Stone* magazine, "It's a lot cleaner than I remember it."

To celebrate Paul McCartney's seventieth birthday on June 18, Paul recorded a version of The Beatles' 'Birthday' and released it as a download for one day only.

On December 19, Paul performed a benefit show at the Hammersmith Apollo in London on behalf of homeless charity Crisis. Olympic Gold medallist, Tour De France winner, guitarist and Paul Weller fan Bradley Wiggins joined Paul on stage to play 'That's Entertainment'. Earlier in the concert, Natt Weller had joined his Dad to play guitar on 'Come On/Lets Go'.

In March 2014, the *Mail Online* published an article headlined, 'The Modfather's Day Out'. In October 2012, whilst on holiday in Los Angeles, Paul was photographed along with his 16 year-old daughter Dylan and both of his two year-old twin sons, John Paul and Bowie.

Paul and Hannah objected to the publication of the unpixellated photographs and took the newspaper to the High Court in London seeking a sum of £45,000 damages and an injunction preventing the use of the photos. The Wellers won the case.

For Record Store Day 2013, Paul released 'Flame Out/The Olde Original'. The seven-inch vinyl came out on Virgin Records as a Solid Bond Production. However, controversy accompanied the single's release because many fans simply couldn't get a copy. It transpired that touts had bought loads of copies and were selling them on sites such as eBay and real fans couldn't get hold of a copy and missed out.

When the news reached Paul he posted on Paulweller.com. "This is a message to all the fans who couldn't get the new vinyl single on Record Store Day and/or paid a lot of money for a copy on Ebay. I agree with all of you who have sent messages expressing your anger and disappointment at the exploitation of those 'limited editions' by touts. Apart from making the record, the rest has very little to do with me, but I am disheartened by the whole thing and unfortunately, I won't be taking part in Record Store Day again. It's such a shame because as you know I am a big supporter of independent record stores, but the greedy touts making a fast buck off genuine fans is disgusting and goes against the whole philosophy of Record Store Day. There were copies of my single on ebay the day before Record Store Day and I've heard stories of people queuing outside their local record shop only to be told there were none left at opening time! It only takes a few to spoil a wonderful concept for everyone else. Shame on those touts. Don't support their trade and don't let them use Record Store Day to ruin the very thing it's designed to support. Onwards, PW."

However, the following year another of Paul's songs, 'Brand New Toy/Landslide' was released to support Record Store Day. Only 500 copies were pressed, which instantly made it a highly sought-after record. This time around precautions were taken so that the touts didn't get their grubby hands on the records.

On October 19, 2013 Paul returned to the Hammersmith Apollo. Actor with a Mod persuasion, Martin Freeman, was on hand to introduce Paul and his band onto the stage and, later in the set, Ronnie Wood joined Paul on stage to lend a hand with 'Be Happy Children'. It was completely unrehearsed and just a bit of fun but seeing Paul Weller and a Rolling Stone wasn't something that happened every week. The following year, on June 21, Paul played at Bedgebury Pinetum in Kent where he was joined on the open-air stage by Roger Daltrey and performed 'I Can't Explain', 'Substitute' and 'The Changingman'.

Taking the opportunity to explore new territories and express his creative nature in another way, Paul got involved with a fashion line called Real Stars Are Rare. "Clothes and music, music and clothes, for me they go hand in hand. They've helped shape who I am," says Paul.

Explaining the origin of the brand's name, Paul said at the time, "Real stars are rare... they only come out at night. Make of that what you will, but I like it and there's a lot of truth in it." The Real Stars Are Rare launch party was held in London on October 8 2014. But for Paul, all roads lead back to the studio making music. It was time to start working on his next album, *Sonik Kicks*.

Sonik Kicks was released on March 12, 2012, on Island Records. The album was recorded at Black Barn Studios and produced by Paul Weller and Simon Dine. It reached No 1 in the UK chart.

Musicians who contributed to the making of the album alongside Paul Weller included Steve Cradock, Andy Crofts, Steve Pilgrim, Andy Lewis, Simon Dine, Noel Gallagher, Ben Gordelier, Graham Coxon, Aziz Ibrahim, Jan 'Stan' Kybert, Charles Rees, Marco Nelson, Hannah Weller, Leah Weller, Mac Weller, Roger Nowell and David Nock.

Sonik Kicks' opening track 'Green' (Weller/Dine) shows Paul dabbling in a bit of Krautrock. The rumours had been true and, for some diehard fans, a little bit of a headfuck until they finally heard

Paul's new songs in the context of the new album. NEU in German means new and is also the band name of the German duo, and ex-Kraftwerk members, Klaus Dinger and Michael Rother. NEU, like Kraftwerk, inspired the likes of Bowie and Joy Division and, somewhere along the line, Paul too as can be detected in a few of the songs on *Sonik Kicks*, 'Green' being the first of them.

Andy Crofts, now a constant in Paul's band, was naturally drafted in to contribute to the album. "On the opening track, 'Green', you can quite clearly hear my backing vocals and I love that tune," says Andy. "I played guitar on a few and on 'Drifters' and 'Be Happy Children' I arranged strings. There may have been more bits but I never remember plus I don't think about what I do as it's all for the song at the end of the day. It's never just me, though there's a variety of people adding something to the melting pot.

"I loved recording the bonus tracks 'Devotion', 'Lay Down Your Weary Burden' and 'We Got A Lot'. That session was amazing and flowed perfectly. I played a lot on these tracks – backing vocals, bass, guitar, vibes, organ, all types of stuff and it just happened so naturally. Same again for the Record Store Day single, 'The Old Original' and 'Flame Out'. In fact, 'Devotion' is one of my favourite songs, shame it wasn't an album track."

"His most cosmic test so far," said Kitty Empire in *The Guardian* in her review of *Sonik Kicks* and the second track on the album, 'The Attic,' stands as an accurate testament to this. There's something about this song that echoes the genius of music producer Phil Spector; there's an urgency to it. It's as if it wants to get somewhere quick, a sort of 'time waits for no man' attitude. The song lasts barely two minutes.

Andy Crofts was credited for the string arrangement and 'The Attic' was released as a download only single.

Paul can be spiky at times and this side of his personality is reflected in 'Kling I Klang', possibly Paul's strangest titled song. It's brittle and packs a punch and the listener is challenged to keep up.

"'Sleep Of The Serene' is like a Sixties B movie curio," wrote Jude Rogers in her *BBC Music Review* of *Sonik Kicks*. The track is the product of the collaboration of Paul, Charles Rees and Aziz Ibrahim, so it goes without saying that it's full of interesting sounds, noises, strings (by Sean O'Hagan) and keyboards that blend and merge and wrap themselves around each other.

"I remember jamming through 'Sleep Of The Serene' with a peddle board that was about six feet long," says Aziz. "I just seem to move along it pressing buttons. But then that's how my guitar parts came about for that track. Again on *Sonik Kicks*, Paul was working with some quite psychedelic approaches that created some great ambiences."

Aziz appears again and shares the writing credit with Paul on 'By The Waters'. The acoustic guitar and strings again provided by Sean O'Hagan, reflect the tranquil mood of Paul's words, "Come now beside the water sit and rest." Now that the album is a third of its way through, 'By The Waters' serves its purpose and prepares the listener for track six – one of the highlights on *Sonik Kicks* and for many different reasons.

Aziz: "Up until *Sonik Kicks*, I'd got the credits for playing instruments on Paul's songs but 'By The Water' was the first song for which I got a writing credit. This was a song that I instigated by bringing a baritone guitar to Black Barn Studios. I had the guitar made for me and thought I'd show Paul because I wasn't sure if he'd seen one before. I was playing around with it in the control room and coming out with some quite strange and eclectic chords that I'd created. These made Paul's ears prick up and within minutes he handed me a piece of paper and asked me what I thought of some lyrics that he had literally just written down. It wasn't the last time he'd do something like that with me and it's because of things like these that I have a big respect for Paul as a songwriter. He's not just a songwriter, he's a great songwriter.

"Paul showed me the lyrics and wanted to know what I thought.

I read them and told him they read really well. He then told me to get into the recording room and we'd get the song down. Paul was really inspired by it and laid down some fantastic vocals. Personally, I love the way the song works with just Paul's voice and the baritone guitar taking up the depth and then there are those beautiful strings. 'By The Water' became a very organic and natural process and was a perfect track for the *Sonik Kicks* album."

'That Dangerous Age' is up next. The 'Shoo-oop, shoo-oop's' are instantly familiar and engaging and give another nod to that Spector-style swing. The inclusion of some tambourine and handclaps over the chorus also adds a pleasing dynamic.

But it's the song's lyrics that are the most intriguing element. Maybe it's Paul responding to his critics, maybe it's simply observing the experiences of people of a certain age around him. On the one hand, you have a man who, "when he wakes up in the morning, it takes him time to adjust" and "if he could only get it back, how high the world would start to stack" and "any chance he gets to fly he goes far, in his car." And then there's the woman – that dangerous age applies to both genders – "she wears her skirt so much higher, she has the air of a high flyer." We all know someone like him or her, perhaps have even been him or her. 'That Dangerous Age' was released as a single and reached 66 in the UK charts.

Harmonica, deep bass and a dub beat spin – *Sonik Kicks* heads off in an unexpected direction with 'Study In Blue'. Much of the song's vocal parts are shared between Paul and Hannah, her vocals really breathing life into Paul's lyrics, "Afternoon shade, peerless sunlight, in your eyes of blue" and "everything I've ever felt is deep inside of you."

The psychedelic dub reggae of 'Study In Blue' with all its experimentation really draws the listener in. It didn't go unnoticed by the BBC Music Reviewer Jude Rogers who described *Sonik Kicks* as, "An emotional, experimental ride."

On February 22, 2013, a limited edition release of 'Dragonfly/

Portal To The Past' was issued. The song featured two of the Nineties' most talented musicians from two of the Nineties' biggest bands, Blur and Oasis – Graham Coxon on Hammond organ and Noel Gallagher on bass. Paul's daughter, Jessie, gets a role to play too. She provided the lyrics that begin with, "She's like a dragonfly with no fire, diaphanous with no intent." The handwritten lyrics were included on the inner sleeve notes.

"When Your Garden's Overgrown" is Paul's tribute to the memory and brilliance of Syd Barrett. The *NME's* Barry Nicholson wrote, "The ageing legend proves he still has what it takes' and a song like 'When Your Garden's Overgrown' demonstrates just that – not that the faithful needed any more converting. It's a song with a great melody and tune and the listener can't help but to be drawn into the story."

'Around The Lake' is very Bowie-esque, which makes it all the more enjoyable. This Weller/Dine composition has a fantastic driving guitar and melodic keyboard. The video for the song shows a night time mountainous landscape with speedy flashes of light dotted about as the camera pans across the scenery and then dawn appears which offers a different perspective. And all the time the music pushes on. 'Around The Lake' was issued as a download single, Paul's first download only release.

Before 'Drifters' enters the stage, there's a 17-second collaboration between Paul and Steve Cradock entitled 'Twilight'.

'Drifters' has a Sixties psychedelic feel that strangely mirrors the official video (directed by Ben Jones) of Indian warriors in full dress brandishing spears and daggers. The warriors clash like the instrumentation of the song with its swirling strings and smashing drums. "Paul gave me a songwriting credit on 'Twilight' but this was really Paul just being generous," says Steve Cradock. "It was very kind of him. He didn't have to do that. I could have just turned up for the session as a guitar player and got paid for that."

Sonik Kicks was dedicated to the memory of Amy Winehouse and 'Paperchase' was partly inspired by the death of the tragic songstress.

Uncut's Michael Bonner drew comparisons with 'Paperchase' to Blur's 'Beetlebum'. The celeste, vibes and glockenspiel are supplied by Paul's two Andys, Croft and Lewis, while he takes care of all the other instruments. Throughout *Sonik Kicks* Paul makes use of Black Barn's Hammond, Moog, Mellotron, numerous percussion instruments and a Farfisa.

John Weller's presence is never too far away in Paul's life and 'Be Happy Children' is a tribute to Paul's father, friend and manager for so many years. It's fitting because 'Be Happy Children' includes Leah Weller contributing vocals and, at the very end, Paul's young son Mac speaks the words, "Be happy children."

Paul delivers heartfelt vocals with lines like, "Oh, my loved ones, look long into the night, your Daddy's gone, but only for a while" and Hannah fittingly adds vocals to the song with, "Sleep now, safe and tight, think with such joy of what tomorrow might bring, be happy children." *Sonik Kicks* was released just two weeks after Paul and Hannah's twin boys Bowie and John Paul were born, and both will no doubt join Paul on some record or on some stage further down the line.

TRACKLISTING

1.	Green	8.	Dragon Fly
2.	The Attic	9.	When Your Garden's Overgrown
3.	Kling I Klang	10.	Around The Lake
4.	Sleep Of The Serene	11.	Twilight
5.	By The Waters	12.	Drifters
6.	That Dangerous Age	13.	Paperchase
7.	Study In Blue	14.	Be Happy Children

Wake Up The Nation

"Whatever Next"

On stage at London's Earls Court on February 18, 2009, Paul received yet another Brit Award. This time it was for Best Male Solo Artist. The competition included Will Young, Ian Brown, James Morrison and The Streets. Adele presented the award and amidst much laughter, Paul mustered enough composure to say, "Sorry I can't be here tonight, but thank you very much for the award. Have a good night".

The next year the *NME* presented Paul with their Godlike Genius Award. At the Shockwaves *NME* Awards held at the O2 Academy in Brixton on February 24, Paul was presented with the gong by Bobby Gillespie and Mick Jones, and on top of what they had to say – "He's the real deal" (Bobby) and "To this man that we love," (Jones) a large screen showed Noel Gallagher, Sir Peter Blake and Carl Barat also praising Paul. Paul's reaction to receiving the award and hearing what had been said about him was, "What could I say – it's taken them 30 years. I'm embarrassed because people said so many nice things about me... but it's all true!"

During the event Paul also performed six songs, three of which were The Jam's 'Eton Rifles', 'Start' and 'Town Called Malice'. Both awards confirmed what Paul's lifelong fans already knew.

Over a sunny weekend at the beginning of July 2009, Paul appeared at the Hop Farm, Paddock Wood, Kent. He headlined the Sunday with the Editors and Doves providing support. Also appearing that weekend was an up and coming new act called Florence and the Machine. During Paul's set, he played a medley that spanned his career – 'Eton Rifles', 'Shout To The Top', 'Wildwood', 'Peacock Suit' and 'Push It Along' all featured. If that wasn't enough, Roger Daltrey joined Paul on stage to perform 'Magic Bus'.

Throughout the remainder of that summer and in between other performances, Paul decamped to Black Barn to record material for the next album. He then spent the last two months of 2009 touring the UK. That same year, Paul was asked to co-compile an album of rare soul music with legendary Northern Soul DJ and amazing dancer Keb Darge.

Lost And Found included a collection of soul and R&B rarities from such artists as The Tempos, Elsie Wheat and The Brothers Of Soul. Compiling the album was a fantastic opportunity for Paul to dive into his own record collection and, with over 30 years of collecting rare soul, he had plenty to choose from.

"When you hear a great record, the first thing you want to do is play it to your mates," says Paul. It's a sentiment that Paul has carried with him since the days he sat around in his bedroom at 8 Stanley Road sharing his latest discoveries with Steve Brookes, other Sheerwater School friends and then The Jam's Rick and Bruce.

On June 7, 2010, two of Paul's old Sheerwater School friends, Sam Molnar and Vic Falsetta, organised a fund raising concert for the Sam Beare Hospice. More than 1,200 crammed into the Woking Leisure Centre to watch Paul play a two hour set at what was called 'Wake Up Woking'. An unexpected and special treat, and certainly a major talking point, was when Bruce Foxton joined Paul to play 'The Butterfly Collector'. On the night, Steve Brookes and his band supported Paul and the event raised almost £60,000 for the hospice. Inspired by the response, Sam and Vic have been organising 'Wake Up Woking' fundraising events ever since.

The album *Wake Up The Nation* was released at a time when society was at one of its lowest ebbs. The 2010 General Election resulted in a coalition government and the threat of terrorist attacks dominated the media. The album came out on April 19, 2010, through Island Records. It was recorded at Black Barn Studios and produced by Paul Weller and Simon Dine. The musicians that appeared on the album included Hannah Andrews (soon to be Weller), Bev Bevan, Steve Cradock, Bruce Foxton, Steve Pilgrim, Andy Crofts, Andy Lewis,

Mark Boxall, Barry Cadogan, Clem Cattini, Rosie Danvers, Terry Edwards, Charles Rees, Laura Rees, Sally Jackson, Jamie Johnson, Roger Nowell, Karenza Peacock, Emma Owens, Kevin Shields (My Bloody Valentine) and the Woking Gay Community Choir.

According to *Pitchforks'* Joshua Klein, "'Moonshine' finds Weller in a ramshackle, rough-around-the-edges VU territory." But maybe this isn't a view shared by all. 'Moonshine' is rough and gruff, strong and tough. Paul's song writing partner throughout the album was Simon Dine. Dine had approached Paul and described the sound he wanted which was urban, tough and quite metallic sounding. *Wake Up The Nation* certainly achieved that.

Barry Cadogan from Little Barrie is back in Black Barn and the Weller camp with his six-string and Andy Crofts plays bass on 'Moonshine'. The drums are provided by Bev Bevan, who is best known as a member of The Move and ELO. Not such an unlikely choice considering Paul's comments about inviting Bevan to appear on the album. "Simon (Dine) and I are big psychedelic music fans, so it was a real buzz. I was back being a 10 year-old Move fan again."

Referring to the track 'Wake Up The Nation', Paul says, "It's a bit of a clarion call for our nation. It's saying we should rise up against the sea of mediocrity, and get some greatness back into this country." And Paul is certainly one individual who has never been guilty of settling for anything that is mediocre. His pursuit of excellence, quality and the extraordinary is what has helped to keep people interested in what he does. Discussing the point further, Paul says, "The media, TV, music, politics, they've all become bland." And many of us would agree.

Whilst Bev Bevan gets the drumming duties, Steve Cradock gets the percussion job and Essex born musician Terry Edwards, who has worked with the Blockheads and Department S, gets drafted in for the saxophone part.

'No Tears To Cry' was Paul's nod to the great Gothic Pop (copyright Lois Wilson) of acts like The Walker Brothers. Clem Cattini was asked to play drums on the song because Paul knew that he'd played on the original songs that 'No Tears To Cry' was inspired by and the song most definitely has that special Sixties vibe about it. Apparently, Cattini 'nailed' the recording of the song in just two takes, which shouldn't surprise anyone. Londoner Cattini cut his teeth drumming with The Tornados before becoming one of rock 'n' roll's most sought after session drummers. In his career, Cattini had worked with a who's who of greats including Dusty Springfield, Georgie Fame, Lou Reed, Jeff Beck and Joe Cocker.

The additional instrumentation on 'No Tears To Cry' is provided by the Wired Strings (Sally Jackson, Kerenza Peacock, Emma Owens and Rosie Danvers). The backing vocalists are Steve Cradock, Hannah (Andrews) and Laura Rees. 'No Tears To Cry/Wake Up The Nation (Live)' was released as a single and climbed to a respectable 26 in the charts.

And then from out of the blue the unimaginable occurs. One of Paul's former bass players features on track four, 'Fast Car/Slow Traffic'. Talking about Bruce Foxton's inclusion on the album (Bruce also played bass on 'She Speaks'), Paul told *Mojo* magazine, "There was no big plan, it was easy, a laugh.' It was the first time that Paul had worked with Bruce since they recorded *The Gift* back in 1982. Elaborating further on how their relationship had been resurrected, Paul said, "We'd both lost loved ones and without getting too spiritual, that was the spur for it." Paul was referring to the loss of his Dad and Bruce's wife Pat, whom he'd known since The Jam days.

In the sleeve notes, *Wake Up The Nation* was dedicated to absent friends John Weller, Pat Foxton and Robert Kirby. John Weller died aged 77 on Wednesday April 22, 2009. He'd been suffering from vascular dementia. John spent his last days in Runnymede Hospital, Chertsey. John will be remembered fondly for many reasons, a rough diamond with a big heart for Paul, his family, friends and fans and he gave us one of the greatest rock and roll introductions that any band could wish for, "Put your hands together for the best band in the fuckin' world." And John believed it too.

'Fast Car' b/w 'Slow Traffic/Fast Car/Slow Traffic (the Primal Scream remix)' was issued as a single. The song is full of abrupt stops and starts which mirror what it's like being a car on British roads in this century and massive Jam fan Steve Cradock got to play alongside another 'Woking wonder'.

What's true about *Wake Up The Nation* is that each song has a completely different vibe. It's an album with no stone left unturned. 'Andromeda' is another track from another world. "'Andromeda' not only sounds like Bowie, it features a lyric in which Paul Weller mans a spaceship and flies away," wrote *The Guardian's* Alexis Petridis. The listener may not be sure exactly what lyric was being referred to here, but there is a mention of planets growing darker and moods getting a lift because of gravity's pull.

Roger (Trotwood) Nowell gets the credit for the synth guitar. Nowell had worked with Paul before as one of the crew and he also worked as a backline technician for Oasis and Ocean Colour Scene. Charles Rees took the drummer's seat and Cradock played 12-string guitar, while Hannah is present on backing vocals.

It's a swirling piece of music that scoops the listener up as it breezes by and that's also the impression the next track, 'In Amsterdam', leaves. This could quite easily have been a moment when you blink and find yourself sitting in front of a grinning Paul Weller, Mick Talbot and Steve White, as the song uncoils like a Style Council snake.

"Down watery steps to the oceans roar, a team of wild horses, play to thunderous applause." The magnificent opening lines of the next song that Bruce Foxton appears on, 'She Speaks'. At times the song really does thunder forward like a team of wild horses. A second guitar comes courtesy of Kevin Shields. Shields, best known for being in My Bloody Valentine, has also worked with Primal Scream and Patti Smith.

'Find The Torch Burn The Plans/How Sweet It Is To Be Loved By You' was also taken from *Wake Up The Nation* and released as a single. For a second time, Charles Rees gets out his drum sticks and Cradock his guitar. Andy Crofts appears with a Stylophone!

"Sessions are always creative with Paul obviously taking the lead," says Andy Crofts. "We try different things and they do or don't work but Paul's free style of recording gives others a chance to speak up and try a little thing here or there. When we were doing 'Find The Torch' on *Wake Up The Nation* I just said could I just try this little bit on the Stylophone. I did it and he loved it and that's kind of the way he works. The biggest part of the song is always done by Paul first so the song has a backbone to build on."

The backing vocals are provided by the Woking Gay Community Choir on the track that pushes and shoves and elbows out of the way anything that stands in its path. "I played on 'Find The Torch, Burn The Plans', but I didn't get a mention for it on the record (I think they just forget about me when they wrote the sleeve notes)," says Steve Brookes." I played some slide guitar on it which they then played around with in the studio. Again, it had been a matter of me just being in the studio one day and Paul asked if I wanted to play a bit of slide guitar on a track he had."

'Aim High' is the funkiest track on *Wake Up The Nation* and one of its most fresh and exciting tunes. It's helped along by Steve Pilgrim's drumming and Andy Lewis' bassline. The addition of the Wired Strings also serve to add an unexpected, yet enhancing dynamic. Let's all aim high and save ourselves!

'Trees' was a song inspired by what Paul observed in the hospital where John Weller was staying before he passed away. "I was trying to imagine what those people's lives were like," he explains. These observations manifest themselves in lines like, "Well, once I was a lover with beautiful long brown hair," and, "Once I was a man, my cock as hard as wood."

The listener could almost expect Jools Holland to be present on this track. Instead, Paul is on piano and guitars, Mark Boxall guitar, Hannah backing vocals and Charles Rees and Steve Pilgrim drums.

The song has moments when it's really beefed up and driven. Paul is a master at slipping up or down a gear and keeping his band on their toes.

"'Trees' was a song Paul wrote around the time my uncle John was in hospital," says Mark Boxall. "When Paul visited, he would notice the other patients wandering around the ward in their varying states of being unwell. He saw people that at one time had been invincible and confident but were now being reduced to someone almost unrecognisable to their former selves. It was Paul's observations of this that he based 'Trees' around.

"It wasn't a song directly to do with John but at the time he was very unwell and Paul tapped into something that motivated him to write a song. I'd grown up knowing John as one of those invincible sort of men, he was always full of beans and confidence and when he walked into a room he would fill it with his presence. John was a great character.

"I was sitting in on one of the *Wake Up The Nation* sessions and 'Trees' was introduced. I hadn't heard the song before. Paul invited me to play guitar on the second movement; there are like four different movements in 'Trees'. There's some guitar that gets introduced. It's very Who power-chord-ish. I grabbed Paul's Gibson SG and started smashing around on that.

"When I added the guitar, the drums, bass and vocals had already been recorded. The guitar part that Paul wanted me to do had been left until the end. I think this had to do with the track being made up of the four different parts which then had to be joined up in the mix and mastering.

"It was a real honour to play on 'Trees' because of the sentimental reasons relating to John. It meant a lot to me being asked by Paul to play on the track. I think 'Trees' is a very underrated song. I mean, if you forget the tune for a minute and just read the lyrics it makes perfect sense and you can get where Paul is with it. There's a lot going on in the song which leads up to that beautiful piano part near the end. I wish Paul would play it more live. Maybe it's not a song for the die-hard Weller fans but 'Trees' is one of those songs that's all about Paul moving forward and you either go with him or not. Paul has and will never be one for resting on his laurels and 'Trees' is Paul pushing on. For me, it's the work of a genius."

'Grasp And Still Connect' is flavoured with its own unique brand of pub rock R&B, that Wilko Johnson would happily digest. Terry Edwards, Andy Crofts and Steve Pilgrim are all back in the fold.

Bells and chimes and an autoharp played by Charles Rees, who also provides the drum part, and the listener gets a dose of 'Whatever Next'. This instrumental dips into the dark vaults of Paul's past. Back in his Jam days he recorded a demo of an instrumental that has since been called 'The Sweeney' (not that Paul, Rick or Bruce knew it as that). Basically, it's a piece of music that would happily serve as a theme tune for some TV drama.

'7&3 Is The Strikers Name' evolves from 'Whatever Next'. It's a vibrant and quirky track and worked when it was issued as a single-sided record. Kevin Shields is back to play more guitar and so are Hannah and Laura Rees for backing vocals. The track presses on like a hungry army, relentless, chaotic, attacking – "Curse those fuckers in the castle, they're all bastards too'. '7&3 Is The Strikers Name' is a force to be reckoned with.

Steve Cradock's presence is strongly felt on 'Up The Dosage'. He plays the drums, bass and guitar. Hannah and Laura Rees are also on hand to give the song a lift with some additional backing vocals. Bowie-esque rock 'n' roll hovers over the song and the opening line, "There's 12 steps to Eddie Cochran," intrigues. But the Fifties reference doesn't fool the listener into thinking this isn't a song with a Seventies feel. The luxury of having time in a fully working studio with an adept team evidently contributes to this creation.

Wired Strings are back for 'Pieces Of A Dream' and Charles Rees is on guitar (he also shares the drumming with Cradock). Paul's very own, not-so-redundant Supremes are brought in to supply the backing vocals and Andy Crofts, Andy Lewis and Steve Pilgrim do a sterling job. The bass part on this track goes to Jamie Johnson who has worked alongside Robert Wyatt over the years.

The song contains some of Paul's most interesting lyrics:

"Like pieces of a dream, all shattered on a screen
Refracted into shapes, explore this new landscape
Like pieces of a dream, disturbingly serene
Comforting at once and yet, nothing you can connect,
Can't put my finger on it, can't put its figure on me
Can't fix my mind upon it, this feeling captured me."

And to finish the album there is the hectic and very punky 'Two Fat Ladies' on which Paul is clearly having a field day. He invited Barry Cadogan back to Black Barn to record the bass and some extra guitar.

And so ends Paul's tenth solo album. But on and on and on he goes...

TRACKLISTING

1. Moonshine
2. Wake Up The Nation
3. No Tears To Cry
4. Fast Car/Slow Traffic
5. Andromeda
6. In Amsterdam
7. She Speaks
8. Find The Torch, Burn The Plans
9. Aim High
10. Trees
11. Grasp And Still Connect
12. Whatever Next
13. 7&3 Is The Strikers Name
14. Up The Dosage
15. Pieces Of Dream
16. Two Fat Ladies

22 Dreams

"Why walk when you can run?"

On February 14, 2006, Paul took to the stage at Earls Court wearing a navy blue double-breasted pin-stripe suit and sporting a haircut that would get copied by countless Weller acolytes. He performed a short set that included: 'Come On/Let's Go', 'The Changing Man', 'From The Floorboards Up' and 'Town Called Malice'. Paul's band, consisting of Steve Cradock, Steve White and Damon Minchella, played a rip-roaring set in front of three enormous backdrops that showed Paul in the late Seventies, mid-Nineties and as he looked then.

That night he'd been handed a Brit Award for Outstanding Contribution to Music. It had been ten years since John Weller had accepted Paul's award for Best British Male on his son's behalf, passing on Paul's apology for not being at the event himself and adding that he felt like "The proudest Dad in the world today."

To see out 2006, on November 7 Paul released a limited edition single via V2 Records called 'Wild Blue Yonder/Small Personal Fortune/The Start Of Forever (acoustic version)'. This was to be Paul's only release of the year.

One new addition to Paul's circle of musicians was bassist and DJ Andy Lewis. They would collaborate on a song together called 'Are You Trying To Be Lonely?'. Talking in the book *From Ronnie's To Raver's* (Snowball/Deabill) about how he and Paul's relationship began, Andy said, "Paul liked my first solo album *Million Pound Project* that I did for Acid Jazz in 2005. At the time, I was working as a roadie for a band who was out on tour for him and I just got chatting to him about what I did. I then gave him some demos for another album I was doing and thought nothing of it.

"A few weeks later I got a phone call from him in the middle of the night saying he loved the stuff I was doing and said he had something he thought was really good and then he started singing it down the line. We made a date to meet up in the studio and that tune became 'Are You Trying To Be Lonely?' I already had the music for it so that was good. And so now whenever there is a Weller after show party, I end up doing some deejaying too."

'Are You Trying To Be Lonely?' was released in September 2007. In 2007, Paul also collaborated on another single, 'Why' with Gabrielle, the singer who had risen to the top of the charts in the Nineties with songs like 'Going Nowhere' and 'Rise'. Paul also played with Blur's Graham Coxon, releasing a single called 'This Old Town/Each New Morning/Black River'. The single was first issued by Regal Records only as a download on July 2, 2007, and then as a seven inch later that month. It got to No 39. 'This Old Town' had also been recorded by Ocean Colour Scene but it had differences and was called 'For Dancers Only'. Paul had performed on the Ocean Colour Scene song which was also on the band's album *On The Leyline*.

In 2008 a particularly significant event unfolded in Paul's personal life. Paul's relationship with Samantha Stock, his long-term partner of 13 years, ended. Paul met Sammi when he was recording at the Manor Studios in the Nineties. During their years together they had two children, Jesamine, who was born in 2000, and Stevie Mac, born in 2005.

Another of Paul's long term relationships also came to an end in 2008. After some thirty years as Paul's tour manager, Kenny Wheeler, who Paul affectionately referred to as, "A grizzly bear with a heart of gold," retired, but not before handing over tour manager responsibilities to his son Bill.

Any album that Paul produces will be full of variety with obvious nods to the Sixties and Seventies and less obvious evidence of the Fifties. The astute listener will detect evidence of soul, funk, jazz, folk and virtually every other genre of music. What's more, he's never been one to shy away from experimentation. Paul wanted to create an album that was intended to be listened to in one sitting, just like *Sgt. Pepper* or *Pet Sounds*. He achieved it with *22 Dreams*.

"Don't be scared of the new, don't get bogged down in one era, or the clichés of 'Oh it's not as good as...' or you'll miss out on what is NOW," wrote Paul in the sleeve notes to *More Modern Classics* in 2014. It's undeniably been his mantra for more than 25 years. *22 Dreams* in many ways was an opportunity, not just for Paul, but for his faithful fans too.

"It felt to me that Paul's *22 Dreams* album was a very bold move for him to do at that time," says Lewis Wharton. "He pretty much had a new band that he was working with. It felt fresh. I also recall people's reactions when they found themselves having to get used to Paul's new sound after having been used to what he'd been doing before. *22 Dreams* was an exciting album and that's where Paul was at that time."

The musicians on *22 Dreams* included Steve Cradock, Hannah (Andrews), Andy Lewis, John McCusker, Barry Cadogan, Billy Skinner, Lewis Wharton, Simon Dine, Charles Rees, Robert Wyatt, Steve White, Models OWN, Graham Coxon, Noel Gallagher, Gem Archer, Pete Howard, Aziz Ibrahim, Terry Kirkbridge, Arlia de Ruiter, Lorrie Lynn Trytten, Mieke Honinh and William Friede.

22 Dreams was recorded at Black Barn Studios and production credits were ascribed to Paul Weller, Simon Dine, Steve Cradock and Charles Rees. The album was released on June 2, 2008, on Island Records and it became Paul's third solo No 1.

'Light Nights' is the track that whisks us off into the first dream. Steve Cradock's 12-string guitar mingles with the cello played by Andy Lewis (who then became a band member and would tour and record with Paul for several years) and John McCusker's violin. Vocalist Hannah Andrews performs her supporting duties with all the sweetness that the song demands. *22 Dreams* was simply dedicated to "Everyone and everything I love" with a special message from Paul to Hannah Andrews, "I could not have made this without you."

The stringed instruments coil themselves around Paul's lyrics like vines on the trunk of a tall and proud English oak tree. The song entices, "Come out to play, come out to play, now that the light nights are here." The *22 Dreams* have really begun.

In '22 Dreams', on which Paul collaborated with Simon Dine, it has a freak beat edge to it which comes as no surprise because Little Barrie's guitarist and songwriter Barry Cadogan, bassist Lewis Wharton and drummer Billy Skinner had all been parachuted in to help record the song. Little Barrie, who had songs from their own two albums to promote, would go on to support Paul live on a number of occasions. Cadogan left shortly after to play with Primal Scream. "There's a lot of dreams – enough for everyone," Paul reminds us, before parting with a repetition of "Save my soul, save my soul."

"Me and the other members of Little Barrie got introduced to Paul via Simon Dine," Lewis recalls. "Simon was very supportive to Little Barrie, he'd come and see us and help us out whenever he could. When he was looking for some musicians to play on the '22 Dreams' track, he thought of Little Barrie and gave us a call. And that opportunity wasn't something we were going to say no to.

"Simon made a demo of the song and that was something put together very precisely. We only got to hear it on the day we got to Black Barn Studios. Black Barn is great, it's the kind of studio you'd like to have if you could have your own space. It has everything you'd need and it has quite a homely feel and a comfortable vibe.

"We then learnt the song quickly on the day. But something wasn't quite working out. I think Billy, who was our drummer at the time, was a bit nervous, well, we all were. I mean, we wanted this to be a good day.

"We worked on the track and as time went by it was getting there, it was okay, but it wasn't quite gelling and we were getting frustrated. But then Tony, one of our good friends and sometimes tour manager, suggested something to Paul, which resulted in Paul doing some singing in the vocal booth and that was when it started to gel and come together. From that point we all relaxed and started to really enjoy the experience.

"It turned into a really good day spent recording with Paul – someone who I really looked up to. It was everything I hoped it would be. We had turned up on that day not really knowing what the agenda was going to be. It wasn't like working in studios that we usually find ourselves in, where money and time is an issue. On that day, with Paul, we all went out for dinner, had a few drinks, went back to the studio and everything loosened up.

"And being around Paul was a special experience. He had so much exuberance about him and this is someone who has spent most of his adult life going in and out of recording studios. He still has such a feeling of excitement and enthusiasm about what he's doing and you just don't always see this in people who have been in music for that same length of time.

"I think Paul is someone whose judgement you have to trust. He has done some things which at the time seem mad, like splitting up The Jam and going off in a completely different musical direction. But it's always worked. He hasn't allowed himself to get beaten down by others or the industry and his feeling about making music is genuinely still very strong and passionate in him. I think people can misunderstand Paul sometimes. Yes, he can come across a bit brash sometimes and he will speak his mind which is not what people want to hear all the time, but it's not being disrespectful."

'All I Wanna Do (Is Be With You)/Push It Along' was released as a single and sneaked into the top 30. It's a song with a strong melody and a mid-Nineties period Paul Weller feel. Steve Cradock on guitar is the band member from that time. Andy Lewis performs bass and Black Barn's Charles Rees plays the drums.

"I'm not out to convince you," sings Paul and when it comes to song writing he doesn't need to. *22 Dreams* was Paul's ninth solo album and his twentieth studio album to date. It was already a massive achievement.

"Out of the blue one day, Paul phoned me and said he wasn't going to make music anymore," says Steve Cradock. "He basically told me that he'd had enough of it. It lasted for about two months and then he phoned again asking if I'd go and do some demos with him. These became the *22 Dreams* demos.

"I walked into Black Barn and Paul was playing his guitar along to a click track for 'Have You Made Up Your Mind?'. Paul played guitar, I played a sort of ska-sounding riff on it and he also played bass and I ended up playing the drums. I turned the snare drum off for it which gave it more of a Cuban type sound and I think Paul's bass is quite reggae sounding on it too. I had walked into Black Barn at about 11am and by three the following morning, the track was finished. By the time we left the studio Paul was smiling and he had the bug again."

"Have You Made Up Your Mind?/Echoes Round The Sun" was the first single from *22 Dreams* and reached 19 in the UK. Cradock features strongly on the song; he plays the drums, guitar and a celeste, an instrument that looks very much like an upright piano, but is in fact an idiophone. Cradock also helps out with additional vocals, which are very noticeable on the chorus, sitting easily behind Paul as he sings the song's title.

'Empty Ring' is the next song on the album and the second with a writing credit to Simon Dine. Simon also provides the orchestration and percussion. The drums have a big sound, as does the ride cymbal that is played constantly throughout and blends well with Paul's piano part. 'Empty Ring' is soulfully rich and well crafted, with a hint of a Seventies style arrangement.

'Invisible' is simply Paul with his piano and expressing in his vocals all the experience of his age (Paul turned 50 the year of *22 Dreams*). "Invisible is a sparse love song worthy of mid-period Elvis Costello," wrote *The Guardian's* Amy Raphael. The song conjures up an image of Paul sat behind a piano in a room with a window that looks out across the English countryside. It's both reflective and incredibly moving. Paul Weller at his finest.

'Song For Alice' is dedicated to the beautiful legacy of Alice Coltrane – jazz legend John Coltrane's second wife and brilliant musician in her own right – who had died the year before *22 Dreams* was released. 'Song For Alice' has jazz elements helped along by rambling percussion played by Simon Dine and a trumpet part delivered by Robert Wyatt. The walking bass line grabs your hand and leads you on the journey. Paul, Cradock and Dine all get a credit for this free-spirited song. Cradock and Wyatt also get a nod for contributing piano parts too.

Steve White played drums on 'Cold Moments' and it would be Steve's last recording venture with Paul to date. Paul's old faithful drummer drives the song forward, keeping it all pinned down while Cradock adds congas alongside his guitar. There's some Hammond organ too that Style Council fans wouldn't fail to notice and both the piano and guitar solos create a sense of smooth soul filling all available spaces. "Sha la la, sha la la la, where I'm heading I don't know," are lyrics that reflect yet another turning point in Paul's career and it's all captured in *22 Dreams* and his new line-up.

The 42 seconds of 'The Dark Pages Of September Lead' is an orchestral piece full of drama and further adding to Paul's attempt at trying to capture the mood of the changing seasons. What really comes through are the vocal parts provided by both Hannah and Paul. *The Guardian's* Amy Raphael said the vocals sounded like early Bowie. And then the song slips away leaving a space for 'Black River' to fill. With peacock voices adding to the quirkiness of the song and Graham Coxon providing further flavour on drums, 'Black River' carries the dreams along, ever closer to their destination.

'Why Walk When You Can Run?' has Paul delivering a message that many of us might benefit from heeding – "No turning back, no giving in". Paul also offers encouragement to someone closer to home, "Run like the wind, run like the wind my son" and "In the years to come I will still call him son."

'Push It Along' is one of the catchiest tracks on *22 Dreams*. The rhythm mirrors the lyrics, "Ride the train baby." Pete Howard, who had a stint drumming for The Clash, lays down the drums that enhance the 'go with it' feel. Cradock also plays some drums. Hannah Andrew spices things up with additional vocals and Dine rightly gets a credit for the "Oo-ahhs."

Next up is a punchy instrumental called 'A Dream Reprise' that again features the three members of Little Barrie. It's an extension of the frantic freakbeat of '22 Dreams', only with more horns.

Lewis Wharton: "At the time we were just playing on and it got recorded. Little Barrie are prone to doing this in the studio anyway. Sometimes, when we're not necessarily going for a take or trying to get something recorded properly, we'll just play. It's often an instinctive reaction, we look at each other and just feel something it happening. Whilst this was happening in Black Barn, Paul and Simon liked what they heard and it got recorded, Paul then added to it at a later stage and it made it onto the *22 Dreams* album.

"Paul has taken Little Barrie out on tour with him quite a few times over the years. The Hyde Park concert was an early one. There was also the Royal Albert Hall and a particularly memorable one at Brixton Academy. I really enjoyed that gig. I remember there had been some problems with the guest list and things got very hectic before the show and whilst trying to sort all this out, the call came that we had to go on. We ran out on stage hyped-up with angry energy and it turned out to be a really fun gig.

"Paul has been a really good support for us. When we've been out on tour with him he's always taken the trouble to look after us and make the effort to remember everyone's names. He does things which really aren't his role and I've always found him to be a man of his word. And he remembers everything. Also, when you do something that sparks an interest in him he really takes an interest and it's above and beyond what an average person does."

'A Dream Reprise' serves as an appropriate bridge into 'Echoes Round The Sun'. Noel Gallagher gets a writing credit on the track and also plays Wurlitzer, bass, piano and Mellotron. It's a song with a wild edge and unique craziness, which is further fuelled by the guitars of Gem Archer and Steve Cradock and Terry Kirkbride's drumming. Kirkbride was the former drummer with Proud Mary and he also worked with Noel Gallagher.

"'Echoes Round The Sun' was a song that slowly evolved," says Noel Gallagher. "Paul and I were talking about doing a song together for ages but for whatever reason it never came off. We'd never get stuck on anything. And then he started to make an album, which at the time wasn't called *22 Dreams*; he was just making another record. There was no talk of it being a double album, nothing.

"I'd been messing around with a drum loop for ages, but I couldn't think of anything to write around it although I loved it. That drum loop came from a song which at that point had never been released. It later came out as my solo 'Stop The Clocks' and was a demo from that. So Paul asked again if I fancied writing something together and I said, 'Yeah, and I've got this drum loop, why don't I send it to you?'

"So I did and he had it for a good couple of months. He came back saying he'd work on it and then book us a day in the studio and we'll knock it out. A couple more months passed and the date's looming. I get down to the studio and as I walk in the drum loop's playing, so I'm thinking great. I then ask him what he's done with it and he says, 'Nothing'. I say, 'Whaddya mean nothing?' and he replies, 'Well fucking nothing.'

"Now I was expecting him to have at least a couple of chords and we could make a start on it. But nothing! Now for some reason Gem (Archer) and Steve (Cradock) were there. So Paul's says, 'What shall we do then?' and I'm like, 'Well fucking hell, I came up with the drum loop. It's your move next.'

"Anyway, I then suggest putting a bass on it and the next thing Paul's handing me the bass guitar. I messed around on it and someone said, 'That's good, do that.' So I got the bass down and we looped it and let that go round for ages. Now all the while this was going on I didn't realise that Paul was sat on a couch behind me. He was wearing a hat at the time, a fedora like Malcolm Allison wore in the Seventies. Paul was writing words down but I didn't know that at the time. So he's writing down words, and me, Gem and Steve are fucking about with chords. Then Paul got on the piano and put some chords on it and then he started singing, which added a kind of a vibe.

"Paul then took that demo away and played around with it, but it still really didn't go anywhere. Then a couple more months passed before we went back down to the studio to finish it off, by which time Paul had written the rest of the song.

"The real genius of that song was that we did a demo of it, which was insane. I'd love to hear it now; it had stylophone on it. That demo was fucking mad. It was Steve's suggestion to play the drums and he came up with this double time type thing and that was when the song really took off. I think it's Steve's part that really makes the song. It goes from being a song that's a bit trippy and weird to being a rock song."

Steve Brookes played Spanish guitar on 'One Bright Star'. It had been many years since Paul had played with one of his oldest and closest friends. Committing to tape must have been a thrilling experience for Steve, especially as that element of his musical relationship with Paul had mostly eluded him way back in the days when the two friends were still wearing their white satin bomber jackets, kipper ties and loon pants. Simon Dine adds some mandolin and Hannah additional vocals on this track that captures all the drama, passion and tension of the Latino rhythm that spurs the song forwards.

'Lullaby Fur Kinder' is a short instrumental with Paul demonstrating his prowess on the piano. Old *Studio 150* friends William Friede, Mieke Honinh, Lorre Lynne Trytten and Arlia De Ruiter also put in appearances. Incidentally, Fur Kinder is German for children.

Paul's piano takes the lead role again in 'Where' Ye Go', and is backed by John McCusker's violin. "Where ye go, that we'll never know, but as long as you come back, that's all that really matters," sings Paul with all the heart and soul of an accomplished songwriter who can turn his hand to folk music at the tip of the straw hat. Paul continues with lyrics that could well be a reflection of himself, "But that's who you are and we have to expect," before concluding with, "You lose track of time, it's alright, it's really alright, because we couldn't bear to be without you."

Aziz Ibrahim provides the spoken word over the track which Paul simply called 'God'. Hannah flavours the tune with her haunting vocals and Cradock is ever present with his acoustic guitar.

"Paul's *22 Dreams* album was the first time that I'd done vocals," Aziz reveals. 'Like on 'By The Water' Paul produced some lyrics and showed them to me and they were for the track called 'God'. I'm a Muslim, which Paul knows, and we'd have various discussions on faith. I think Paul is happy to involve me in songs that have a spiritual content. He showed me the lyrics for 'God' and asked me what I thought about them. I read the lyrics as a story and I liked them. I had no objection to them as a Muslim and I had empathy towards the subject matter.

"I think Paul then recorded a version using Steve Cradock as the vocalist but when Paul spoke to me he said, 'I think God is a Manc'. I don't know exactly why Steve's spoken word didn't work but whatever, it was Paul who felt my accent would work better. So I ended up doing the spoken word part. I went into the studio and that part was done in one take. When it was played back Paul said, 'Yeah, God is a Manc.'"

Noel Gallagher: "Paul asked me to narrate the 'God' track but I told him no because I'm not in any way into 'God'. But he kept asking and giving me loads of reasons why I should do it. But in the end I turned to him and said, 'Here's a fucking idea, why don't you do it?' but he refused. If he'd said to me 'I think Gods a Manc,' I would have done it!"

'111' is another Weller, Dine and Cradock composition. Dine plays the Moog and Cradock the Mellotron. It's a short instrumental piece and another bridge over gaps in the dreams' journey. The dreamer stirs gently, eyes open, just a little, but it's not time yet, the dreamer's body is already wrapped up in sheets, he turns and the sheets tighten, the sandman has his grip, won't let go, neither the dream nor the night is over yet. Sleep on. Dream on!

Steve Cradock: "I was around Black Barn quite a lot when Paul was doing *22 Dreams*. I think it was the first album where Paul recorded everything at Black Barn. The Barn became his playground again. It was like Paul had his own Manor Studios. He had his manor and there were no rules and because of this, it was a really creative time. There was one session with only Simon Dine, Paul and me. One minute Paul would be asking someone to play the Moog and the next the Mellotron. I remember asking him what key the tune was in and he was like, 'I'm not telling you,' so I just played around with it, then we all went into the mixing booth and we all had a reverb pot and pan pot and just fiddled with them. It was like playing Space Invaders. I remember John Weller dropped by the studio and we played it to him and all he could say was, 'That's fucking rubbish.' It was a brilliant moment. In the end that song became '111'."

'Sea Spray/22 Dreams' was also taken from *22 Dreams* and got to No 59 in the UK Singles' chart. It's a foot tapper and the first song that Hannah got a credit for. She's also credited for supplying the hornpipes. Cradock is having a field day in Black Barn as he contributes drums, percussion, guitars, mandolin and bazooka to this uplifting cracker of a song.

The final dream is 'Night Lights'. It's an extension of 'Sea Spray', which explains why Hannah also gets a songwriting credit on this track, along with Cradock and Charles Rees, suggesting it's another one of those songs created within the wooden walls of Black Barn. The song contains guitars, piano, celeste, Moog, harmonium, but it's God who has the final word with the sounds of thunder and rain...

TRACKLISTING

1. Light Nights
2. 22 Dreams
3. All I Wanna Do (Is Be With You)
4. Have You Made Up Your Mind?
5. Empty Ring
6. Invisible
7. Song For Alice
8. Cold Moments
9. The Dark Pages Of September Lead to the New Leaves Of Spring
10. Black River
11. Why Walk When You Can Run
12. Push It Along
13. A Dream Reprise
14. Echoes Round the Sun
15. One Bright Star
16. Lullaby Fur Kinder
17. Where'er Ye Go
18. God
19. 111
20. Sea Spray
21. Night Lights

As Is Now

"To the start of forever"

On February 11, 2005, Paul appeared at a Tsunami benefit concert held in Cargo, London. Paul had been booked to play a few days earlier but the gig had to be rescheduled owing to a slight illness. On the night of the show, Keb Darge was on hand to spin some Northern Soul tunes from his vast record collection. In 2011 Paul would find himself performing at another tsunami fundraiser, this time on behalf of a recent Japanese disaster. The concert was held at Brixton O2 Academy on April 3 and also featured Beady Eye, Graham Coxon, Primal Scream, The Coral and Richard Ashcroft.

Also in February Paul played the Royal Court, Liverpool, and two dates at the Apollo, Manchester. On July 16 he performed at Guilfest, Stoke Park, Guildford. The remainder of the year was spent playing concerts in the UK, Holland, Germany and Italy.

It was on the journey home from Europe that Paul told Steve White he wanted to write a record that sounded like one continual piece. This idea evolved into *As Is Now*. Once it was set in motion, Paul described the process in the *As Is Now* DVD filmed by Lawrence Watson. He said that the songs, "Kinda came to me. I felt like a conduit for the tunes."

As Is Now was produced by Paul Weller and Jan 'Stan' Kybert and was recorded at Wheeler End Studios in Buckinghamshire and mixed at Studio 150 in Amsterdam. It was Kybert's idea to record the band as soon as possible after they had been touring together. He knew this would help capture a unique feel. All the songs on *As Is Now* were written by Paul Weller.

As Is Now was released on October 11, 2005, and released by V2 Music. Musicians on the album included Steve White, Steve Cradock and Damon Minchella. The album reached No 4 in the charts.

In the sleeve notes Paul, as per usual, took the time to say some thank yous. He referred to the Studio 150 and Amsterdam 'family' (the horns on the album were provided by Dutch musicians) and photographer Lawrence Watson. Paul endearingly wrote "Lol Watson – a truly great photographer."

Paul dedicated *As Is Now* to Jim Capaldi, calling him one of the greatest drummers ever. During a musical career that spanned several of the golden decades, Capaldi was most famous for being a member of legendary band Traffic but he also played regularly with the likes of Eric Clapton and George Harrison.

"Equality rather than ego in a band has always been important to me," says Aziz Ibrahim. "Paul has always shown me that. The press hasn't. For example, if they write about one of Paul's albums they only select certain musicians to pick up on, Noel Gallagher or Graham Coxon for example, and other musicians that contributed don't get a mention. But Paul has always done his utmost to do the right thing. For someone with that status and that calibre he is still very down to earth and he will step out of his way for people.

"I did a show with Paul in Camden, a tribute concert for the Traffic drummer Jim Capaldi. Paul invited me to play guitar with him on a couple of Traffic songs. Some of the organisers didn't treat me well, like dirt actually, and when we went on stage they only introduced Paul. But as soon as Paul got to the microphone he took the trouble to introduce me and that gesture has always stuck with me. It's a respect that not everyone has, certainly not in the music industry, but Paul does.

"My friendship with Paul has always been a series of events. I was on holiday in LA and while I was on Santa Monica beach I bumped into Steve Cradock. He told me that he was on tour with Paul and he and the band were in a hotel not too far away. So I went to say hello and then Paul asks me if I want to do the support for his show in LA. I didn't have a band but put one together over a few days and played the support. He also invited me to play a song with him during his set."

On August 31 1981, young Jam fan and amateur photographer Derek D'Souza was invited to shoot Paul, Rick and Bruce in Chiswick Park. Some of the photos that Derek shot were used on the 'Absolute Beginners' sleeve cover.

Derek's handiwork with a camera had initially come to the attention of Paul after Derek sent him some photographs he'd taken at Jam gigs – he used to sneak his camera into the shows – and Paul liked what he saw. Before he knew it, Derek was being collected from Woking train station by Ann Weller in her Fiat X1/9 and taken to the Weller's home to discuss an invitation to shoot The Jam. It was the start of a long and fruitful relationship.

Derek set up his own website – blinkandyoumissit.com, and 'Blink And You'll Miss It' is the opening track on As Is Now. A tight overdriven guitar riff kicks the album into gear. Steve White's drums work closely with Damon Minchella's superb bass playing to give the song a funky edge. These two brilliant musicians demonstrate their talents constantly throughout the album. Their bond is special and they went on to play together in the bands Trio Valore and The Family Silver.

As the chord rings out from track one, track two slips in effortlessly. 'Paper Smile' has that 'Lazy Sunday' beat to it – a stomper rather than a stormer (they come later). "What's in a life if you don't live it?" asks Paul as he navigates his way into the new album which, in Paul's opinion, was good as anything he had ever done.

'Come On/Let's Go' begins with an acoustic guitar which sounds like it could turn into 'That's Entertainment' but instead develops into a good rock song – "Sing you little fuckers, sing it like you got no choice." This track has so many of Paul's influences contained within. Not surprisingly 'Come On/Let's Go/Golden Leaves' was issued as a single and reached No 15.

'Here's The Good News' b/w 'Along/Super Lekker Stoned' was the third single taken from the album. It's piano led and wouldn't sound out of place on a Faces record. The trombone solo, played by Louk Boudesteijn, adds an interesting dimension just after the verse "Ah millions march back on their feet, still no sign from those who preach." There's also a trumpet part played by Jan Van Dulkeren and that combines with the whole West Coast jazzy feel of the late Seventies. This in turn makes way for Paul's last words, "Can I get a little peace for me?" And now we're deep into the album.

Enter 'The Start Of Forever' and a beautiful acoustic guitar. For a moment it suggests an 'English Rose' for the Noughties. The lyrics are instantly engaging, "Hold tight angel, morning will soon be here, washing your pillow in swathes of gold and red." Big cymbals and strings are added to create further atmosphere before the song launches into an unexpected funked-up soul jazz jam.

The next track, 'Pan', fades in slowly and it's evident the band have permission to stretch their legs. "He is not the god of creation, but he is the lord of the morning light," sings Paul over his piano part. The piano is augmented by a cello played by Rosie Walters. In just two minutes, Paul has made his point and changed the course of the album.

"As Is Now was made over the space of two weeks in March, April and May, the spring months recorded in a beautiful wooden barn, all played live as you hear it now," says Paul. It was a joy to make, so many good memories and fun'. 'Pan' is a testament to Paul's words.

'All On A Misty Morning' is introduced by Paul playing an acoustic guitar beside a violin, viola and cello. The song conjures up images of lush green English fields at the crack of dawn – "All on a misty morning, I come to you with love…"

"I thought 'From The Floorboards Up' was amazing," Paul proudly admitted a year after As Is Now's release. He wrote the song after a gig in Glasgow and the next day Paul, Steve White, Damon Minchella and Steve Cradock rehearsed and recorded a demo of it. A few nights later the song was included in the set. "It's a song about playing live to an audience where, on a good night, the power seems to come up from the ground through the stage, through the band and out into the audience where the energy hangs in the air," says Paul. "You can't see it but boy, can you feel it."

Talking to Paul De Noyer in Amsterdam at the time, Paul enthused about Chuck Berry, Little Richard and Bo Diddley coming to perform in the UK. He said he felt rock 'n' roll was back and that trail of thought led to 'From The Floorboards Up' being a "rockin' song."

'From The Floorboards Up/Oranges And Rosewater' was also released as a single and became a favourite live. The image of Paul raising his arm high into the air after the words, "It sings in the air and dances like candle light," will be familiar with anyone that caught Paul performing around the time of the album's release.

The piano and bass on 'I Wanna Make It Alright' slows the tempo of the album down again. Throughout the song, Paul is in a reassuring mood. "I wanna make it alright, I don't want you feeling blue and I wanna put things right." Lyrics like these carry a depth of meaning that resonates with so many of his fans. If anything can be said about Paul's lyrics, it's that he helps us articulate our own feelings that sometimes we struggle to find the words to express. 'I Wanna Make It Alright' is all about expression.

A warming mood has been set by the time 'Savages' takes centre stage. The song has an introduction that Noel Gallagher could have had a hand in (he's not on this album) and it's one of the outstanding tracks on As Is Now. The piano allows the song to breathe freely as do the lyrics, "You have no love, it has all gone cold on you." Paul was inspired to write 'Savages' after the Beslan School Siege of 2004 when 385 people, 186 of which were children, were killed by Islamic militants,

As the song 'Fly Little Bird' progresses, it turns into a Beatle-esque psychedelic indulgence complete with swirls and backwards guitar. This all merges into one with the vocals, "Fly, fly little bird, when you fly… you give the world to be, when you start to breathe, you give the world to dream, when you start to live." 'Fly Little

Bird' is strong, emotional and powerful and demands the listener to surrender to its charm.

'Roll Along Summer' really showcases Steve White's drumming. The rest of the band can only follow him on this number. Lyrics like, "Roll along summer, breathing life into the world, creating space that wasn't there before," and the sax solo, fashion a Style Council feel with images of long hot summer days in the Eighties and white jeans, pastel coloured jumpers and day trips to Paris.

'Bring Back The Funk' is another opportunity for Paul's band to stretch their legs. It has echoes of the freshness Paul captured during his Paul Weller Movement period and Steve White's 'Philly hi-hat', as Paul liked to call it, really drives the track along. At seven minutes, it's one of Paul's longest songs.

And then it's time for the wonderfully sounding 'The Pebble And The Boy', and what a great track to wind down *As Is Now*. The song could have been plucked right out of the 'Confessions' album sessions with its strings and piano.

Paul's lyrical delivery is breathtakingly beautiful, "Can you tell the difference between a pebble and a boy... Can you see the future with each step you take?"

After hearing a song like this, it's easy to see why Paul rated his new album so highly.

TRACKLISTING

1. Blink And You'll Miss It
2. Paper Smile
3. Come On/Let's Go
4. Here's The Good News
5. The Start Of Forever
6. Pan
7. All On A Misty Morning
8. From The Floor Boards Up
9. I Wanna Make It Alright
10. Savages
11. Fly Little Bird
12. Roll Along Summer
13. Bring Back The Funk (Pts 1 & 2)
14. The Pebble And The Boy

Studio 150

"This album is dedicated to my loved ones,
of which, thank god, I have many"

On March 15, 2003, Paul and Steve Cradock performed at an anti-war concert held in Shepherds Bush Empire. The event was an attempt to raise awareness about the impending Gulf War.

Towards the end of March, a compilation album called *The Sound Of The Style Council* was released. It included a collection of obvious tracks like 'Speak Like A Child' and 'Long Hot Summer', but mixed in with the classics were more surprising choices like, 'The Piccadilly Trail', 'Ghosts Of Dachau' and 'Spin Drifting'.

In early summer Paul was invited to present Ray Davies with a Silver Clef Special Achievement Award. The event was held at the Intercontinental Hotel in London on June 27. Four years later, Paul would receive his own Silver Clef Award.

On April 8, 2004, Paul appeared at the Ronnie Lane Memorial Concert held at the Royal Albert Hall (in 2004 alone, Paul performed five times at the Royal Albert Hall). Paul and Ronnie Wood joined Slim Chance, a band that included Ronnie Lane's brother Stan, to play 'Ooh La La', 'The Poacher' and 'Spiritual Babe'.

The event, called 'One For The Road', was organised by John Hellier, the driving force behind the respected Small Faces fanzine *The Darlings of Wapping Wharf Launderette*. For several months, John grafted away to produce an outstanding event that also included appearances by Pete Townshend, Ocean Colour Scene, Midge Ure, Glen Matlock, Mick Jones and Mollie Marriott. Kenney Jones, playing with his band Jones Gang, also made an appearance. Their set included a version of 'Stay With Me' and 'All Or Nothing' where they were joined by Chris Farlowe. The three-hour concert was recorded and the DVD was sold via the *Darlings of Wapping*

Wharf Launderette website.

A triple CD box set, *Fly On The Wall*, was released in July 2003. The 38 track collection included a selection of B-sides, rarities remixes and unreleased tracks from Paul's solo career like 'Here's A New Thing', 'Steam', 'The Riverbank' and 'Ohio'. It came with a booklet about the history and context of each song together with a stunning collection of Lawrence Watson photographs.

Also in July 2003, Paul signed to V2 Records, having parted with Independiente in March. The label was founded in 1996 by Richard Branson and Stereophonics had been the first signing. Universal purchased V2 Records in 2007.

Since Paul had been a teenager, he'd been making mixtapes for friends. When considering *Studio 150*, he saw it as an opportunity to do something similar for his fans. The tracks included were not his favourite songs, but they were songs that had he knew he could "make his own" and this he achieved.

Studio 150 was released on September 14, 2004, on V2 Records and entered the charts at No 2. It was recorded at Studio 150 in Amsterdam and produced by Paul Weller and Jan 'Stan' Kybert.

"I saw Paul the day after he recorded some demos at Wheelers End Studios for those *Illumination* sessions and we talked about maybe doing some more work in the future," recalls Jan. "I didn't hear anything for about six months and then my phone rings and a voice says, 'Hello Stan its Paul Weller, do you want to do a record then?'

"We went on to do some work with Simon Dine at both Wheelers End and Black Barn and then along the way he said he didn't want me to engineer on a record, he wanted me to produce it and that became *Studio 150*. To be asked to produce was a real leg up for me. For someone like Paul Weller to come in and say that gave me a huge opportunity for my career and I'm very grateful to him for that."

In the sleeve notes Paul wrote, "This album is dedicated to my loved ones, of which, thank god, I have many."

The musicians on *Studio 150* included Steve Cradock, Steve

White, Damon Minchella, Lorre Trytten, Louk Boudesteijn, Eliza Carthy, Carleen Anderson, Mieke Honingh, William Friede, Jan Van Duikeren, The Stands, Petra Rosa, Sam Leigh Brown, Herman Van Haaren, Bastiaan Van Der Worf, Aimee Versloot, Ray Bruinsma, Stefan Schmid, Frans Cornelissen, Claude Fontaine, Martin de Ruiter, Bill Newsinger, Seya Teeuwen, Pauline Terlow, Sarah Koch.

Nolan Frederick Porter wrote the following words in the introduction for the book *Black Music White Britain* (Snowball/McKenna) in 2013: 'Considering I saw my first R&B television review produced in Britain in approximately 1958, I realised that Britain's love affair with black music and black musician's was there way before I came on the scene. England has kept alive so much of the old R&B and their love for the artists has given hope and gratitude to many of the performers who are still around today, myself included. It's hard for me to measure the impact that it has had on the UK but I can measure the profound effect it has had on my life. I feel that my music found a home in the UK and we have become musical friends forever. When I perform in the UK I feel I've come to my musical home. My heart beats faster there!'

In Paul's own way, on *Studio 150* he was also keeping alive much of the great music that has been produced by black musicians from America.

Nolan Frederick Porter, or N F Porter, was born in Los Angeles in 1949. In the late Sixties and early Seventies, he released two albums, *No Apologies* and *Nolan* and produced two tracks that the Northern Soul scene especially embraced – 'Keep On Keeping On' (back in the days when Joy Division were called Warsaw they based their song 'Interzone' on 'Keep On Keeping On') and 'If I Could Only Be Sure'. Paul was familiar with both songs but chose the latter to record.

Paul's version of 'If I Could Only Be Sure' moves along at a smooth, mellow tempo. The organ gives the song a rich soulful edge and both the organ and guitar solos remind us that Paul is making the song his own and he does it triumphantly. What's more, Paul may have been responsible for turning more people on to the amazing N F Porter.

At the Fonda Theatre, Los Angeles in 2015, Nolan Porter joined Paul on stage to perform a version of 'Heatwave'. Actor Martin Freeman was also on hand to introduce the acts that night.

Following the show, Nolan wrote, "WOW!! Two nights ago, I had one of the best experiences of my musical journey! I was able to be on stage and sing a song with the great Paul Weller and his absolutely together band!! My wife Patrice and I went to see Paul the night before I sang with him. As soon as we got backstage, I could feel the warmth and respect that people had for me as a fellow musician. I was also asked about the passing of Frank Zappa's widow, Gail Zappa. Patrice, being Frank's sister, really appreciated the condolences and concerns that were expressed backstage. Paul Weller, his family and staff, were kind and I felt that I was among old friends. I was very comfortable. Most of the material Paul played those nights was new and many people in Los Angeles had never heard it before. They loved it! And usually L.A. audiences are very cynical about new material.

"The best part of that experience to me personally was to be able to thank Paul Weller for recording my old tune 'If I Could Only Be Sure' and helping to breathe new life into my music career, even at this stage of my life. A special shout out to Neil Jones of Stone Foundation and Marv Mack of Soulside Productions for helping to facilitate this meeting. Neil always tries to support me and it was great working with Marv. Good on both of you! Much love."

Sweeping cymbals and strings open Paul's version of 'Wishing On A Star' before some subtle drum programming arrives which is soon joined by Steve White. Paul's voice sounds mature and soulful and, backed by the string arrangement, the song generally sounds full. It captures a mood of driving through country lanes on warm summer nights.

Rose Royce had recorded 'Wishing On A Star' back in 1978. The song, written by Billy Rae Calvin and produced by Norman

Whitfield, had appeared on their *In Full Bloom* album. It's been covered many times by artists like Beyonce, Seal and Jay Z. Paul's version of 'Wishing On A Star/Family Affair/Let It Be Me' was released as a single and reached No 11. 'Family Affair' had originally been recorded by Sly and the Family Stone and 'Let It Be Me' was a record by Betty Everett.

Paul counts in the next track, 'Don't Make Promises' and it's an infectious mood upper. Paul and his band give this song a rootsy feel, White pushes the rhythm along using brushes and Danny Thompson plays double bass.

'Don't Make Promises' was written by American folk musician Tim Hardin. The song had been included on his 1966 debut album called *Tim Hardin 1*. Besides Paul, other artists to cover this song have included Marianne Faithfull and Joan Baez.

Paul opens 'The Bottle' with some energetic acoustic guitar and then, pow!, the rest of the band enter. At times it sounds frantic, but it all comes together brilliantly. Of course, there's a wah-wah pedal along with stabbing brass, some thunderous funky bass and flute. Paul's arrangement is dynamic and pushes the song into multiple dimensions.

Gil Scott-Heron and Brian Jackson (Jackson also played the flute on the song) wrote 'The Bottle'. It was included on Heron's 1974 album *Winter In America*. The lyrics are a frank observation about alcohol abuse. 'The Bottle/Corrina Corrina/Coconut Grove' was released by Paul as a single.

"Black is the colour of my true love's hair," sings Paul in his best folksy tone. 'Black is The Colour' is a song that could quite comfortably fit into *22 Dreams*. Eliza Carthy's violin solo brings an authentic folk edge.

"I don't know for certain why Paul got in touch, but it may have been because he'd heard my version of 'Wild Wood' which I recorded for my *Angels And Cigarettes* album," says Eliza. "My management contacted me one day and said that Paul wanted me to play on a couple of his songs, so I was delighted. Then I was sent a CD with the songs on it and set about working out my parts – both fiddle and vocals. When I got into the studio the producer said only the fiddle was needed. That CD contained the original versions of the two songs 'Early Morning Rain' and 'Black Is The Colour'. Until Paul sent me the songs, I'd never really listened to any Gordon Lightfoot either.

"I'd never met Paul before and had been a fan of The Jam, so my experience of going into the studio with him was really special. And working on his material really opened my eyes to what an amazing singer and character he is. I got invited to go down to Black Barn and I loved that experience. It felt like going into another world – a sort of hidden little place. I remember knocking on the door and Paul opening it. He actually seemed quite nervous and quiet to start off with, I think he can be quite shy, but after a while it was okay. On the day there was only me, Paul and the producer Jan Kybert.

"I'd already worked out several parts that I could play. I worked on the notion that if they had too much they could always strip it back. I mean, up until that point I hadn't had any direction from Paul at all. I think Paul knew that to get the best out of a folk musician and capture that folk flavour it's probably best to just let them run with it. Paul allowed me to be myself. I also think I may have been one of the first folk musicians that Paul had worked with too.

"One thing that really sticks out from my time being in the studio with Paul was when I put the 'cans' on and I could hear him singing directly into my ears. It was a 'bloody hell' moment – wow, what a voice! I remember thinking that's why Paul Weller is Paul Weller – that voice is incredible. I discovered something about Paul that I just hadn't known before and now whenever I hear Paul come on the radio I remember that moment."

The first known recording of this traditional folk song 'Black Is The Colour' is by Mrs Lizzie Roberts in 1916. It is believed the song originated from Scotland before becoming popular amongst American folk communities. Other notable artists to have recorded versions of this sweet romantic song include Nina Simone and Joan Baez.

Some of Paul's fans found the next song to have been a strange choice, but it works and Paul delivers a soulful performance. 'Close To You' was written by Burt Bacharach and Hal David and first recorded by Richard Chamberlain in 1963. Dionne Warwick also recorded the song along such greats as Frank Sinatra and Dusty Springfield. But by far the most famous version was by The Carpenters in 1970.

Paul picks up his acoustic guitar again for song number seven and violinist Eliza Carthy re-joins him. Paul's combination of folk and soul totally works on this version of 'Early Morning Rain'. 'Early Morning Rain/Come Together' was released as a single but only just scraped into the top 40.

After waving a close friend off at Los Angeles Airport in 1964, Canadian songwriter Gordon Lightfoot was inspired to write the song. It then appeared on his 1966 debut album *Lightfoot*. Bob Dylan, Neil Young and even Elvis Presley also recorded versions of the song.

Eliza Carthy: "I also did a BBC Special with Paul at Broadcasting House. We performed 'Wildwood' and 'Early Morning Rain'. It was a funny day because after the show we went for a drink in the BBC bar. The small audience watching the performance had been an invite-only affair, so there were all these Paul Weller and old Mod fans and they all came to the bar. It was also the last night of *Strictly Come Dancing*. This meant that in the BBC bar there was one half filled with all these Weller fans and the other all these *Strictly* fans. It was like Brucey baby and all the contestants in one corner and Paul and all his mates in the other. It was one of the funniest evenings I've ever seen.

"I then didn't see Paul for a while, but I have done recently. He was with Steve Cradock and the thing is they are just such nice people. They always make an effort to come over and say hello, they always give you a cuddle, ask you how things are going. They are straight, proper people and I think that's how you last in this industry."

Noel Gallagher wrote 'One Way Road' for Oasis. It was the B-side to their single 'Who Feels Love', a song from the album *Standing on the Shoulder of Giants.* It was a nice touch of Paul to do a cover of one of Noel's songs and his version was used as the theme tune for the TV programme *Lead Balloon.* The male backing vocals were supplied by The Stands, a Liverpool outfit that included drummer/singer Steve Pilgrim.

Paul's cover of 'Hercules' is funk dirt at its finest. The heavy cymbals and a piano part help give it a raw edge and it's clear that Paul is in his element as he struts through this Seventies funk monster. 'Hercules' was originally recorded by American R&B artist Aaron Neville in 1973. Although it was committed to vinyl with the B-side 'Going Home', there were problems with the pressings and so it never got a proper release. As a result, it's a record that sits high on the list of 'must haves' of rare vinyl hunters worldwide.

Sweeping strings, shakers and an unexpected acoustic guitar solo give the next song on *Studio 150* a whole new meaning. In 1979 Sister Sledge had a hit with 'Lost In Music' with 'Thinking Of You' as the B-side. Around the same time, Paul was writing and recording material for *Setting Sons,* so he may not have paid too much attention to Sister Sledge at that time. 'Thinking Of You/Don't Go To Strangers/Needles And Pins' was also lifted from *Studio 150* and released as a single.

Paul's cover of 'All Along The Watchtower' is packed full of acoustic guitar and a smooth sounding organ part. The tempo rolls along with an almost bluesy feel. This version is certainly an original take on a much-loved song and the addition of the backing vocals by Carleen Anderson, Sam Brown and Claudia Fontaine is a bonus.

Bob Dylan penned 'All Along The Watchtower' while he was recuperating from a motorcycle accident in 1966. The song then appeared on his *John Wesley Harding* album in 1967. In January 1968, the Jimi Hendrix Experience recorded a version in Olympic Studios (Brian Jones was present to lay down some percussion). The Hendrix version was included on the *Electric Ladyland* album. 'Watchtower' has also been covered by Eric Clapton, Bobby Womack and Neil Young.

Neil Young wrote 'Birds'. The song was included on Young's third solo album *After The Goldrush*. Paul's piano part is very much up front and Carleen, Sam, and Claudia return to provide some gospel style backing vocals. 'Birds' was a clever choice of song to bring *Studio 150* to a close.

TRACKLISTING

1. If I Could Only Be Sure
2. Wishing On A Star
3. Don't Make Promises
4. The Bottle
5. Black Is The Colour
6. Close To You
7. Early Morning Rain
8. One Way Road
9. Hercules
10. Thinking Of You
11. All Along The Watchtower
12. Birds

Illumination

"Share Your Dream"

In 2001, Paul appeared on a tribute album to The Who called *Substitute: Songs Of The Who* and performed a version of 'Circles'. The album included other music heavyweights like David Bowie ('Pictures Of Lily'), Ocean Colour Scene ('Anyway, Anyhow, Anywhere') and Pearl Jam ('The Kids Are Alright').

On April 20, 2001, Paul appeared at the Astoria in London. The occasion was a tribute concert to mark the tenth anniversary of Steve Marriott's death. Paul's set was helped along by Noel Gallagher and Gem Archer and every song performed was either by the Small Faces or Humble Pie. Other artists who appeared were Peter Frampton, Clem Clempson, Jerry Shirley and Greg Ridley, Kenney Jones and Ian McLagan. A CD of the show, *One More Time For The Ol' Tosser*, was released with performances from the day including the All Star performances – Paul's collaboration with Noel Gallagher, Gem Archer, Steve Ellis, Ian McLagan and Kenney Jones on 'Became Like You', 'Get Yourself Together', 'Here Comes The Nice', 'I'm Only Dreaming', 'Tin Soldier' and 'All Or Nothing'.

Paul spent a chunk of 2001 touring with an acoustic set. The album, *Days Of Speed*, captured a selection of highlights from the tour and kicked off with a version of 'Brand New Start'. This recording was taken from one of Paul's shows at the Shepherds Bush Empire on June 2. 'The Loved' followed, also taken from the same show. Paul then worked his way through a selection of songs from his career – 'English Rose', 'Amongst Butterflies', 'That's Entertainment', 'Headstart For Happiness'. The songs were recorded at venues in Berlin, London, Dublin and Southampton. The album ended with 'Town Called Malice' recorded at the Velvet in Rimini on May 18.

Paul also spent the latter part of 2001 working on material for his next studio album, *Illumination*.

On February 9, 2002, Jimmy Page joined the Paul Weller band on stage at the Royal Albert Hall for a Teenage Cancer Trust fundraiser and they performed 'Dazed And Confused'. Robert Plant also appeared on the bill.

On May 21, 2002, Universal released the double CD *The Jam at BBC*, including sessions with John Peel in 1977, and live at The Rainbow in 1979. The tracks included 'In The City', 'London Girl', 'All Around The World', 'Thick As Thieves', 'Ghosts', 'Precious' and 'Funeral Pyre'.

On July 28, 2002, Paul performed at Hyde Park and the concert was filmed and later released on DVD. He opened the show with 'Sunflower' and the set also included 'Bull Rush', 'Leafy Mysteries' and 'Stanley Road'. For the encore, he returned to the stage to play 'Wild Wood', 'Call Me No. 5' and 'Woodcutter's Son'. A relatively unknown London based band originating from Nottingham, Little Barrie, were one of the support acts.

Illumination was released on September 16 by Independiente. It was recorded at Black Barn Studios and Wheelers End Studios and produced by Paul Weller and Simon Dine. *Illumination* reached No 1 in the charts.

Alongside Paul, the other musicians on the album included Steve Cradock, Steve White, Damon Minchella, Noel Gallagher, Gem Archer, Kelly Jones, Aziz Ibrahim, Jocelyn Brown and Carleen Anderson.

Acknowledging the musicians that contributed to the album in the sleeve notes, Paul wrote, "Many thanks to everyone involved in the making of this record. It takes a team to really create something special and I sincerely hope we have."

"Coz we're going places we never dreamt we could," ushers in the chorus on track one, 'Going Places', a straightforward number without any frills. Paul plays all the instruments apart from the drums that come courtesy of Steve White.

'Going Places' sets the tone – there's something different about the sound. This was the first album that Simon Dine produced for

Paul, and that probably had something to do with it. Simon was a member of the band Noonday Underground. Charles Rees and Jan 'Stan' Kybert were the engineers on *Illumination*.

'A Bullet For Everyone' evokes memories of glam rock. Paul and White take care of all the instrumentation, apart from Damon Minchella's bass, and there's a particularly sharp guitar solo by Paul. "Everybody wanting it, wanting it to stop, the chaos and destruction, the bloodshed on the rocks, the pain and the deprivation, the losses and the grief, the tired worn out promises of the politicians' brief." It was reassuring to hear Paul's sentiments hadn't changed since his teenage days when he screamed his thoughts and fears to other teenagers in sweat-soaked rooms.

'Leafy Mysteries' b/w 'Talisman/Wild Wood (Live)' was the second single from *Illumination*. Steve Cradock plays acoustic guitar on this breezy number where Paul sings, in his best Sixties-style vocals, "Just open up the world I find so small to me, when there's so much to see – so much to be." The outro and final guitar chord sounds like it could've been taken from any of a dozen Jam songs.

'It's Written In The Stars' b/w 'Horseshoe Drama/Push Button Automatic' was the first single released from *Illumination*, reaching No 7. Simon Dine/Noonday Underground were credited with the brass and FX on this chipper of a track. The song evokes memories of the Acid Jazziness of the late Eighties in the way the brass parts loop. The Hammond organ surely must have brought a smile to the ex-Prisoners' James Taylor's face. The "ah ha's" help to pull the listener into the groove.

'Who Brings Joy' is a song about Paul's daughter Jessi, "You, who brings joy into the world, makes me swirl of such love, and all you ask in return is to be loved." Cradock plays classical and Nashville guitar throughout the song while White pins the track down with some simple brushes and cymbal work. The lyrics also provide an insight into Paul's life as a family man and the constant struggle to balance work and family life, "I just want so much to be here with you."

'Now The Night Is Here' is another song where Paul plays all the instruments, apart from the drums. It's definitely the most folk flavoured song on *Illumination*. The lyrics could have been lifted from any traditional folk song, "No velvet dress can compare to your beauty face so fair." It's only as the song nears the finishing line that it changes into a much rockier number.

'Spring (At Last)' is an enlightening piece of music. The simply combination of piano and Paul's vocals is stunning. Aziz Ibrahim plays the sarod and tambura providing some Eastern spice. Aziz had previously worked with Simply Red and the Stone Roses and several of Ian Brown's solo projects.

Aziz: "I think Paul just likes my own unique way of playing and I think he recognises that it's different to him and different to, say, 'Chopper' (Steve Cradock). I've always found Paul to have an open mind. I played sarod on 'Spring (At Last)'. It's an Indian instrument that my brother put me on to and I set about teaching myself to play. Paul actually knew what a sarod was. He lent me an album which was called *Autumn Song* by Vasant Rai and it included a sarod on it (which reminds me, I've got to give it back to him!). At the time of playing on 'Spring (At Last)' I was still learning the sarod, but it worked out okay and fitted in with the psychedelic-type sound that Paul was seeking to capture on *Illumination*."

Noel Gallagher plays drums and bass guitar on 'One X One' and Oasis band mate Gem Archer picks up the acoustic guitar part leaving Paul to fill in the gaps.

Noel: "Paul recorded *Illumination* at my Wheelers End Studios. I remember when he called me up and asked if he could use the studios. I told him of course he could. On the first day, me and Gem went around to his house to pick him up. He came out wearing a hat (another hat) with a 12-string guitar in a plastic bag as it was pissing down. In the car we had a book that had just come out about The Beatles' gear and we showed it to Paul. 'What,' he said, 'they've written a fucking book about the drugs The Beatles took!' But we quietly explained to him that it was about the equipment the band used, not gear as in drugs.

"In Wheelers End it was Paul, me, Gem and Jan 'Stan' Kybert and we did some demos. The first one was 'One X One', the second 'Going Places' and there was a third track too. I played drums on all three of them but Paul only kept my drums on two, Steve White replaced me on the other one. So, we were doing these songs and they were great. Paul wanted to keep this vibe that sounded loose, like they were just demos, to which I said, 'Well, you've come to the right place then, coz with me playing drums they're not gonna get any looser.'

"It was Paul's idea for me to play the drums. We were sat in the studio and I'm behind the drum kit and Paul's sitting with his guitar, playing some chords. I just played along until I worked out the song. I used brushes which he liked so much that when he tried to do the song again with Steve White, he didn't like that feel. The point is, it doesn't matter who or what you are, or even if you play something that is technically wrong or just sounding shit, if it feels right to Paul, it stays. But at the same time, I've been in the studio with him countless times when he said, 'Put some guitar on this.' So I've done it, just one go, and he's gone. 'That's great, that'll do,' and I'm like, whoa, hang on a minute, one take, fucking hell, can't I have another fucking go? and he's like, 'No, no, it's fucking great.' And then the album comes out and it's not on there.

"It was done at a strange time; the last record he made of that ilk. After *Illumination* he did *As Is Now* that he also recorded at Wheelers End. I remember when he was recording it; we were in the studio, and Paul was trying to tell me a parable pissed. He was relating it to one of the songs on the album. He was going on and on trying to tell the parable of these two foxes sat on a hill, a Dad fox and son fox. The son fox says, 'Dad, let's run down to that chicken coop and eat one of those chickens,' but his Dad says, 'No son, why don't we sneak down there and eat them all?' But Paul was trying to tell me this whilst being pissed up and about 45 minutes later he was still going, 'So there's two foxes...' It just descended into chaos and it wasn't until the next day I understood what he was trying to tell me."

'Bag Man' begins with some arpeggio guitar and Paul singing, "You may find me in the street somewhere or maybe floating around the bins." Steve White's drums produce a constant rhythm using brushes and the organ pins the song down. It's one of Paul's most dynamic songs.

Aziz is back for 'All Good Books', this time with his guitar. Damon Minchella is on bass and Paul's well-rehearsed backing vocalists, Carleen Anderson and Jocelyn Brown, are also back in the mix.

The song has lots of Hammond organ-fused soul and the lyrics provide an explanation for the song's title, "If Jesus could hear us now... and if Mohammad could see us now... the violence you've mistaken in the words you took to be taken."

When Paul wrote 'All Good Books', the world was still in a state of shock following the terrorist attack on the World Trade Centre a year earlier when nearly 3,000 people perished. Al-Qaeda claimed responsibility and became public enemy number one. The world woke up to a new level of threat and Christianity and Islam seemed to be at loggerheads.

Paul wrote the music for the next track, 'Call Me No 5' and Kelly Jones penned the lyrics. Jones and his band Stereophonics had signed to V2 Records in the mid-Nineties and went on to become the most successful Welsh band of all time. It's a good rock song and Paul and Jones share the vocal parts.

There's a feel of late-Sixties' Rolling Stones or Small Faces in 'Standing Out In The Universe', a casual mid-tempo rock song. Carleen Anderson and Jocelyn Brown back up Paul's vocals on the track. Damon Minchella plays bass and Steve Cradock gets out his Nashville guitar again.

Cradock: "In the studio there will be an array of guitars available to be used. The Nashville tuning, an octave higher than a normal guitar, worked on 'Standing Out In The Universe'. It's a beautiful sounding guitar that, when you compress it and put a bit of reverb on, sits comfortably in the mix and doesn't take up too much sonic pattern within the track. It's quite mercurial in that sense. Another word to describe it would be lush. A Nashville guitar was also used on 'Sweet Pea' and it works well alongside the normal six string. When a song is evolving, there will be moments when you have time to consider what could work. There'll be times where I'll grab a lap steel guitar and try that."

'Illumination' closes Paul's sixth solo album. He plays acoustic and sings on this comparatively straightforward number. The lyrics are steeped in mystery, "I close my ears and I hear no one, I'm in a moving film, it's black and white and beautiful and it has no end to write."

TRACKLISTING

1. Going Places
2. A Bullet For Everyone
3. Leafy Mysteries
4. It's Written In The Stars
5. Who Brings Joy
6. Now The Night Is Here
7. Spring (At Last)
8. One X One
9. Bag Man
10. All Good Books
11. Call Me No.5
12. Standing Out In The Universe
13. Illumination

Heliocentric

"There's no drinking, after you're dead"

I n 1998, Paul collaborated with Ben Sherman to produce a shirt. He had approached the iconic company and asked if he could design a Ben Sherman shirt in the style of how he remembered them when he was a kid growing up in Woking. Paul submitted a sketch with details that included a large 'contemporary Italian collar', sewn-in pleat and chunky buttons. The retro shirt smacked of quality, a return to what had made the brand so respected in the Sixties and Seventies.

The Style Council album, *Modernism – A New Decade*, was finally released in 1998 along with a Style Council box set. Another release, *Modern Classics: The Greatest Hits*, contained 16 of Paul's 'hits', beginning with 'Out Of The Sinking' and ending with 'Into Tomorrow'.

More Modern Classics was released in 2014. Twenty-one tracks were chosen to represent Paul's output since the 1998 album. *MMC* kicked off with 'He's The Keeper' and included 'Sweet Pea, My Sweet Pea', 'Wild Blue Yonder', 'Starlite', 'Flame-Out' and 'Brand New Toy'.

"Can it really have been 15 years already?" Paul asked, writing in the sleeve notes. "And what has changed in that time? Well, apart from a lot more grey hairs and wrinkles, very little really."

The photographers Lawrence Watson, Julian Broad and Dean Chalkley provided the sleeve design that featured images of Paul, one of which showed him standing below the Ham Yard W1 road sign. Ham Yard, just off Great Windmill Street, had been the site of infamous Mod club, The Scene, in the mid-Sixties. In 2014, a new hotel was built on the spot which, coincidentally, was the venue for The Jam documentary premiere in 2015.

In 1999, *Q* magazine presented Paul with the Best Songwriter award. On the night, the award was handed to Paul by soul legend

Edwin Starr. Paul had performed a version of Starr's 'Big Bird' when he had been with The Jam.

The day after Paul's birthday in May 1999, he gave an interview for the Small Faces fanzine *The Darlings Of Wapping Wharf Launderette*. John Hellier conducted the interview and has kindly allowed us to include it here in its entirety.

JH. When did you first become aware of the Small Faces?

PW. It was around the time of 'Tin Soldier', I think it was late 1967. I remember seeing them on *Top of the Pops* with PP Arnold.

JH. What was the attraction of the band?

PW. All of it for me. They were the most complete band. They had a great look but that alone is no good if you can't play. The whole image thing was a fabrication that just came naturally together. And the music, well, that was just fantastic. Although they were just kids, literally, Steve's voice had a lot of maturity and that was in their playing too. But the look just blew me away, it was unique. It almost looked manufactured, but of course it wasn't.

JH. Which member do you identify with the most?

PW. No-one in particular. I liked all of them. I suppose style-wise it was mainly Steve, but I don't particularly identify with anyone in the band.

JH. What was your favourite Small Faces period?

PW. I suppose '67 onwards. I favoured the Immediate years but I liked the earlier stuff as well. By 1967 the group had grown up. My favourite album is the first Immediate one. There are some great songs on that. I wasn't aware of the album at the time – it was years later that I backtracked on it.

JH. Did you ever meet Steve or Ronnie?

PW. No. I've only met Kenney and Mac. I was in contact with Ronnie once. I wrote him a letter and he wrote me one back. We were gonna meet up but it never happened. I did have the opportunity to meet Steve in 1984 when he did the interview with Paolo Hewitt, but I sort of bottled out. It's not always a good thing to meet the people you admire anyway. It's best to keep a healthy distance really.

JH. How would you describe Steve as a vocalist and musician?

PW. He was a unique talent wasn't he. I don't know how I would describe it. He was one of the great white soul singers, I know it's been said before, but he really was. He's just amazing, especially when you look at the size of him. Also, he was a very underrated guitarist. I've been watching a video of a live gig he did in the Eighties and I was very impressed with the guitar work and the harp as well. The only thing I didn't like was when he was into that kinda screechy stuff with Humble Pie.

JH. What did you think of the offshoot bands: Faces, Humble Pie etc?

PW. There were certain tracks I liked from all of them but I wasn't a big fan of them in particular. Oh, I loved that Humble Pie track 'Groovin' With Jesus'.

JH. What did you think of the Small Faces reincarnation in the mid-Seventies?

PW. I never agree with bands getting back together. That's bollocks, all that. I didn't go to see them or buy any of their records. Without Ronnie it couldn't possibly be the same. Ronnie was on the promo video for 'Itchycoo Park' wasn't he? Apparently, at a rehearsal he popped out for some fags and never came back. I never even heard the comeback albums. I just wasn't interested.

JH. You worked with both Kenney and Mac in recent years: what were they like to work with?

PW. Yeah, they're both brilliant musicians, apart from Kenney's fucking mobile phone! Once he turned that off it was OK. Mac especially, I mean he's kept on working hasn't he.

JH. Did you like Mac's autobiography?

PW. Yeah, it was good. At least he's got a decent fucking memory for someone who was out of it! He remembered all those little details, yet he didn't know 'Get Yourself Together' when I asked him about it.

JH. What did you make of the way Steve's career went? While

people like Rod Stewart became mega-rock stars, Steve ended his days playing in pubs.

PW. I think you make your own choices in life. I don't think there's any kind of sad story there because Steve Marriott didn't want it. That's how it seems to me anyway. Although I'm not convinced they were the happiest days of his career, it's hard to say, I'm not inside the man's head. Humble Pie were massive in America, but he seemed to turn his back on all that.

JH. Did you like what Steve was doing in his later years?

PW. I never heard enough of it to make a fair comment, really. I watched the live *Packet of Three* video and it was like pub rock really. It's not really my kind of thing in some ways but you can't knock it because his playing and singing was still fucking good. It was nearly all R&B covers which is a simple option but again I wouldn't knock it. There was always a bit of magic between him and Ronnie when they were together, like Lennon and McCartney. It didn't matter whoever wrote the songs, the little bit of magic was always there.

JH. Where were you and what were your feelings when you heard about Steve and Ronnie's sad deaths?

PW. With Steve it was just before a gig at the Brixton Academy. We already had 'Tin Soldier' in the set so we played that for Steve. With Ronnie I was at home and Kenney called me. I'd just started writing a song about him called 'He's The Keeper'. I wish I'd brought the lyrics with me for you to print in *Wapping Wharf* (Paul later faxed these to me and they appear on page six). I was quite tearful about it, more with Ronnie than with Steve for some reason.

JH. Do you own any Small Faces memorabilia?

PW. No, just mainly all the European EPs. I've got loads of pictures and stuff but nothing else really. Dean (Powell) was telling me about that guy with the guitar for sale but I'm a bit cautious about that. If someone was to give me a signed picture of all four of them that would be cool.

JH. What's happening with the Ronnie Lane tribute EP?

PW. I don't know, that's a bit of a sore point. It's been going on for a long time now, over two years and even before Ronnie died. We did a couple of tracks. Steve (Cradock) recorded 'Done This One Before' and I did 'The Poacher'. We were going to do another two tracks.

JH. Did The Jam ever feature any Small Faces songs in their live set?

PW. Well, yeah, we did 'Get Yourself Together', I think that was the only one. We've done 'All Or Nothing' before at sound checks. We nicked enough of their riffs though – can you hear 'Don't Burst My Bubble' on *The Gift*?

JH. So how would you sum up The Small Faces briefly?

PW. They were the most complete pop group for me. They had everything. They were amazing players that all had the same influences. The image, the haircuts, blimey they were even all the same height. A kinda dream band that everyone would want to be in.

JH. What are your own immediate plans and what do you see yourself doing in ten years?

PW. Just to make a new album early next year. I can't even think about ten years from now, it's too scary. I just get on with it. Whatever will be will be!

JH. And finally, you used Small Faces miniatures on your *Stanley Road* album sleeve and a *Rave* magazine featuring Steve and Ronnie on an old Style Council LP. Any chance of a *Wapping Wharf* cover appearing on a future album sleeve?

PW. Anything is possible if money changes hands! (laughs).

JH. Thanks Paul, for your precious time

PW. My pleasure mate. Keep up the excellent work with the magazine.

In October, 2005, *Here Come The Nice: A Small Faces Songbook* was published by Helter Skelter. The book was a collaboration between Paul and John Hellier. "Apart from being great tunes," wrote Paul, "you will also discover fantastic words and concepts, melodies and patterns." Paul commented on each of the songs featured in the book.

The Small Faces songbook was not Paul's first book collaboration.

In 2000, he teamed up with Paolo Hewitt, another writer with Mod expertise, to produce *The Soul Stylists*. Paul was credited with the concept for the book and he wrote the introduction where he mentioned Brutus shirts, Levis, DMs, Loafers, Harringtons and Crombies. He referenced English working class kids, trips to Petticoat Lane and hearing 'Sex Machine' for the very first time at Woking Football Club. He captures a youth, *his* youth, as he witnessed the end of the Sixties and the start of the Seventies. These were the foundations upon which he built his own sense of style and influenced countless others.

Paul dedicated the book "To the greatness of black music, black culture and the black race who have given so much to inspire us." Paolo dedication was "To all the Woking suedeheads."

On November 27, 2000, Paul performed at the Royal Albert Hall along with The Who and Noel Gallagher and played 'So Sad About Us'. He also joined in with 'See Me Feel Me'.

Noel Gallagher: "I've got loads of favourite moments playing live with Paul. One time he was performing at some huge concert and I'd gone along just to see him. Now he's done this to me a lot. I'll be in the dressing room before the gig and it's just all handshakes and good to see you. Not another word. All the time I'll be getting shit faced. Then, during the bit between the end of the gig and the encore, he'll ask me to get up on stage with him. I'll be saying, 'Well no not now, I'm too fucking pissed.' But he'll be, 'No come on.' Then he'll ask if I know such or such a song and I'll say yes. But then I'll go on stage, plug my guitar in but switch it off and just mime it. Afterwards people will come and say things like, 'Fucking man, that was brilliant, you was having it.' I've told Paul many times if he's going to do that at least give me a few hours' notice and I'll even bring my own gear.

"And then there was the time when I asked him to get up on stage with me when I was with Oasis at the Shepherd's Bush Empire. I asked him to play the guitar solo on 'Champagne Supernova', but the cunt stood right in the dark, where nobody could see him!

"I did another gig with Paul where he got up with me and we did 'The Butterfly Collector' and 'All You Need Is Love', but acoustically. There was just something in the room that night that was great. I love Paul's tunes but there was another time when he got me on stage and said he wanted to do one of my tunes. He picked an obscure one that I didn't even know. Before I could finish telling him that I hadn't played it in so many years, he's already announcing me on stage. But it's always great getting up with Paul on stage and he's now one of my oldest friends. It's still a buzz and long may it continue."

When Robin Black put the lease up for Black Barn Studios, Paul jumped at the opportunity to buy it. Back in the days of laying down demos for the *Paul Weller* album, he recorded them in Black Barn. Over the years, Paul would enjoy the freedom to come and go to his own studio when he pleased and some of his most experimental music has been created in Black Barn.

The studio also became a second home for some of Paul's band mates. "It's like our church," says Steve Cradock. "I still look forward to going into Black Barn with Paul. It's like our Mecca. It's an amazing place. It's a place that's given Paul a freedom to do his music in a way that he hasn't had before. And it's been like that since *22 Dreams*. In Black Barn Paul is free to be a writer, a musician, an arranger, a composer.

"In the old days, Paul would've sent me a demo of a song and I would learn it before going into the studio. Nowadays, much of we do in the studio is done cold. I'll turn up and it will evolve from there and something will always happen. The process will be pretty much the same, it's just that there might be more people in the studio on that particular day. Paul will be giving direction and listening to people's ideas at the same time. He's very encouraging and he is a great conductor and arranger. He can see and hear things that no one else can.

"I've been thinking about this recently and I don't believe he sees himself as being that much of a musician but judges himself more as a songwriter and a singer. You can see the ideas that he has when you get to have a peek at his notebooks. By the time the first day of recording comes, he's already got a lot of stuff down in his note book and in his head. Once the session is underway, it becomes very work-mode like. Everyone is trying to capture what's happening live and fluid and breathing. The lead might be taken by the vocal and if that's the goer then everything else will be finished around that – but it's still a very mercurial process.

"In all the years that I've been working with Paul, the thing that hasn't changed is that he wants to create the best thing that will blow everyone's head off. He still wants to be able to play someone, anyone, the song and say 'get on this you fucker.' It means a lot to him.

"And as the years go by he's become more liberal in the studio, so anyone that just happens to be in there at the time can become part of the melting pot of that day. And if you're lucky enough to be there on the day it's a buzz. This arrangement really works for Paul.

"When I work with him in the studio there are two things going on. He has an idea what he wants and he's also open to anything new too. Paul is like that with anyone he works with.

"He's always open to new ideas."

Noel Gallagher: "Black Barn is great and he also has a good little firm of people around him. The clock's not ticking in his own studio. He's also able to stay down there, so he's kind of able to be immersed in it all. It was similar when we had Wheeler's End. We could take all day just fucking about. And having Black Barn works for Paul because he's the type of guy that will try anything and everything and he'll even get to the end of the week, rip the song up and start again and I suppose he can do that because he doesn't have to be out of his studio by nine o'clock. I envy him that."

Heliocentric was released on April 10, 2000, on Island Records. It was produced by Paul Weller and Brendan Lynch and was partly recorded at Heliocentric Studios. Paul's simple dedication in

Heliocentric was, "To the ones I love."

"We recorded some of *Heliocentric* at Heliocentric Studios," says Paul. "The studios were owned by Chris Difford of Squeeze and located in Rye in Sussex. He lived next door. It was a nice place to work and we got a lot done down there and again tried to record everything that retained that live feel."

The musicians who played on *Heliocentric* were Steve White, Steve Cradock, Damon Minchella, Brendan Lynch, Cliff Stapleton, Mark Boxall, Dominic Kelly and Robert Kirby.

The opening track, 'He's The Keeper', is about Ronnie Lane. In April it was issued as a single (backed with 'Heliocentric/Bang Bang') which was, "so undervalued at the time" according to Paul.

Of Ronnie Lane, Paul says, "His intentions were sweet and noble. He was a shining example for any songwriter." By 2000, Paul had met many of his idols – Pete Townshend, Stevie Winwood and Ian McLagan amongst them – but he never got to meet Ronnie Lane. He had no personal relationship with Lane but his lyrics suggest, if only... "In the backlog of conversations we never had."

'He's The Keeper' is a perfect album opener. Paul's band, consisting of White, Cradock and Minchella, sound tight and passionate as they breathe life into the song. Brendan Lynch is also present, and not just behind the mixing booth. Lynch plays glockenspiel on this track.

"I actually sampled each note from a glockenspiel that had been used in a studio that The Clash recorded in," says Brendan. "We'd been using 'glocks' as far back as the *Paul Weller* album. Using samples that we'd made ourselves have been an important contribution to many of Paul's albums. Often they've been very subtle but they all work and I think they helped the songs sound much more contemporary to whatever period of time we were in."

The 'Heliocentric' track marked the beginning of Paul's friendship with musician Aziz Ibrahim, as he explains. "I first met Paul when I was with Ian Brown in Paul Smith's shop in Covent Garden. By chance Paul (and Steve White) came into the shop and we were

Paul Weller, live on April 13 2017, at the Rivermead Centre in Reading

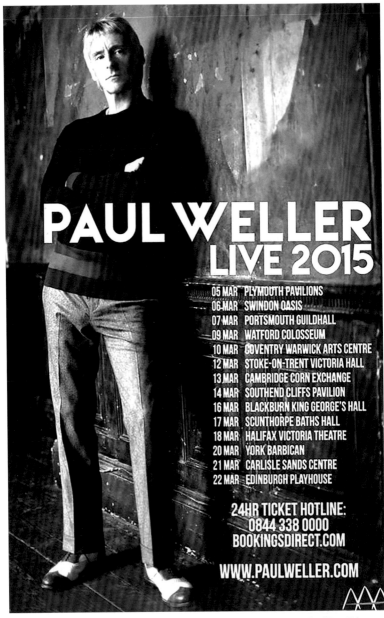

Above: Poster for Paul's 2015 UK tour. Opposite: a collage by photographer Tony Briggs, showing Paul alongside Oasis and Steve Cradock, recording their cover of The Jam's 'Carnation' (top); Paul and Liam Gallagher, same location (bottom)

Paul Weller behind the keyboards,
at the 'Carnation' recording session.
Photo: Tony Briggs

Above: the author with Sir Peter Blake (right) creator of the *Stanley Road* album sleeve
Below: Paul has been a long-time favourite at festivals. Photo: Tony Briggs

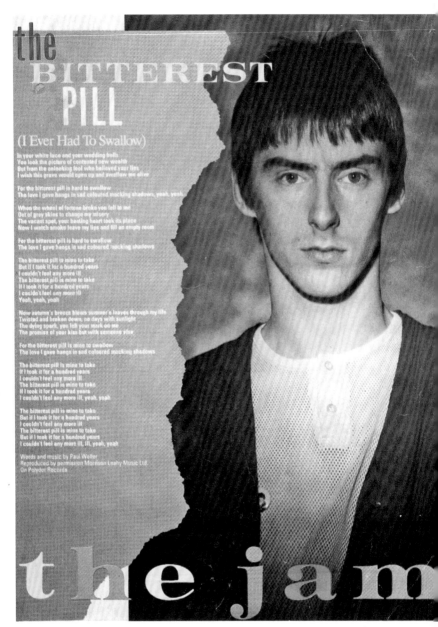

the BITTEREST PILL
(I Ever Had To Swallow)

In your white lace and your wedding bells
You look the picture of contented new wealth
But from the onlooking fool who believed your lies
I wish this grave would open up and swallow me alive

For the bitterest pill is hard to swallow
The love I gave hangs in sad coloured mocking shadows, yeah, yeah

When the wheel of fortune broke you fell to me
Out of grey skies to change my misery
The vacant spot, your beating heart took its place
Now I watch smoke leave my lips and fill an empty room

For the bitterest pill is hard to swallow
The love I gave hangs in sad coloured mocking shadows

The bitterest pill is mine to take
But if I took it for a hundred years
I couldn't feel any more ill
The bitterest pill is mine to take
If I took it for a hundred years
I couldn't feel any more ill
Yeah, yeah, yeah

Now autumn's breeze blows summer's leaves through my life
Twisted and broken down, no days with sunlight
The dying spark, you left your mark on me
The promise of your kiss but with someone else

For the bitterest pill is mine to swallow
The love I gave hangs in sad coloured mocking shadows

The bitterest pill is mine to take
If I took it for a hundred years
I couldn't feel any more ill
The bitterest pill is mine to take
If I took it for a hundred years
I couldn't feel any more ill, yeah, yeah

The bitterest pill is mine to take
But if I took it for a hundred years
I couldn't feel any more ill
The bitterest pill is mine to take
But if I took it for a hundred years
I couldn't feel any more ill, ill, yeah, yeah

Words and music by Paul Weller
Reproduced by permission Morrison Leahy Music Ltd.
On Polydor Records

the jam

Above: *Smash Hits* printed the lyrics of chart hits every issue, and The Jam's 'The Bitterest Pill' was no exception. Opposite: Mick Talbot and Paul Weller show off their dapper threads from C&A and Top Man for a magazine feature in April 1983

YOU CAN'T buy style — either you have it or you don't. Paul Weller, founder of The Style Council, favours a blend of classic separates from C&A and Italian shops, a feeling echoed by Tracie and the Questions who are signed to his Respond label. You don't have to be a millionaire to look sharp — and here are the clothes to prove it.

PAUL WEARS: White
shirt
£13.99 from C&A.
Stripey
cardigan, about £15 by
Palmero
Carlo. Trousers made
specially.
Shoes, £30 by Rider.

MICK WEARS: Black
trousers
£19.99 from Top Man.
Grey
jumper, 'about 12 quid'
from
Jockey. Diamond
jumper, about
£18 by Aitch from Top
Shop.
Shoes, £34.99 from

THE JAM

Jam File

Verbal Jam Sound Effects

Photo Faces of the 80's

The Jam File, a one-off
Jam special magazine

introduced. At the time, the Stone Roses had split and I was co-writing material with Ian and those songs appeared on the *Unfinished Monkey Business* album. We got on together instantly and Paul was fully aware of the work I had done on Ian's album. I remember he especially seemed to like the 'My Star'.

"I, of course, was very aware of Paul's work but finding out that he was also aware of my work was very strange. So from the off we got on and discovered a mutual respect and that was the same for Steve White who is a great musician and human being.

"Paul invited me to Jacob's Studio to do some recording. I played on a track that Paul put out from *Heliocentric*. It was the B-side to 'He's The Keeper' and also called 'Heliocentric'. Steve White and Brendan Lynch played on that track. At the time, I was also recording my first solo album *Lahore To Longsight*. Other musicians that played on that album included Andy Rourke and Mike Joyce of The Smiths, Steve White, Denise Johnson of Primal Scream, Mani and also Paul who sang on a track called 'Middle Road'.

"After the session, Paul asked me to play support for him and the opening show was at the Royal Albert Hall. This was the beginning of our friendship that has continued to this day. Paul is a good guy, he shows interest in people and the support bands and all credit to him."

The next track on the album, 'Frightened', is introduced at an easy pace with Paul playing the piano. Strings are provided by the Robert Kirby Orchestra. "I'm more frightened, white lightening, so sudden and blinding, yet no more enlightened, just a little more frightened" is the song's chorus. This was not going to be an album packed with three minute pop songs.

'Sweet Pea, My Sweet Pea', b/w 'Back In The Fire (BBC Radio version)/There's No Drinking After You're Dead (Noonday Underground Mix)' was released as a single in August. It's a song about Paul's first daughter, Leah.

It begins with a gentle acoustic guitar and minimal bass drum strike, and then the song really gets going. "I write for you and I to try… sweet thing, loving you is easy." Paul's words invoke that special bond between father and daughter.

Following the middle eight Paul sings, "The future, it's looking at you, it only exists because you're alive." In the inner sleeve, Paul agreed to have four photographs of Leah included, one giving the peace sign standing by the kitchen sink, another grinning away while perched on a white Lambretta, one standing in a garden with the caption 'Leah in the sun' and one other sat at a table. On *Heliocentric*, Paul was more than happy to share with the world some of the special things in his life.

In 2014, Leah modelled for DAKS. For one of the AW14 campaign photoshoots, Paul joined her in Brighton.

More acoustic guitar sets 'A Whale's Tale' on its way, this time played by Mark Boxall who also provides the backing vocals. Across the years, Paul would return the favour by playing on several COW tracks.

"I play in a band with my wife Maxine called COW and we have now recorded three albums and Paul has played on about fourteen of our tracks," says Mark. "It was Paul who offered to play on our songs. Steve Cradock also offered his services. At the moment, we're working on a project that includes Steve Ellis of Love Affair and Paul. Paul plays some very Style Council type guitar and keyboards on the songs."

'A Whale's Tale' swims along at a steady pace with an electric guitar wailing gently beneath the current. The lyrics, "You don't even know me, but you hunt me the same," may have been directed at journalists who Paul had been surrounded by for years and were constantly fishing around for a bite.

Mark Boxall: "Around the time of *Heliocentric*, I was playing in my own band called Weaver and Paul was looking for a new guitar player. He offered me the job, which I obviously told him I'd love to do. Paul was already demoing tracks for *Heliocentric* and I went down to Black Barn and got involved with them. 'A Whale's Tale' was one of the tracks that we worked on during those sessions. We did a demo of the track at Black Barn but then took it to another studio near Guildford called Jacobs and it was there that we put the final mix down. There was me, Paul, Steve White and I think Damon Minchella too.

"I played guitar on the track. I was tossed a style of guitar that I wasn't used to at the time. It was a guitar that is smaller than a normal acoustic and tuned to the Nashville country sound, which meant it had a particular kind of twang. The sound is especially noticeable at the start of 'A Whale's Tale' and it works really well throughout the track. I also did some of the backing vocals on the track's verses and choruses.

"On the day of recording, I turned up at Black Barn and Paul told me that I would be playing on one of his demos. I had no idea which one. He wrote the chords down on a bit of paper and I was directed into the recording room. Paul, Steve White and Charles Rees were all there and it was a bit daunting. I remember playing through the chords and Paul saying, 'No Marky, that's wrong, you're not playing the right chords.' I told him I was playing exactly what he'd written down.

"Anyway, it went on like this for a bit and it wasn't working, then Stevie White came over to me and looked at the bit of paper on which Paul has written the chords down only to discover that Paul had written the wrong ones! After we sorted that out, everything worked just fine.

"Those *Heliocentric* sessions were the first time I had done any proper work with Paul. He was very encouraging and he was so easy to work with. He knew exactly what he wanted, but if there were any mistakes and he liked them, he'd use them. There's no messing around for Paul, it's always only for the good of the song."

'Back In The Fire' ambles along, there's no need to rush. Brendan Lynch appears again, this time playing the mini-Moog. Paul vents his spleen throughout – "I'm not handcuffed to some wanker who doesn't know me" – and signs off with, "Your three wishes expired, now you're back in the fire."

'Dust And Rocks' is yet another song that begins with an acoustic guitar and the words, "Well she's waiting by the window, with a fading tear. It ends with, "Still she's waiting by the window, she has no fear."

It's essentially a folk rock song with a production that makes the acoustic drums sound big. There's some haunting slide-guitar during the choruses and more piano and the Robert Kirby Orchestra returns to bring the song to its conclusion. But just as the listener believes it's finished, it returns as if to say I'm not quite finished yet until it eventually fades away.

Next up is 'There's No Drinking, After You're Dead' – "And time is but an essence, encased upon the wall, that brings our day of reckoning much closer to us all." Since Paul was a teenager, alcohol has played a big part in his life. Rick Buckler described drinking as The Jam's favourite sport, not that Paul drank his way through The Jam years. Indeed, for some of them he avoided alcohol completely. But things changed and for a period in Paul's life alcohol had a firm grip on him. Talking to the *NME* in 2012, he admitted he thought he was an alcoholic. A few months earlier he said in *The Times* that he'd given up drinking because he believed his hedonistic lifestyle might actually kill him. At the time of writing this book Paul had been sober for over five years.

'Time And Temperance' sees Brendan back to play some more mini-Moog and glockenspiel, and strings return too. White gets to unleash his talent and the guitars really beef up the song whilst Minchella's bass is ever steady and interesting. The orchestra goes wild as the song finishes, "As you lose your mind, something else in time, and faces strange, rearrange."

An organ introduces 'Picking Up Sticks'. Dave Brubeck also had a song with the same title. The organ and band give the song a jazzier feel, not heard elsewhere on *Heliocentric*. The droning sound comes from a hurdy-gurdy played by Cliff Stapleton. The track also provides White with an opportunity to impress with a brief drum solo.

For the last track, 'Love-Less', Paul sets a slow pace at the piano, and the orchestra returns to provide support – "Midnight star, light the way, for thoughts that change, like night to day, and bless the course that runs in time, no matter how far, shine my way." 'Love-Less' is Paul yet again writing poetry and setting it to music.

TRACKLISTING

1. He's the Keeper
2. Frightened
3. Sweet Pea, My Sweet Pea
4. Back In The Fire
5. A Whale's Tale
6. Dust And Rocks
7. There's No Drinking, After You're Dead
8. With Time and Temperance
9. Picking Up Sticks
10. Love-Less

Heavy Soul

'Minds alive'

In February 1996, Ocean Colour Scene released the song that placed them firmly at the top of the Britpop scene. Supported by Radio 1 DJ Chris Evans, 'The Riverboat Song', from the band's second album *Moseley Shoals*, was also used to introduce his television programme *TFI Friday*. Paul played on the song.

On June 9, 1996, Paul played in London's Finsbury Park. Over 30,000 people enjoyed a lazy Sunday afternoon and soaked up some of Paul's new songs. On August 18, Paul performed at the V96 Festival in Hylands Park, Chelmsford.

In November, Paul recorded a version of Traffic's 'Feelin' Alright'. He donated the track and the royalties to the *Tenth Anniversary Childline Charity Album*. The CD also included tracks by Ocean Colour Scene, Menswear, Salad and East 17.

On July 13, 1997, Paul played at T in the Park held at Kinross, Scotland. Also performing that weekend were Placebo, Ocean Colour Scene, Travis and Kula Shaker. Paul reappeared at the festival in 2014.

Also in July, Paul visited the Cardinal pub in Woking to watch Dave Liddle's band Blue Express play. He joined Liddle on stage to play 'High Heeled Sneakers'. Paul's old friend Steve Brookes was also present that night.

In the closing months of 1997, Paul toured the USA, Japan and Europe. He was firing on all cylinders and writing some of the best songs of his career. His fans just couldn't get enough of him.

Heavy Soul was released on June 23, 1997, on Island Records. The album was recorded at Woolhall Studios (owned by Van Morrison) in Bath and produced by Paul Weller and Brendan Lynch.

Lynch on production duties for *Heavy Soul*: "We captured quite an edgy sound for *Heavy Soul*. We turned up the treble for that album.

We didn't change the recording format in any way, it was still all done live. The only difference was that we recorded *Heavy Soul* in Woolhall Studios. We moved there because the Manor Studios had closed down. It had been owned by Richard Branson but he sold it off. We were gutted because it was like our spiritual home. But there was a nice vibe in Woolhall and everybody was relaxed. I enjoyed working there."

Not as such a dedication, but in the sleeve notes Paul wrote, "To my people, you know and so do I. To anyone whosoever slated me, fuck you!"

The musicians who played on *Heavy Soul* were Steve Cradock, Steve White, Mark Nelson, Brendan Lynch and Jools Holland.

In 2011, the ninth edition of a Mod fanzine, run by Adam Cooper for today's sussed generation, was published. It featured an article about Paul and the front cover included a picture of him from Jam days. No one was surprised to find Paul still getting massive attention from Mod zines, even after so many years. Cooper's fanzine was aptly called *Heavy Soul*.

'Heavy Soul (pt 1)' kicks off the album with a guitar strum that suggests the song is heading in a certain direction, but then it changes its course as Paul delivers the first lyrics, "We're words upon a window, written there in steam." And then the band step up. It's a basic four-piece outfit that sounds grounded and established. White flavours the song with some of the most interesting drum fills ever committed to tape and Cradock and Nelson keep the song moving along as Paul explains, "I've got a heavy soul, it's a joy to know."

As the track ends, 'Peacock Suit' bursts into life and comparisons to the Small Faces are immediately drawn. 'Peacock Suit/Eye Of The Storm' was released in August along with a promotional video that showed Paul, White, Nelson and Cradock performing the song in the basement of Nomis Studios. Paul wasn't wearing a suit "In my peacock suit, I look so cute," but a floral shirt while he played his Rickenbacker 'Wham' guitar. Oh, and someone was filmed walking the streets of London dressed up as a peacock, as you do.

'Up In Suzes' Room' is a unique song in so many ways. The ukulele played by Nelson, the mini-Moog played by Lynch and the strings by Wired Strings all contribute to that uniqueness. The lyrics also intrigue, "Yellow strands mingle into red, warm air blows, down upon her soft bed, she licks my face and the feeling spreads."

Brendan Lynch and Max Heyes were responsible for the experimental sounds included in 'Brushed'. "The song was a sort of continuation of stuff we had tried before on a track like 'Whirlpools End' and some of my own remixes," says Lynch. "The suggestion was not to do a remix as such but instead to record a song and put some of the elements of what might go into a remix into it. It was a matter of taking the basic form and manipulating it using what's available on the mixing desk. But it's still a live band playing."

The addition of a psychedelic feedback guitar provides a feel, as does the way Paul delivers his vocals with all the gruffness and energy that got him through his Jam days. The song is tough, and every moment of it screams life. 'Brushed/Ain't No Love In The Heart Of The City/Shoot The Dove/As You Lean Into The Light (acoustic version)' was also lifted from the album and issued as a single.

The acoustic guitar and softer vocals from Paul give 'Driving Nowhere' a palatable sweetness. "Driving nowhere, going no place, I'm just drifting." Nelson plays sitar on this mid-tempo track (the type of tempo that Paul said he wanted to get away from at the time of making As Is Now) and in just over two minutes this pop song is over.

'I Should Have Been There To Inspire You' is literally one of the most inspired songs on Heavy Soul. The use of piano, played by Paul, and accordion, played by Lynch, along with the naturally sounding drums, turns the song into a warm breeze blowing through an open window.

"I should have been there to inspire you, not paint your world a cold, cold blue... I should have been there to inspire you, I could have told you truthful too, that I believed in you."

Towards the end, the song evolves into an unexpected instrumental section that employs chords that have a dark side. This section is jazzed up with a piano all over it, and that in turn develops into a kind of dub reggae feel.

'Heavy Soul (pt 2)' fades in, an interesting slice of sound with Paul playing vibes, Nelson on sitar again and Rosie Wetters adding extra vocals. Wetters was also responsible for the various string arrangements that are found on some of the tracks on the album.

"Minds alive! On Friday Street" sings Paul at the opening of track eight. It's another song that Paul, Nelson and White pin down. As Adam Cooper adopted *Heavy Soul* as the title for his Modzine, so a Mod outfit based in Glasgow borrowed 'Friday Street' as the name for their club nights.

"Friday Street was named after a small village which is not far from Dorking," says Paul's Mum, Ann. "Paul used to drive through it. He can write stories and when you think back to The Jam days, he was still only young to be writing such lyrics. He's a bit like Ray Davies, who also wrote stories about what he saw around him, y'know, something like walking over Waterloo Bridge. When Paul was young he used to go into London with a pen and paper and write down things that he saw. He's a good storyteller, he really is."

'Friday Street/Sunflower/Brushed/Mermaids (Live)' was released as a single in September 1997.

It's the use of White's rimshots that provide the basis for the rhythm of 'Science'. It's certainly a toe-tapper. The simplicity of the instrumentation allows the song to breathe while all the time pushing forwards. Paul's vocals are soulfully British, "I've got a pen in my pocket, does that make me a writer?" and, "Standing on the mountain doesn't make me no higher... putting on gloves don't make you a fighter." Superb!

The Wurlitzer on 'Golden Sands' is provided by Jools Holland. The beat is similar to 'Science', but 'Golden Sands' has a different vibe.

It's fun and upbeat and Holland's presence is really felt. His *Later...* *with Jools Holland* show started in 1992 and over the years Paul has been invited back many times. On Sunday February 25, 1996, an entire Jools Holland show was dedicated to Paul who performed 16 songs including 'Foot Of The Mountain', 'Sunflower', 'Man Of Great Promise', 'A Year Late' and 'Out Of The Sinking'.

This is the slowest song on *Heavy Soul* and Brendan is back to supply some more mini-Moog. The tempo of the song certainly drops the mood down a notch as do the opening lyrics, "Gentle rain, here it comes again." There's simply no need to rush a song like this.

According to Paolo Hewitt, 'As You Lean Into The Light' was written for him and it's easy to understand that to be the case when you consider such lyrics as, "If I could be the rain, I'd rain from your eyes, and I'd wash away the emptiness you feel inside." Paul knew all about Paolo's background growing up in children's homes around Woking; an upbringing that was so very different from his own.

'Mermaids' backed with 'So You Want To Be A Dancer/Everything Has A Price To Pay', was issued as single in November. For some reason, Paul decided to give Roy Wood a mention beside this song in the sleeve notes. It's a joyful track to sign off *Heavy Soul* and is stuffed with infectious "sha la la la las."

TRACKLISTING

1. Heavy Soul (pt 1)
2. Peacock Suit
3. Up In Suzes' Room
4. Brushed
5. Driving Nowhere
6. I Should Have Been There To Inspire You
7. Heavy Soul (pt 2)
8. Friday Street
9. Science
10. Golden Sands
11. As You Lean Into The Light
12. Mermaids

Stanley Road

'The more I know the less I understand'

On December 4, 1994, a memorial gig was organised for Joe Awome at the Shepherds Bush Empire and Paul was a willing performer. Joe had been a member of The Jam crew. In those days, each member had been assigned a security guy. Paul had Kenny Wheeler, Rick had Chris Adoja and Bruce's guy was Joe who had once been an aspiring boxer and had even faced Muhammad Ali in an exhibition fight. Paul had known him since the days of playing Michaels in Woking because Joe had worked at the club. He'd been suffering from a brain tumour and had tragically died on the operating table.

On June 25, Paul performed on the main stage at Glastonbury and had his new songs from *Stanley Road* to impress the Glasto audience. Also gracing the festival's various stages that weekend were Oasis, The Verve and The Charlatans. This was the summer when Britpop peaked.

The battle of Britpop between Oasis and Blur would come to a head in August, when both bands fought over getting their new singles – 'Roll With It' and 'Country House' respectively – to No 1. Britpop (a dirty word amongst those artists lumped in with it) did, nonetheless, help to attract a new generation of young people to Paul's songs.

Referring to the musicians that got 'lumped in', Paul says, "They were people of similar musical vision." That vision was especially noticed by Paul in two Mod-friendly young bucks, Noel Gallagher, the main songwriter with Manchester band Oasis, and Steve Cradock, the hugely talented guitarist who was one of the founder members of Birmingham band Ocean Colour Scene.

Noel would become a close friend and collaborate with Paul on several songs and projects and Cradock's connection with Paul resulted in him being asked to join Paul's band. Steve, a life-long

Weller fan, jumped at the chance and since being included on *Wild Wood* has stayed with Paul for over two decades while still managing to keep his beloved Ocean Colour Scene afloat too. The Weller/Cradock partnership has certainly been a fruitful one.

On April 17, Paul was featured on Channel 4's *The White Room* and was joined by Noel Gallagher. Paul and Noel's paths would cross several more times throughout 1995 including the 100 Club on June 1, the Phoenix Festival on July16 and the Brixton Academy on November 30.

July saw the release of *Long Agos And Worlds Apart: A Tribute To The Small Faces*, an album on which Paul was pleased to contribute. Joining the Kenney Jones' All Star Band, Paul recorded a version of 'Almost Grown' with Kenney Jones, Mick Talbot and Marco Nelson. Other acts that contributed were Primal Scream, Dodgy, Ocean Colour Scene and Gene.

On September 4, 1995, *The Help Album* was released. It included contributions from Blur, Oasis and The Smokin' Mojo Filters cover of 'Come Together' that Paul and his supergroup band mates recorded in Abbey Road Studios.

In October, Oasis released their second album *(What's The Story) Morning Glory*, which included the brilliant 'Champagne Supernova', on which Paul played lead guitar and sang backing vocals.

On October 28, Paul performed at the Unite Against Racism concert held in Manchester and organised by the TUC. Also in October, the book *Days Lose Their Names And Time Slips Away* was published. It was an illustrated account of Paul's career between 1992 and 1995 and a collaboration between Paolo Hewitt and Lawrence Watson.

Paul spent much of the last three months of the year dipping in and out of Europe playing concerts before performing on the *Jack Dee Show* on December 16. Dee, a huge Paul Weller fan, respectfully introduced Paul playing piano on 'Stanley Road'. Dee would go on to co-write a series called *Lead Balloon* and the show's theme tune, 'One Way Road', was written by Noel Gallagher and performed by Paul.

Stanley Road was released on June 7, 1995, on Go Discs. It was recorded at the Manor Studio, Oxford, and produced by Paul Weller and Brendan Lynch.

"Going to Manor Studios was great just to get away from London," recalls Brendan. "Getting away meant removing ourselves from all the other distractions that life throws in the way. Being in Manor Studios meant we could just concentrate on writing and recording. It was a quite a chilled-out place to be, we all liked being there and we liked the sound that we got. As a studio and a place to record an album it had everything going for it. We would all stay there too. Everyone had their own room. Sometimes we'd be there for three-week stints and this set up meant we'd get a load done.

"A typical day in the Manor would include everyone getting into the studio for about 11am. We would set everything up that we needed and get ready to record. But before the actual recording, the band would run through the song a few times and normally before lunch. By this time everything would be fine-tuned and ready to go. After lunch, we would start laying down takes of the song.

"What we would find is that the takes would get better and better as they went on. There might be up to seven or eight takes and then we'd have a break, sit with it for a couple of hours before choosing the best take and that would end up the final version. The remainder of the day would be spent doing overdubs, having an evening meal and then continue to work on to about 11pm. Usually once the backing tracks have been done the band can go, and then I'm there to continue with Paul. A lot of the mixing was also done down at the Manor and that would be just me, Paul and Max. Each song would take a couple of days.

"In the early Nineties, everything was recorded with clicky bass drums and very processed sounds. A lot of the Indie bands at the time recorded in a way that sounded like they'd gone to a gig and were playing through a live PA and put lots of top on the bass drum. But we didn't want to record like that; we wanted to record everything more naturally. We tried to use the microphones to capture the natural sounds of the instruments. To do this we would spend a lot of time setting up the equipment in the studio.

"We would spend a long time setting up the microphones around Steve White's drums and getting them just right. It was only when everything was ready that we'd go for a take and, pretty much what I heard in the studio, that live take would end up the recording on the actual record. Apart from a few live overdubs that is.

"Paul playing an instrument whilst he sang could really affect his vocals and really enhance the track. Paul can get little inflections that wouldn't be there if he had just sung straight without playing anything. The thing with Paul is that he doesn't do rehearsals: with him it's always a performance and it's always the most important one.

"He just doesn't do anything half-hearted. It's a great quality that Paul has and because of it we captured some great moments in time. I have very fond memories of working with Paul on some of his albums. The *Paul Weller* album means a certain something because that was the first time I got credited as the producer on a Paul Weller record and that for me was like a dream come true. But then *Stanley Road* is also important to me because that album represents all the years of hard work up to that point. We recorded about 17 or 18 songs for that album in just nine weeks and that included the mixing. It was hard work and pretty good going."

Talking about *Stanley Road* in 2006 Paul said, '*Stanley Road* was the peak of my writing abilities – at least up to that point."

Paul said that *Stanley Road* was about growing up in Woking. "I had a great childhood living in my house in Stanley Road." Sunday mornings were spent playing with his Dad in the nearby woods while his Mum made Sunday lunch.

"Paul wrote the *Stanley Road* album about the places he knew that from around Woking," says Mum Ann. 'At the time of writing it he was living up in Send Hill. He wrote 'Wildwood' about a house which is on Newlands Corner. The house is still there but the house name is painted on the wall now because people used to steal the name plaque."

The *Stanley Road* artwork was created by Peter Blake. "Paul was a fan of The Beatles and a fan of Sgt Pepper and he talked to someone about the idea of me doing the art work for his album," says Peter. "Paul got my phone number and he gave me a call. He phoned out of the blue, he was very polite, he always called my wife, Chrissy, Mrs Blake; he was very gentlemanly. We chatted on the phone and he asked me if I would do his album cover. At that time I hadn't done an album cover for quite a while, so I was happy to do it.

"Paul and I met up and I had an idea I wanted to put to him. The idea came from another album cover that I was going to do but never happened and that was the concept of a child holding a photograph of themselves as an adult. And then there was the idea of including 'favourite things'. I asked Paul to give me a list of his favourite things.

"Paul gave me a long list. Some of them we changed for the album cover. The footballer Paul gave me was Peter Osgood but along the line we changed it to Georgie Best. The thinking behind that was that Georgie Best was more of a cult figure and Osgood wasn't. But Osgood is now, and if we were doing it now then it would be Osgood we'd use. But back then the classic football icon was Georgie Best.

"As I read through Paul's list it made sense to me. It was a list that meant things to Paul. There's a picture of his Mum Ann and Dad John and there's a young Paul and his sister Nicky. There's the Stax Records logo and two miniature models of members of the Small Faces. Paul gave me the models, for some reason he only brought me the two, and we took photographs of them. The Mod on the scooter was of obvious interest to Paul and worked as a symbol of something that's been important to him.

"There's the John William Waterhouse painting of 'The Lady of Shalott' and this being on the list surprised me at first. I was also quite surprised that Paul wanted a poem by Wilfred Owen. After Paul explained to me why he wanted it on the cover it made perfect sense.

"The green bus represented something from his past. I presume it took him from Woking to somewhere. I remember Green Line buses – they were very glamorous and more expensive. When I went to art school in Gravesend, I could only use the normal bus but there was a Green Line bus that was kind of an express but cost more money and I couldn't afford it.

"I had a collection of postcards and that was where the image of London came from. It seemed suitably kind of nostalgic. Paul gave me the Empire State Building ticket, I think he must have been up there at some point. John Lennon was an obvious reference, same with Aretha Franklin and so was the Eiffel Tower, also something from Paul's past.

"The five-pointed star, heart and target are motifs that I have used before. The target worked on the album because that had become the Mod symbol. Paul chose the number eight. I think the Wellers lived at number eight Stanley Road. I sourced the number eight from an old circus poster.

"The only thing I added was the bus ticket. It was an in-joke about collages. When I first knew what a collage was, I discovered Curtis Fritters and he always included a bus ticket in his work.

"I painted the picture of Paul as a child in front of the Stanley Road sign. I had a very indistinct photograph to work from. I invented the bricks and Stanley Road sign. There was an idea that there'd be a limited edition LP and then there'd be a limited edition CD and the painting of Paul holding his adult self would be raised slightly above the surrounding art work. I don't know if those were ever done in the end.

"And on the back cover, Paul wanted some very simple kind of faint water colours. I did that using the basic colours then wrote the song titles onto it.

"The album cover is a piece of art work. Nowadays it's conceivable that I would do something like this on a computer, but I can't use a computer. I cut things out and arrange the pieces around. I have the original artwork somewhere.

"For something like this I use a nine-square grid. I use that quite often. There's a centre piece and then squares around it. Each square is then broken and made different and I look for a balance. The red on the star is far enough away from the red in the target and the design comes together.

"It was Paul's suggestion to use a certain kind of lettering for his name. I had a collection of Victorian board games and they had the lettering I used on the album. It's not the same as the scrabble pieces as some people think. The scrabble letters have a number in the corner so when people rip me off sometimes they use scrabble but it's not what I used."

The musicians on *Stanley Road* included Steve White, Steve Cradock, Yolanda Charles, Noel Gallagher, Stevie Winwood, Mick Talbot, Carleen Anderson, Helen Turner, Brendan Lynch, Dr Robert, Joy Hawley, David Liddle, Mark Nelson and Constantine Wier.

In Paul's thank yous to the various people that helped to make the album possible, he added "…and my audience for seeing it through good and bad, thank you. PW."

In his dedication he wrote, "I dedicate this record to my Mum and Dad, who've always been there for me and always encouraged me to follow this path. It's also for my wife Dee and our beautiful children and loves of our lives, Nat and Leah, so many things I'd like to say to all of you, so I'll just say I love you."

Paul got the title for 'The Changing Man' after hearing his daughter Leah refer to one of her dolls as, 'The changing man'. Not that any of the lyrics in the song indicate this. Instead, the opening line, "Is happiness real, or am I so jaded? I can't see or feel, like a man been tainted," is pretty bleak. The song also includes one of Paul's deepest lyrics, "And the more I see, the more I know, the more I know, the less I understand." A curio-ponder indeed!

Steve White, Steve Cradock, Carleen Anderson and Dr Robert give a strong performance and manage to create a Small Faces sound and feel – after all, the miniatures of Ronnie Lane and Steve Marriott feature in the sleeve design. Paul delivers a blistering guitar solo that gives the song a strong edge.

'The Changing Man/I'd Rather Go Blind/It's A New Day, Baby/I Didn't Mean To Hurt You (Live)' was released in April 1995. The promotional video featured Paul strumming his Gibson guitar in a very Steve Marriott way and going through a few costume changes including a very stylish tan coloured leather jacket. The video is packed with pop art and mod iconography reminiscent of the *Stanley Road* sleeve design.

The lyric in 'Porcelain Gods', "Too much will kill you, too little ain't enough," is not a drug reference, as many assumed at the time, but about success and fame. "More empty words" and "Beware false prophets, take a stand," is Paul having a dig at the "Prophets, seers and sages" from across the centuries and he revealed the lyric also related to Dee C Lee.

'Porcelain Gods' is a song that captures the ambiance of the Manor Studios. Paul's feeling for the studio is cemented in every note. He sings, "How disappointed I was, to turn out after all, just like a porcelain god, that shatters when it falls," so sweetly and so soulfully. It's a blinder of a song.

'I Walk On Gilded Splinters' was written by Mac Rebennack, better known as Dr John, and appeared on his debut album *Gris-Gris* in 1968. Cher recorded the song in 1969 and Humble Pie did a version in 1971.

Noel Gallagher joins Paul's band to add some additional acoustic guitar and Mark Nelson plays bass, while Constantine Weir provides the extra vocal part. Paul's version captures a deep soulfulness which pushes its way to the front of the queue. It's easy to understand why Paul chose it to cover.

"I was in Manor Studios when Paul was doing *Stanley Road*," says Noel. " I was only there for a couple of nights, but the others were there for months on end. They obviously felt some kind of magic there. For me, I've gotta say it was just another studio. But

I guess if you're in a studio and you're recording what you feel is your best work, you're gonna feel something for that studio. It was a good studio and I had a good time down there doing 'I Walk On Gilded Splinters'. And it was great being around hearing the coming together of *Stanley Road* months before anyone else and, thinking wow it's gone somewhere else again since *Wild Wood*. It was like a real privilege.

"But all those old residential studios are gone now; it's a whole part of the music making culture that's died. All those great bands that we were brought up loving like Led Zeppelin would all stay in those studios and spend four months recording those albums. But nowadays it's just a matter of record something and crack on sharpish, and I think it affects the quality of the music. And Paul's from the Seventies so it's in his DNA to be like those bands and approach recording in that way too.

"I was mixing a live Oasis concert using the Rolling Stones' mobile studio, which at that time was parked up at the Manor House Studios. I needed to go down and oversee some mix and was told Paul was booked into the Manor House at the same time. I thought great, it couldn't be any better. I'm there doing my stuff and he's doing his and we're hanging out and then Paul asks if I wanted to play on a track, to which I was like, 'Yeah, do I.' Paul then says, 'Do you know Dr. John?' and I say, 'Of course.' But I'd never fucking heard of Dr. John. Then Paul asks if I knew the 'Gilded Splinters' song and I say, 'Of course,' while thinking I don't have a fucking clue what he's going on about. This was in the days before you could quickly check your iPhone, look the song up and come back with, 'Yeah, what a belter, one of my favourites.'

"Luckily, the song was all in E but I'm saying to Paul, 'So what do you want me to play?' and all the time I'm trying not to let it be known that I've never heard of the geezer or the fucking track. Anyway, Paul tells me to just play whatever I want. But I'm going, 'Yeah but what sort of thing do you want me to play?' I've still no idea what kind of a song 'Gilded Splinters' is. I ask if he wants something a bit flowery and he tells me that it doesn't matter because it's all in the same key anyway. So now I'm thinking, cool, got it and so then it was just a case of playing something."

Some piano and sparse strikes on the ride cymbal provide the introduction to one of Paul's best loved songs, 'You Do Something To Me'. It's undoubtedly one of Paul's classic ballads, gentle and full of emotion. Paul plays piano and the guitars, including the guitar solo, Yolanda Charles plays bass and Helen Turner the organ. One of Paul's most memorable lyrics is contained in the song, "Dancing through the fire just to catch a flame, just to get close to, just close enough, to tell you that you do something to me, something deep inside."

'You Do Something To Me/My Whole World Is Falling Down/A Year Late/Woodcutter's Son (Live)' hit the charts in July and became one of the anthems for the Britpop generation.

On 'Woodcutter's Son', Steve Winwood was invited to play on the first of two tracks on *Stanley Road*. Birmingham-born Winwood had played in the Spencer Davis Group, Traffic and Blind Faith, so Paul was very familiar with his musicianship and lasting contribution to rock music. The song itself is influenced by Sixties rock and R&B. Dave Liddle, who'd been working with Paul since The Jam days, plays slide-guitar on the track.

"Steve Winwood came down and played on a couple of tracks," recalls Brendan Lynch. "I hadn't met him before so that was great. He was very easy to work with. It was a matter of him turning up and asking us what we wanted him to do. I think he'd heard a demo of a couple of songs but that was all. We told him to play the piano live with the band and that really surprised him. I think he thought he'd just be doing a couple of overdubs."

Steve Cradock has his own recollections. "I remember watching Paul teaching Stevie Winwood how to play a piano part and thinking this is wrong, Paul should be playing it. It was a no-brainer to me. I told Paul too but he replied, 'No, I like what Stevie's doing with it.'

Helen Turner returns to play organ and Dr Robert the bass on track six, 'Time Passes'. Again, the piano intro is supplied by Paul and it sets this gentle song on its way. Paul delivers his words with meaning, words that tell a story of departure, connection and separation.

Paul wrote 'Time Passes' during the 1994 Christmas break. He made his first demo on January 2 1995 at the Manor. Apart from one line in the middle eight, he considered the song to be almost 'perfect'.

'Stanley Road', with its psychedelic intro, shuffles and grooves along at medium pace. It has a real Sixties feel that mirrors the decade where Paul grew up in the family home in Stanley Road and learned to play guitar in his bedroom while listening to Beatles records and wrote some of the earliest Jam songs and dreamed his dreams, "A dream to meet, going on and on."

Alongside Yolanda Charles on bass and Helen Turner on organ, Brendan Lynch plays some mini-Moog.

'Broken Stones' b/w 'Steam', was released as a single in September. Mick Talbot was invited to play Fender Rhodes on 'Broken Stones' and Brendan Lynch accordion. "It was really nice getting 'Wings Of Speed' recorded and after it we all went for a drink and I thought that was it, time to wind down," says Mick Talbot.

"We went and had a meal, sat around talking about the old times and it was a really nice atmosphere. It was quite late into the night and we'd downed tools a good few hours, and then, out of the blue, Paul says to Brendan, 'I forgot, I wanted Mick to play on 'Broken Stones' too'. I was on the verge of thinking I was ready for bed but we ended going back into the studio and recording the track there and then.

"Just before I played my part, I remember Paul played me what he had. He'd already laid down some Wurlitzer and after hearing the first two bars I turned to him and said, 'This sounds like the track 'If I'm On The Late Side' by The Faces." "Trust you!" Paul replied.

"But it was. The backbeat was similar to something that Kenney

Jones played. It's also like the 'Tin Soldier' beat. I really liked 'Broken Stones'. It had an early Atlantic Records feel about it. At the centre, you had Paul on the Wurlitzer. I think he laid down some Hammond too, Marco (Nelson) played a James Jameson style bass line, which worked with what Steve (White) was playing and Brendan played on it too. It was soulful. Both Paul and Brendan said they were keen not to have any guitar playing on it. It sort of went against the rules but it worked. It was similar to the way Gil Scot Heron played alongside Brian Jackson because of the way Paul had put the song together and it was so solid, it freed me up to be more decorative. It was beautiful and it clicked and it had a certain type of charm to it. The fact that 'Broken Stones' hasn't got any guitar or horns made it really work.

"The Manor was like a whole other character in the scenario of what Paul was producing around that time. It brought out a lot of good things in Paul and the people he was working with at that time."

Paul's Hammond organ works well with White's rimshots to give the song a soulful feel. The track is a great example of British blue-eyed soul.

"I played accordion over the solo on 'Broken Stones'," says Brendan. "I took it into the studio one day and Paul suggested that I play it on the song. I tried something and it came out sounding a bit like a harmonica and it worked. It was an amazing feeling being asked by Paul to play on songs, I did feel like part of the band. It was really a matter of everyone doing what they could to make the record sound great."

'Out Of The Sinking' was Paul's attempt at writing a great English Mod love song. The lyric, "across the water," alluded to London's River Thames, a sight very familiar to Paul. 'Out Of The Sinking/Sexy Sadie' was the first single released from Stanley Road.

'Pink On White Walls' is the second song that features Steve Winwood. He plays the piano part while Paul takes care of the Hammond. It's a highly interesting track with evocative lyrics, "The sun shone pink on white walls and the trees stood so tall, defiant, proud and loud."

'Whirlpool's End' begins with an acoustic guitar before lurching into high gear. Paul and Steve Cradock join forces to deliver the "sha la la" backing vocals, a great favourite at live shows.

'Whirlpools End' is an exciting, solid, straightforward track with hard-hitting lyrics, "A bomb exploding in another town, children choking on a poisoned cloud."

'Wings Of Speed' sees Paul describing how the painting 'The Lady of Shalott' by John Waterhouse moved him – "In dreams, she floats on a stream, with Jesus at the helm, the water reeds that her boat along the way, as she comes to me." Mick Talbot appears for a second time on the album, playing pipe and Hammond organ. There's a cello too, provided by Joy Hawley, and Paul delivers the words whilst playing piano.

"Paul invited me down to Nomis Studios saying he wanted me to play on some new songs," says Mick. "At the time, Helen Turner was in the band which I pointed out to him but he said there was loads to do and wanted me involved. I ended up playing on 'Woodcutters Son' and 'Pink On White Walls'. The intention was that we'd then all go down to the Manor Studios and cut them properly. In the end, Stevie Winwood played on them and those versions made the album.

"However, there was another song he wanted me to play on and that was 'Wings Of Speed'. I went down the Manor and when I got there I was taken to a church that was just down the road. The crew had run cables all the way from the studios to the church and this meant the band could all play at the same time. There was an old reed organ in the church and that's what Paul wanted me to play. I remember it was very cold in the church and I felt so glad I'd taken my duffle coat. Dave Liddle was with me and, bless him, went and got a little portable heater and spent the session running around me, topping me up with the heat.

"It was a challenge playing that organ but it was an instrument that was unique to that track. Getting the best for the track was the priority, just like the ethos we'd had in the Style Council.

"It had been Paul's idea to use the church organ – maybe he'd spotted the church when he'd been out for a walk. I recall him saying the song had a hymn-like quality to it, so I suppose using the church organ made sense. I also think Paul liked the challenge of pulling it off, so all the band played together at the same time."

Carleen Anderson provides a stunning vocal part – "Fly on wings of speed that will bring you home to me, I'll never be free from the darkness I see, as I wait for your smile."

In 2010 a woman named Isabell Crundwell was cremated in a small chapel in Kent. She died far too young, just 41, under tragic circumstances. 'Wings Of Speed' was played as the curtains closed on her coffin and the mourners wept. Isabell had been a Paul Weller fan since her childhood. She would've loved the idea of the song being used to conclude her funeral service.

TRACKLISTING

1. The Changing Man
2. Porcelain Gods
3. I Walk On Gilded Splinters
4. You Do Something To Me
5. Woodcutters Son
6. Time Passes
7. Stanley Road
8. Broken Stones
9. Out Of The Sinking
10. Pink On White Walls
11. Whirlpools' End
12. Wings Of Speed

Wild Wood

'I write this now while I'm in control'

I n 1993, Paul was featured on the front cover of the *NME* alongside the headline, 'My Regeneration'. It had been seven years since he last appeared on the cover of a music paper. Paul was clearly back in favour.

By 1993, Paul was also back riding a scooter. Photographs by Lawrence Watson showed Paul on a scooter while giving lifts to his son Natty and another young boy. In 'Wild Wood's inner-sleeve, Paul gripped the handlebars of his white Lambretta while Steve White and Marco Nelson rode pillion.

Italian influences have given so much to the British Mod scene – shirts, shoes and scooters. The Lambretta and Vespa were adopted by the original Mods as their preferred choice of transport. Their clean, smooth shapes reflected the Mods ambitions and intentions. Paul got his first scooter when he was still a teenager and years later he wrote 'Lambretta Love Poem', "Gleaming bright/white SX."

This was the year that Paul's solo career really started to take off, especially after he returned to play Glastonbury.

Paul had known Eddie Piller since the days of The Jam and he was very supportive of bands linked to Piller's Acid Jazz record label. One band from the Acid Jazz stable was Mother Earth and in 1993, Paul sang backing vocals on Mother's Earth's 'Mr Freedom' that was released in April.

"I first met Paul at one of our gigs in Subterranea around late 1992," says Mother Earth guitarist and singer Matt Deighton. "He came backstage and ponced some cigarettes off us. After that we would see each other around places like Denmark Street, where people like myself and the other Acid Jazz lot would hang about. There was a woman called Ann-Marie who worked at Acid Jazz Records and she was good friends with Dee C Lee, so they'd be out and about and

Paul would come and see them and we'd all meet and mix.

"Paul then came and performed on a Mother Earth track, 'Mr Freedom'. I think we got him because he was visiting the studio one day. He was quite in with the Acid Jazz crowd and would often visit the label's headquarters. The studio where the Acid Jazz artists also recorded had a mixing desk that had once been in Solid Bond Studios. I think the day Paul came into the studio we were trying to record 'Autumn Stone' by the Small Faces. Someone must have just asked Paul if he'd be willing to sing some backing vocals on 'Mr Freedom' and he said yes. It was great. I had a lot of respect for Paul even though I wasn't a big Jam fan and I told him that. However, a track I really liked by The Jam was 'Shopping'.

"Paul gave me a birthday present once – performing on my *Common Good* album. I'd been touring with Paul and his band which included Steve White. I asked Steve if he'd play some tracks on my solo album and he agreed. There were others like Marco Nelson and Mick Talbot who also played on that album. Paul said to me, 'I've got you a birthday present and that's a couple of days recording down at Black Barn.' It was a really nice thing for him to do and then he came and played guitar on some of the album's tracks. He also played a Mellotron on a track too. I remember on one of the days when Paul was recording he was also being photographed by Tom Sheehan. I think he was doing an interview for *Q*."

Matt Deighton would also work again with Paul and this time with a Small Faces member. "Acid Jazz organised some event that involved a load of their acts getting filmed," says Matt. "Bands like Corduroy were there. Kenney Jones of the Small Faces' son worked as a tape operator at Acid Jazz Records, he was only young at the time, but somehow I got invited to do some recording with Kenney. He'd phoned me and asked if I could help out recording a version of 'Rolling Over' and that Paul Weller had also agreed. What we did got filmed, but it's never been on general release. This was around 1995."

In July, Paul gave one of his songs, 'The Loved' to *The Big Issue* to be used as a flexidisc. It was given away free in the 35th edition of the magazine. In the first week of the issue's publication over 80,000 copies were sold. Paul had been holding onto this song since 1991, although in its earliest demos it had flutes and vibes on it.

Wild Wood was released on September 6, 1993 on Go Discs. It had been recorded at the Manor Studios. "The manor was a very special place, with magical qualities about it. It was in the wood and the stone-everything," says Paul. He always spoke of the Manor Studios with affection. It was the right place for him to be during that period. In the sleeve notes Paul wrote, "A big thankyou to all at the Manor for their kindness and help, we had a great time."

Wild Wood was mixed at NOMIS, which is Simon spelt backwards as the owner was Wham manager Simon Napier-Bell. It was produced by Paul Weller and Brendan Lynch and reached No 2 in the charts.

"The process of working in the studio with Paul varies," says Brendan. "Sometimes, Paul will come into the studio with a song that is already pretty complete, as in he will have all the production ideas in his head. Other times he would turn up with an acoustic version of a song and we would work out the other parts from there.

"With the *Wild Wood* album we did about four demos for each track. Usually the first demo would be a matter of quickly getting the song down and bung in loads of ideas and not think about it too much. This might take 40 minutes and would be a very rough mix. The second demo would be a bit more refined. The third one would be adding other instruments like percussion and the fourth demo would be pretty much what was going to be recorded. Everything was done live and by the time of recording everybody involved knew exactly what they would be playing. This approach began on the *Wild Wood* album and continued after that."

The musicians who helped Paul make *Wild Wood* included Steve White, Marco Nelson, Yolanda Charles, Jacko Peake, Brendan Lynch, Helen Turner, Robert Howard, Dee C Lee, Max Beesley, Simon Fowler,

Mick Talbot and David Liddle.

"To our saucepans and the universal," wrote Paul in the sleeve notes.

Paul said he got the riff for 'Sunflower' while practicing a guitar scale. He wondered what it would sound like if he simply reversed it. He tried, liked what he heard and 'Sunflower' was born.

Ann Weller: "When Paul lived at Limberlost, he would look out of his windows and see the fields filled with sunflowers. That was Paul's inspiration for this particular song."

"I write this now while I'm in control." At this time in his life, Paul was writing prolifically. The songs were flowing from him and it can't be denied that throughout the Nineties Paul wrote some of his greatest songs.

'Sunflower' was recorded in April. Paul played Mellotron and Moog and Jacko Peake the flute. In July 1993 'Sunflower/Bull-Rush-Magic Bus' was the first single to be released from *Wild Wood*.

'Can You Heal Us (Holy Man)' starts with a piano played by Paul. He also plays guitars, Hammond, Mellotron and bass. White plays drums while the percussion is shared between Paul, Brendan Lynch and Max Heyes. Martin 'Max' Heyes had been working closely with Brendan Lynch as a studio engineer for some years. He was one of the Lynch Mob and would work on several of Paul's albums throughout the Nineties. The song is a fine example of funk rock, Weller style.

"'Wild Wood' was my attempt at trying to write a very modern day folk song," says Paul. The entire track is constructed around Paul's vocal contribution where he reminisces about the "magical memories" of places he frequented in his youth.

'Wild Wood' was also the name of a house that Paul would frequently drive past when travelling back and forth from London on the A3. The lyrics originated from Paul's thoughts about elements of Dee C Lee and Paolo Hewitt's childhood experiences. Paul played it solo in public for the first time on the *Highlights and Hang Ups* documentary. At the time of filming, Paul had just written the song. 'Wild Wood/Ends Of The Earth' was also a single and was released in August.

'Wild Wood', a particular favourite of the Smiths' Andy Rourke, included Helen Turner on organ, Marco Nelson on bass and Brendan Lynch on Mellotron. White played the simple but effective drum part, which was all the song required. While Paul's acoustic guitar and vocals carry the song, it's the simplicity of 'Wild Wood' that gives it a magical charm.

"On the 'Wild Wood' track I played Mellotron which is a keyboard and one of the first kind of samplers," says Brendan. "Each key has a tape loop that plays a sound you've taped. It can provide other-worldly sounds and it's a really interesting instrument. The idea of using a Mellotron came about after we'd been down the pub. It was when we got back to the studio I said to Martin 'Max' Heyes, who was engineering, that I wanted to get down some ideas I had. I recorded three Mellotron parts and doing so I remember John Weller coming into the studio and saying, 'Don't break the tapes Bren.'

"The following morning, we played back what had been recorded and it actually sounded great and ended up staying on the part at the end of the song. The best thing about working with Paul is that if someone suggests an idea or wants to try something, he would always let them have a go. This helps provide a really creative atmosphere."

Next up is a short instrumental piece simply called 'Instrumental (Part 1)'. It's a jazzy funk piece that could have come out of the Paul Weller Movement period.

'All The Pictures On The Wall' then fades in with White's funky drumming that persists throughout the track keeping everything upbeat and breezy. All other instruments on this song were played by Paul. He got the idea for the song after visiting a pub where the landlady explained that the pictures on the wall were of her ex-husband.

"The clock hands ticking on the wall are just reminders of it all." The song is about a relationship that has lost its lustre and what were once good memories are now nothing but dim recollections of a time that was "full of love." It was at Glastonbury in 1993 that Paul also told Steve White that his marriage to Dee C Lee was falling apart.

On 'Has My Fire Really Gone Out?' Paul takes a swipe at his critics. "Put an end to all your doubts, has my fire really, really gone out?". *Wild Wood* is a bridge between Paul's Style Council and Paul Weller Movement phase, and an enticing horizon. Some members of the music press simply needed to understand that. Beginning with a drum roll introduction, the song sees Paul playing a Wurlitzer, Robert Howard on guitar and Marco Nelson and Max Beesley on backing vocals in the choruses.

Before 'Country' starts, there's a short interlude with sound effects that could have been lifted from *The Dark Side Of The Moon*. But then an acoustic guitar casually drifts in and 'Country' slows everything down. Paul and Robert Howard take care of the guitars and Brendan Lynch the stylophone and that's all the instrumentation needed to support Paul's lyrics, "I know a place not far from here, where's life's sweet perfume fills the air."

'Instrumental Two' comes and goes in 50 seconds and then it's straight into '5th Season' which finds Mick Talbot playing Hammond and Dee C Lee on backing vocals.

Talbot: "Paul sent me a cassette of '5th Season' and asked if I could play some Hammond on it. I think we cut it live. Paul sang his vocal live whilst he played piano. I think Dave Liddle played guitar on it and Dee added her part at a later date. I believe '5th Season' was one of the last tracks to be recorded for *Wild Wood*.

"It was nice to do and nice to catch up with people. There was Marco Nelson and Steve White and with Paul they had a real good thing going on as a trio. One of my favourite live performances, as that line up, was on the *White Room* show when they performed 'Sunflower'. I thought it was really powerful and everything that was needed was there. The song felt like it was bigger than the sum of all its parts.

"We recorded '5th Season' at the Manor Studios and that was a really great place. It was already Paul and his band's little kingdom. By the time I went down to record the track, they'd been there for a while and it was coming towards the end of the sessions, so they were all very happy – a kind of end of term spirit. They literally showed me around their manor! I remember thinking it was like a little holiday camp.

"Because I already had a demo of the song and knew what I was meant to be playing, I didn't think recording the song would take that long. But they had all gotten into that recording-the-song-will-be-as-long-as-it-takes mood. I'd been used to being a session musician and working in studios where everyone was conscious that the meter was running, but in the Manor Studios it wasn't like that at all. They even had catering there and it seemed to me that every five minutes a gong was being banged and we'd all down tools and go and get something to eat. I would be like, 'But I thought we were about to lay down a take' and Paul would be like, 'Yeah, but we're going for dinner.' In the end, I stayed with them at the Manor from Monday to Friday. It was a laugh and a very sociable time.

"Getting to hear *Wild Wood* before it got released was great and I remember Paul asking me what I thought of it. I told him it was going to be a really important album for him."

Paul is forever the wordsmith – "The serpent tangles in the lions claw, a cloud of darkness hangs over all as fires soar in search of sky. So blow embers like fire flies, hoping love is where they'll lie and the season change us too." '5th Season' is a fine example of quality blue-eyed soul with the piano and organ part creating that feel. There's also an additional guitar performed by Dave Liddle, Paul's guitar technician of many years.

'The Weaver' b/w 'This Is No Time/Another New Day/Ohio (Live)' was released as the third single from *Wild Wood* in October 1993. It was the first song of Paul's on which Simon Fowler and Steve Cradock of Ocean Colour Scene were included. For Steve Cradock, this was the start of a journey and dream he couldn't have imagined when he first went knocking on the doors of Solid Bond Studios a few years earlier.

"I worked on 'The Weaver' before Paul had asked me to join the band," says Steve. "I was staying with a girlfriend who lived in London at the time and Paul phoned up saying he wanted to play me something and could I go around to his place. I was so nervous, properly shitting myself, so I swallowed a load of dope. By the time I got to Paul's front door it was really hitting me, sweaty hands and everything.

"Paul opened the door and I stepped inside and then I see Dee C Lee and by this point I'm tripping. I'm thinking, shit it's Paul Weller and Dee C Lee. Paul then showed me up to one of the bedrooms and he gave me a Small Faces album. Within minutes I'm smoking something and in his room he had this lovely plush carpet and I drop a bit of what I'm smoking on it and burned it. He was fine about it though.

"But while all this was going on, Paul played me a demo of 'The Weaver' and that version had a 'gob iron' (harmonica) on it. It just sounded amazing to me. I said he should just release it as it was. But Paul said he wanted me to play some guitar on it and he wanted me to go down to the Manor Studios to do that.

"The Manor Studios was incredible. It had a lovely set up with a bohemian feel to it. There was a beautiful lake there and Paul's scooter was there. And what was nice, no sense of any clock watching. The studio itself was like a temple and when you went in there you kinda got cloaked by its atmosphere. It was bit like how Mani describes being in the Stone Roses in the early days. He said it was like the four of them were inside an egg. I think the Manor definitely contributed to the vibe of what we were doing.

"There was also a grand piano and a big snooker table there and people would be playing them whilst someone put on Traffic and Joe Cocker albums. There was always great music being played. And then we'd sit around a huge fire. I was like, 'Fuck, this is the way to record albums.'"

Thirty-four seconds of 'Instrumental One (part 2)' continues in the rich vein of acid jazziness – rare groove, Seventies funk and soul before allowing 'Foot Of The Mountain' to join the proceedings. The folky feel of Paul's acoustic guitar and vocals brings to mind artists like Neil Young and Nick Drake. "At the foot of the mountain, such a long way to climb, how will I ever get up there, though I know I must try." Paul manages to capture all the earthiness of folk music and the Nineties in one song.

'Shadow Of The Sun' greets Dee C Lee again with some extra vocals as Paul sings, "I plan to have it all while I'm still young, and chase the fields across my dreams, in the shadow of the sun." With the addition of the instrumental section at the end of the song, this track is the longest on *Wild Wood*.

'Holy Man (reprise)' is a short burst of funk of which Curtis Mayfield would've approved with a heavy bass line supplied by Marco Nelson.

Paul got the idea for 'Moon On Your Pyjamas' as a result of the effects of the mobile over his son Nathaniel's (Natty) bed. The lyrics are soft and pure and revealing, "Was that a shooting star I saw? It's rare for me to make a wish at all."

It's only right that Dee C Lee contributes to this song as it's very personal to her family. 'Moon On Your Pyjamas' wouldn't have been out of place on a Style Council album. Max Beesley plays Wurlitzer on the track. Max was around during the time of the Paul Weller Movement and he also played with the Brand New Heavies and Incognito before carving out a successful career as an actor.

'Hung Up' b/w 'Foot Of The Mountain (Live)/The Loved/Kosmos' was released as a single in spring 1994. It was the only song on *Wild Wood* that wasn't recorded at the Manor. Instead it was recorded in June 1993 at one of The Jam's old haunts, Nomis Studios. 'Hung Up' was also the only track that Marco Nelson didn't play bass – he was replaced by Yolanda Charles.

The three-piece band of Paul, Steve White and Yolanda Charles is all that this two-and-a-half minute song needs – "Hidden in the back seat of my mind, some place I can't remember where, I found it just by coincidence an' now I'm all hung up again.'

TRACKLISTING

1. Sunflower
2. Can You Heal Us (Holy Man)
3. Wild Wood
4. Instrumental One (part 1)
5. All the Pictures On The Wall
6. Has My Fire Really Gone Out?
7. Country
8. Instrumental Two
9. 5th Season
10. The Weaver
11. Instrumental One (part 2)
12. Foot of the Mountain
13. Shadow of the Sun
14. Holy Man (reprise)
15. Moon On Your Pyjamas
16. Hung Up

Paul Weller

'Into tomorrow'

One evening in the summer of 1990 at Ronnie Scott's while watching Cuban band Irakere, Paul asked Steve White if he'd help him record some demos at Solid Bond Studios. "As long as there are no bloody drum machines," replied Steve. Having the ever faithful White beside him was just the injection that Paul needed to move forward.

On November 1, 1990, Paul performed his debut gig as a solo artist to an intrigued audience at Dingwalls in London. No one could have predicted that he'd insert a mixture of Jam and Style Council songs into the set.

For the remainder of the year, Paul played shows in Italy, Germany, Leicester University and finally on December 5 he played at the Town and Country Club in London.

Once Paul's new set-up was match fit, he played a handful of low key gigs in venues like London's Subterranea. Baz and Dan, two long-time Weller fans, stood in the crowd waiting for Paul to come on. From out of the darkness, John Weller sidled up to them. John, who didn't know the two fans from Adam, did most of the talking. He said to them that the gigs Paul was doing were going to make or break him. And then he disappeared leaving the two fans bewildered but eagerly awaiting to hear Paul's new songs.

"Those early Paul Weller Movement gigs weren't very well attended at all," recalls Ann Weller. "Sometimes there would only be me and Nicky and about 40 other people. John (Weller) used to go and chat with people in the audience asking them what they thought. He was always looking for feedback.

"I especially remember the gig at Subterranea because that was a brilliant show and things really went off after that. Up until that point it had been a strange period for Paul. Nobody really knew what was happening in that time between the last Style Council album and getting dropped by Polydor. It was good for Paul when Andy Mac of Go Discs stepped in but for a while it was like being in the wilderness. In many ways that period was a bit of a blur."

Nicky Weller: 'I loved 'Into Tomorrow' and I had so much fun on that tour. It was Russell Reader that designed the stage set. It was our idea to add the rainbow theme which we placed around the drum kit and keyboards."

Next up, Paul and his band flew to Japan to play some gigs to what turned out to be hugely welcoming and appreciative audiences. It was just the boost that Paul needed. "Those gigs were me trying to find my feet," says Paul. "And I found direction again."

Following a second visit to Japan, Paul went to the States. Whilst playing a gig in the Greek Theatre in LA, Ian McLagan joined Paul on stage. It was the first time Paul had shared a stage with a Small Faces' band member. It wouldn't be his last.

Back in Solid Bond Studios, Paul recorded a version of The Beatles' 'Don't Let Me Down'. It was his contribution to an Oxfam campaign to help victims of famine in Cambodia. The song appeared on the 1991 album *Revolution No.9 – A Tribute to The Beatles in Aid of Cambodia*.

In early May, 1991, Paul, with the Movement, appeared on the Jonathan Ross Show. Ross introduced Paul as, "One of Britain's finest pop and rock merchants," and then the band performed 'Into Tomorrow'. When the song finished, Paul put down his battered looking Fender Stratocaster and headed for his seat, ready to be interviewed by Ross.

Wearing a black tee-shirt with a chain and crucifix hanging around his neck, black trousers and some stylish black and white loafers, Paul was enthusiastically welcomed by the studio audience.

Ross began by asking Paul about his regular performances at benefit concerts and on charity records and referred to Live Aid's 'Do They Know Its Christmas'. Ross focused on the way some of the other artists arrived for the studio session in helicopters and limousines while Paul walked up to the studio carrying an umbrella.

"I'm just not a person who's into helicopters and yachts," Paul replied. "I don't do it to be street-cred, that's just nonsense."

It was abundantly clear from the audience's reaction that Paul had their respect. Ross then introduced the topic of punk and fashion and asked Paul if he was obsessed by style. "No, I'm not style-obsessed, I'm just into what I'm into. I don't make a big thing of it. To me it's like a religion, a code. It gives something to my life. I'm still a Mod, I'll always be a Mod. You can bury me a Mod."

Ross then asked Paul what his plans were for the Paul Weller Movement and it was obvious that Paul honestly didn't know. He talked about the small venues the band had been playing and said his band was, "a mixture of the two things," referring to The Jam and The Style Council.

Ross then talked about a Clash song being used in a jeans advert at the time and asked how Paul would feel if a Jam song was used in the same way. Paul said it wasn't something he'd like to see happen. Then Ross quizzed Paul about reforming The Jam. "Definitely not," was Paul's predictable reply.

Paul looked genuinely sad when he told Ross his band would close the show with 'Tin Soldier', saying that Steve Marriott had died only a couple weeks earlier. On Saturday April 20, 1991, Paul had walked onto the stage at Brixton Academy and informed the audience that Steve Marriott had just died, before launching into 'Tin Soldier'.

This national TV exposure was timely for Paul and his new outfit. The interview went down well and the public could see that Paul was back and armed with some new material. The British public was primed for Paul's return.

In the summer of 1992, Paul signed a contract with Go! Discs. He had already signed an agreement with Japanese label Pony Canyon that resulted in *Paul Weller* being released in Japan six months earlier than in the UK. The album also got to No 1 in the Japanese charts.

Paul Weller was Paul's debut album as a solo musician. It was released in the UK on September 1, 1992. Paul dedicated the album to Nathaniel and Leah, adding, "Little arrows from our bow, may you soar high and always free."

The *Paul Weller* album was produced by Paul Weller and Brendan Lynch. The musicians that Paul employed on the album included Steve White, Jacko Peake, Carleen Anderson, Dr Robert, Camelle Hinds, Dee C. Lee and brother Marco (the admirable lord Marcus Nelson).

'Uh Huh Oh Yeh' contains a sample from Hot Rod Poppa by Marsha Hunt. Beginning with some phased guitar supported by brass stabs and some funky ghost beats, 'Uh Huh Oh Yeh' b/w 'Fly On The Wall' was released as a single in August 1992 and made the top twenty. The promotional video was mostly filmed in Woking, no surprise as the opening lyric was, "I took a trip down Boundary Lane, try an' find myself again." Paul also mentions, "A lazy bridge on a hot afternoon."

'Uh Huh Oh Yeh' is a song about Paul finding his way again. In many ways, this feel continues throughout the entire album. Paul makes no attempt to hide this fact, just like he never tried to conceal the difficult period he had been going through musically since the end of The Style Council and being without a record label. The song certainly contains echoes of The Style Council, but with something new added.

Paul was building on what he had and knew – "Dear reminders of who I am, the very roots upon which I stand." Woking, The Jam, The Style Council had contributed to, "All the dreams I had to dream, were really something, not make believe." Paul's new album was his first step into tomorrow.

Some gentle sounding organ and mellow rimshot introduce 'I Didn't Mean To Hurt You'. While Paul had been grappling with the uncertainty of his career, he had a supportive family and loyal friends behind him. He wasn't always easy to be around either. But in this song, Paul does sing about being grateful, "You built me up when

I was falling down." Those closest to him saw and felt the effects that the last two years had on Paul, both personally and professionally.

In the sleeve notes Paul wrote, "Thanks and love to Dee, my (fairly) long standing and (frequently) long suffering wife, who's stood by me when I've been way down and hateful with it, for putting up with all my many moods and still believing in me."

Paul continued, "Love and thanks to my father and manager, always there steadying the course and help chart new ones." He added, "My Mum and 'Juney' for helping out with the kids and my sis for doing likewise."

'Bull-Rush' begins with some swirling organ before Paul enters "In a momentary lapse of my condition." White again comes to the fore. This song, like the whole album, was tailor-made for his style of drumming. Backing vocals are supplied by Dr Robert and Dee C Lee and the influences of jazz, soul and funk are never far away, especially so in the soulfully psychedelic finale of flute, guitar and hand claps.

'Round And Round' is another Style Council-influenced number. It could quite easily have been snatched up by some soul songstress like Anita Baker. Dee C Lee and Camelle Hinds give the song a smooth edge. A Jacko Peake saxophone solo blends with Paul's jazz soaked guitar while White's drums embrace both with love and affection.

Dee C Lee is a natural fit for 'Remember How We Started', a song about a pair of lovers' first tentative steps into ecstasy, "Remember how we started on a summer's night, too young to know about what might." The song has a mellow groove that breaks into another swirling sax solo from Peake.

Just before 'Remember How We Started' ends, the song dips into a subtle Seventies' funk.

Enter one of Paul's most well-loved songs, 'Above The Clouds', "Autumn blew its leaves at me." The song unfolds like a rose kissed by the breeze whisked up by White's drumming and a hint of bongos. Paul patrols the grooves with a disciplined bass.

"Above the clouds, what's to be found, I have to wonder, will I be around?" 'Above The Clouds/Everything Has A Price To Pay' was the third and final single from *Paul Weller* but, surprisingly, just scraped into the top fifty.

The put-the-needle-on-the-record generation will recognise the beginning of the next track, 'Clues'. Paul's guitar dances with Peake's saxophone before White's snare arrives breathing dragon fire. In the sleeve notes, Paul said, "My eternal gratitude goes to White and Peake for their outstanding contributions, inspired playing and belief in my songs." 'Clues' is testament to that. The song relies on dynamics with ebbs and flows and lifts and dips and "stumbles and falls like a fool in love," and artfully sets the scene for the next track, 'Into Tomorrow'.

Released in May 1991 on Paul's own Solid Bond Productions funded label Freedom High, 'Into Tomorrow' was his first single release and only just made it into the top 40. But he was back where he belonged – up front and personal and in the public eye. The first recording sessions for 'Into Tomorrow' took place across two days in the last week of February 1991 after Paul and Brendan Lynch got snowed in. This provided them with time to work on the track.

"I first met Paul because I was doing some engineering with him on the last Style Council album *Modernism – A New Decade*," says Brendan. It was just after that period that Paul got me involved with some new demos that he wanted to do and we did them at Solid Bond. I saw and worked with Paul as he went through that transition period.

"Even though Paul was in a sort of limbo period, he was still constantly writing. Ideas were still flowing and then what really sparked everything off was 'Into Tomorrow'. That song was almost a template for what happened afterwards.

"We started recording the *Paul Weller* album in Solid Bond but during the making of it we moved to another studio, Black Barn, which years later he eventually bought.

"The 'Into Tomorrow' sessions came about because we got snowed in at Solid Bond. The weather was especially bad so we just stayed in the studio for a few days and worked on the songs. Being forced into that situation actually helped because the songs really came together. I think by the end of the sessions, Paul knew he had something really special.

"At the time, the Young Disciples were recording their album in one of the other rooms at Solid Bond. It was a nice feeling; everybody knew each other and were friendly and just generally it was a really good time."

It didn't go unnoticed to Paul's more savvy fans that 'Into Tomorrow' makes references to two legendary British Mod and soul clubs – the Mojo Club, "Your mojo will have no effect," and the Twisted Wheel, "Round and round like a twisted wheel." The Mojo Club was located in Sheffield and had been run by Peter Stringfellow. In the Sixties, bands like the Small Faces and The Who performed there. The Twisted Wheel was originally based in Brasenose Street, Manchester between 1963 and 1971.

'Amongst Butterflies' was written as a poem inspired by Paul's own memories of the Shah Jahan Mosque in Woking and the Muslim burial ground at Horsell Common, where the video for 'Funeral Pyre' was shot. Ann Weller had once worked at the Shah Jahan Mosque as a cleaner. "I had five cleaning jobs around Woking – posh people's homes!" laughs Ann.

"I also cleaned the Shah Jahan mosque on the Oriental Road and used to take Paul with me. Nicky had to come too and she was still in the pram then. On one of these visits, Paul managed to fall into the pond there. One of the women came running into the mosque shouting that he'd fallen in the pond, so I ran out to get him. The people that were responsible for the mosque were lovely. It was actually the first mosque to have been built in the UK."

The Shah Jahan Mosque was built in 1889, the first of its kind in Britain. The monument at Muslim burial ground marked the resting place of 12 Muslim soldiers who had died in WW1 and WW2. In 1968, the bodies of the soldiers were moved to Brookwood Cemetery because of damage caused by constant vandalism. The monument was restored in 1993. A teenage Paul carved his initials into the wall that surrounds the cemetery and you can still see 'PW' to this day.

All the songs on *Paul Weller* were written by Paul except 'Strange Museum', a Weller/Talbot composition. The song was based on a Tony Marchant play called *The Attractions*. It begins with a simple organ, "Come on in, admissions free, I won't refuse those that wanna see."

Mick Talbot: "Paul and I had written a track called 'Strange Museum' and it was included on Paul's debut solo album. However, I didn't play on that version. There was something missing on the demo and Paul wanted to meet up and do something with it. We went into the studio and he asked me to remind him of certain parts that had been done, but he'd forgotten and he said he wanted to do something with it for his album. I think the song came out of sessions from those last days when we were still the Style Council. At that time we were working on three albums. There was Dee's *Slam Slam*, we were doing one with Dr Robert and we had *Modernism – A New Decade*. Plus, I was starting to work with the Young Disciples. There was a lot going on and 'Strange Museum' was just a part of it.

"I think the *Paul Weller* album was a really underrated record. I think it's really good. It was an album that reflected what Paul was being influenced by at that time and leading up to it, that whole Acid Jazz thing was really getting going. Paul was always going up The Fez and he was hearing a lot of those Acid Jazz records and seeing what was going on.'

'Strange Museum' is a laid back breeze of a song with organ, guitar and rimshots all easing along gracefully. The presence of Brendan Lynch's direction and production techniques is obvious. This was a sign of things to come.

The penultimate track on Paul's debut solo album, 'Bitterness

Rising', starts with an acoustic twirl wrapping itself around Paul's vocals like Christmas paper before being joined by other instruments. Dee C Lee and Carleen Anderson wring out the backing vocals, "(It's just) bitterness rising, taking you off, bitterness rising, gotta shake those feelings off." The song oozes determination.

'Kosmos' winds up the album. Maybe writing the songs for *Paul Weller*, Paul found answers to questions that had been troubling him, "Dying to know, who am I? What am I? Wherever am I to go…?"

TRACKLISTING

1. Uh Huh Oh Yeh
2. I Didn't Mean To Hurt You
3. Bull-Rush
4. Round And Round
5. Remember How We Started
6. Above The Clouds
7. Clues
8. Into Tomorrow
9. Amongst Butterflies
10. The Strange Museum
11. Bitterness Rising
12. Kosmos

The Style Council Years

"*Paul is somebody who is constantly soaking stuff up. He will allow anyone and anything to influence him. I'm often embarrassed when people wrongly say that I introduced him to some forms of music that people couldn't hear in The Jam. Paul has got a far deeper knowledge of most kinds of music than I have and he has a much, much bigger collection of records and he's still an avid collector. I certainly can't keep up with him. He stays aware of very modern, cutting edge music and when he's on a roll, what's moving in him is strong and powerful.*

"*I often think back to my first year with Paul. The Style Council recorded many songs and I feel it was a pleasure and a privilege. What Paul provided me with was a lot of raw material and it was there for me to express myself.*

"*Another thing about Paul is that he is very encouraging. He's always got a lot of faith in other people's ability. Paul sees something in people, he's done that to me, and I've seen him do it to other people and it's when people are trying to do something that they're not sure about and are on the brink of giving up. That's when Paul will take the time to talk to you about it and he'll leave you having the belief in yourself that you can do it. He'll have great faith in your ability even if you haven't and that's a special thing to be around. Paul can be very nurturing like that.*

"*The godfathers of British R&B, people like Alexis Korner and Cyril Davis come to mind. It was people like them that encouraged and nurtured the players like Eric Clapton and Peter Green. I think Paul has been like that for the generation that he was a part of. And it comes naturally in him.*"

Mick Talbot

Modernism – A New Decade

"In my mind different voices call"

In 1988, just before the *Modernism* album experiment, the Style Council released a song via Acid Jazz Records called 'Like A Gun' under the alias of King Trueman (AKA Paul). The eight minute plus song was typical of Acid Jazz from that period – soulful organ, saxophone and vocals that could have been lifted from any of Funkadelic's albums.

The 12-inch vinyl included four different versions of the same song (the sax mix, the dub mix and the radio edit mix were the other versions). However, there were issues with Polydor surrounding the release and the record was blocked. According to Acid Jazz label owner, Eddie Piller, around 100 copies made it into the shops, 50 to DJ's, 20 to the press and about 30 white labels were also pressed. 'Like A Gun' is considered to be one of the rarest slices of Paul Weller vinyl and nowadays the record is a much sought-after collector's item.

At the beginning of 1989, the cultural landscape of the UK was changing. A new youth movement was gurgling like a volcano, ready to erupt. When it finally did, Britain's youth fell under a spell of hypnotic trance-like beats and bass lines and an array of brilliant psychedelic imagery. The hitherto underground scene of Acid House was preparing its assault on the mainstream. Paul's keen instinct sensed it. And what was more, he saw himself playing a role in it.

And that role materialised in *Modernism – A New Decade*.

In an edition of *Go Go* magazine from 1986, Paul reassured his fans, "I still come from a modernist approach, and always will do." In 1989 he still was. Nothing could change that.

Paul's interest in Mod began a few years before The Jam were signed to Polydor and his interpretation of what Mod was constantly evolving. While researching the topic of Mod, he'd discovered Pete Meaden's infamous words – "Clean living under difficult circumstances." There was also the brilliant book *Mods* by Richard

Barnes, that enlightened avid young wannabes by informing them that Mod was, "Being a concept, a collection of ideals and was never meant to have been a movement or mainstream, but if it was to be, then there were certain boundaries, rules even, to make it work properly."

The evidence that Paul understood what Meaden and Barnes meant is there for all to see in his music and sense of style,

In 1974, Paul bought a Lambretta, his first scooter. During his time in the Style Council, he would be filmed and photographed zipping about on these sleek Italian machines.

As a teenager, Paul wanted to learn more about Mod clothes and style. When everyone around him had long hair, wore flares and listened to Bowie, Bolan, Sweet and Slade. Paul's interests lay elsewhere. He was already familiar with such brands as Fred Perry, Brutus, Ben Sherman and Levi. The French and Italian influence became more perceptible during the Style Council era.

Paul soon realised that Mod was a unique, inherently stylish way of life, its finger constantly on the panache pulse. All of this suited Paul's personality and attitude and his love of clothes, music and British youth culture.

Modernism – A New Decade was Paul's third album title that included the key letters MOD along with *This Is The Modern World* and *All Mod Cons*. All three records said something about Mod in their own way and reflected Paul's position on his Mod journey at that time.

"When I get into any style of music, that's what I want to play at that time," says Paul. In 1977 it had been Punk, in 1983 soul and R&B and in 1989 it was House.

In February 1989, the Style Council released 'Promised Land' b/w 'Can You Still Love Me?', a version of the Joe Smooth House classic. The second single was 'Long Hot Summer (89)' b/w 'Everybody's On The Run' that wonderfully reflected the mood of that ecstasy-drenched summer. Sticking with the dance music theme, Paul also worked with Dee C Lee on the *Slam Slam* project. A sole single, 'Something Ain't Right' was released in September.

On July 4, 1989, the Style Council performed their last ever gig at the Royal Albert Hall. The audience's response was volatile. Some fans tore up their programmes, threw them to the floor and stormed out. Mick Talbot recalls being "Booed and abused" throughout their entire set.

Nicky Weller also witnessed the concert. "I don't actually remember much about it other than people not getting it and walking out. It would be interesting to see it again. A friend of mine got permission to film it, so somewhere that concert is on film."

"I think people overreacted to the last Style Council gig," says Mick. "I didn't think it should have been that much of a surprise to people, especially those that had been around us since we'd started. I think Paul and I had always tried to do something different. In the early days we'd do off the wall things like open the gig, put the support band in the middle and then we'd close the gig. We liked to try things that broke with convention. So, yes, some people seemed aggrieved by what we tried in the end but our way of thinking had been there from the beginning. Unfortunately, some people didn't see it that way.

"By the time we recorded *Modernism*, Paul and I had already said it was going to be our last album and that had been agreed before the record label had told us they weren't going to release it. The Style Council stopping wasn't because of the album not getting released; we already felt we'd done as much as we could and we were already of the mindset of winding the Style Council up."

Nicky Weller: "By the time *Modernism – A New Decade* was being recorded things were changing for the Style Council. I liked that album. It was very much of the time. I remember thinking that things were going a bit mad when Paul asked me to dress the band. Paul had been on tour in Japan and when we came back I went and bought all these different coloured patterned tee shirts and Bermuda shorts from Fenwicks. It was partly psychedelic and partly what people were wearing in the Acid House scene – all the kids were chanting 'acieed'. Paul was very aware of that music and he liked it too and that led to *Modernism – A New Decade*."

The set list from that Albert Hall concert was: 'Can You Still Love Me?', 'Move (Dance All Night)', 'Promised Land', 'Sure Is Sure', 'Everybody's On The Run', 'Tender Love', 'It's A Very Deep Sea', 'I Can't Deny Myself', 'Little Boy In A Castle', 'Mick's Blessings', 'A Woman's Song', 'Now You're Gone', 'Mick's Company', 'Cost Of Loving', 'Waiting On A Connection', 'Depth Charge',' Like A Gun', 'Changing Of The Guard', 'You'll Find Love', 'That Spiritual Feeling'.

Paul, talking in August 1989, "I wouldn't like to be forced into a position where I have to compromise and make records just because that's what the public or the record company want to hear."

Sound familiar? He'd said as much in the summer of 1982 after the announcement of the end of The Jam. Nevertheless, Paul called time on The Style Council, the band that had seen him sail upstream through the Eighties.

Modernism – A New Decade was submitted to Polydor in 1989 but they rejected it. For Paul, this was an unexpected and devastating reaction from the label that helped launch his career.

During the months that followed, Dee C Lee described Paul as being "miserable and lost and his confidence gone." He found himself in a situation that to some extent was out of his power to change. This sense of powerlessness was uncharted territory for Paul, but he didn't give up. As fate would have it, the next stage of his career was already being ushered in.

Mick: "I was hanging around Dingwalls and appreciating what Norman Jay was doing when listening to his pirate radio station. Norman embraced a lot of different music and it all seemed to make sense. He was one of the main guys in the rare groove scene that then led into the early rave thing. Norman would have played Joe Smooth's 'Promised Land' and that's where I would have heard it.

"We liked House music. We appreciated the finer details of what came out of certain places like Chicago and New Jersey. And then there was Detroit, but I think that was more techno. Chicago had that church thing going on, it was more soulful. With House, there were acts producing good music that wasn't so Kraftwerk influenced and for me it had a link to the late Philly sound. It was good four to the floor stuff. For us, House music was the new soul, it was where we saw soul was going. And many of the pioneers of House music had been soul boys.

"Paul was on top of what was happening in the House scene. He was always going into City Sounds getting the latest imports. We both liked those records and we appreciated the vocals in those songs. The guy that sung in Ten City had a brilliant falsetto voice that could have been Curtis (Mayfield) or one of those soul names.

"At the time of doing *Modernism*, House music was still underground and it wasn't that well known. For me the Style Council doing those songs on Modernism wasn't that far removed from the Stones or the Beatles covering soul songs on their first albums. If a song like 'Promised Land' had more of a profile, I doubt we would have covered it."

'A New Decade', the album's opening track, sets the tone. Recorded at Solid Bond studios, it has all the ingredients of a stomping garage groove that was still alien to many of Paul's fans. But there was more to come.

'Love Of The World', with a drum pattern not too dissimilar to 'Break For Love' by Raze, also includes the Cappuccino Kid adding some vocals, "Amore, amore, amore" and Dee C Lee spices up the song with some "Oh oh yeahs."

When Polydor's A&R man and friend of Paul, Dennis Munday, quizzed Paul over some lyrics that he couldn't quite decipher from 'The World Must Come Together', Paul couldn't recall what they were. It's a soulful House track with the heavy, fuller sound favoured by many at the time.

For those involved in the underground Rave scene of 1989, it did,

146   Paul Weller: Sounds from the Studio

to some extent seem as if 'the kids' were uniting. An underground
Rave scene had one foot in the north in clubs like the Hacienda and
the other foot in fields and warehouses just outside London on the
edges of the M25. In one hot summer, Rave swept aside much of what
had gone before. It was punk for the school of '89. The music was
fantastic, the drugs brilliant, the mood light-hearted and friendly.
But all good things come to an end.

Criminal elements recognised a lucrative opportunity and
swooped. And so did the authorities. Parties were ambushed by
both and as quickly as it arrived, Rave ground to a halt, at least the
field and warehouse parties did. The scene, albeit watered down,
had no choice but to move back into clubland if it was to survive
and that gave rise to the superclubs like the Ministry of Sound. Even
the thousands of ravers that attended the Freedom To Party rally in
Hyde Park in the summer of 1990 protesting against the Criminal
Justice Act of 1988 that prevented them having their parties, did
little to dissuade the government's attitude. The days of smiley face
tee shirts and bandanas were numbered. But against this backdrop,
Paul's own song writing was mirroring what he saw and what he felt,
and, in Paul's opinion, "House was the new Mod music."

'Hope (Feeling Gonna Getcha)' has echoes of 'No Way Back' by
Adonis and captures the feel of the mid-Eighties Chicago House
scene. It wouldn't be out of place played to thousands dancing the
night and most of the morning away in some farmer's field in the
Home Counties.

Without doubt, one of the stand-out tracks on Modernism is 'Can
You Still Love Me?'. Any raver worth their salt would relate to the
lyric, "I look into your eyes and suddenly see the changing colours of
a world of mystery." At the time of writing and recording Modernism,
Paul hadn't experienced the drug Ecstasy. But thousands had and
when an E was good it was really good, the best feeling in the world
and perfect to dance on without any inhibitions or self-conscious
shackles. Just before the introduction of Ecstasy, Acid House kids

were wolfing LSD and "Worlds that changed colours and worlds full of mystery," were being experienced every weekend. Paul and Dee C Lee's vocals work perfectly on this track.

Paul once said, "I believe in God." Whatever the case, those feelings have certainly inspired some of his song writing. 'That Spiritual Feeling' is full of percussion, keyboards, drums and brass supplied by members of James Brown's very own brass section including Fred Wesley, Robert 'Kush' Griffith, Pee Wee Ellis and the legendary Maceo Parker. If Paul hadn't known of Parker's previous works in the Sixties and Seventies, he would certainly have heard his music in Soho's Wag Club, a place he frequented when it was at its hottest in '86-'88). 'Cross The Track (We Better Go Back)' had been a stormer on the Wag dance floor in 1987.

'That Spiritual Feeling' would appear as the B-side on Paul's debut solo career single 'Into Tomorrow' in 1991.

The song writing credit for 'Everybody's On The Run' was shared between Paul and Dee C Lee. It has the infectious rhythm you would expect on a good funky House track. Its vibrancy is reminiscent of 'Trans Global Express'.

And finally, there's 'Sure Is Sure', another standout track. It includes a piano riff that sits on top of the drum machine, bass line and synth sounds. It's another deep House track with soul and gospel-like vocals that help drive the song along. 'Sure Is Sure/Love Of The World' was intended to be released as a single in July but due to Polydor pulling out, it never got its chance.

TRACKLISTING

1. A New Decade
2. Love Of The World
3. The World Must Come Together
4. Hope (Feelings Gonna Getcha)
5. Can You Still Love Me?
6. That Spiritual Feeling
7. Everybody's On The Run
8. Sure Is Sure

Confessions Of A Pop Group

'But now I just laugh and sing'

The single 'Life At A Top People's Health Farm' was released in May 1988. The Style Council's new album, *Confessions Of A Pop Group* was released the following month.

On the album cover, Dee C Lee was strategically positioned so that her tummy was hidden as she was pregnant with Nathaniel at the time of the shoot. Nathaniel was Paul and Dee C Lee's first child. Mick Talbot sat crouched over a piano while Paul stood in full view wearing a very dapper Eighties double- breasted suit, his hair bleached. Beneath the words, the Style Council there were four more: New York, Gstaad, Tokyo, Marble Arch. Gstaad was a town in Switzerland and the Marble Arch reference related to the location of Paul's Solid Bond Studios.

Production for *Confessions Of A Pop Group* was credited to both Paul and Mick Talbot and the album was released on June 20, 1988, reaching a respectable No 15. Not bad considering the British pop charts were dominated that year by the likes of Kylie Minogue, Tiffany and Whitney Houston.

In parts, *Confessions Of A Pop Group* is a dreamy Eighties emulation of 'Yellow Submarine' and wouldn't be out of place as a film score. The album is an eclectic mixture of genres ranging from classical (Paul was listening to a lot of Debussy at the time), jazz, R&B, soul, funk and pop. It was only the contemporary production sound that gives the songs any sense of the era from which they come.

The musicians on the album included Paul, Mick Talbot, Dee C Lee, Steve White, Camelle Hinds, Paul Morgan, Dick Morrissey, Frank Ricotti, Nick Brown, Chris Lawrence, Little Joo Ruocco and The Swingle Singers.

Confessions Of A Pop Group begins with '(Piano Paintings)

It's A Very Deep Sea'. Piano and rich sounding cymbals give the impression of depth, an ocean's depth. "I'll keep on diving till I reach the ends," sings Paul. Instrumentation is minimal but what is included works to create the watery atmosphere, as Paul continues to sing, "I'm diving, oh I'm diving." Sounds of seagulls float in and out. "Perhaps I come to the surface and come to my senses," closes the song.

'The Story Of Someone's Shoe' is about the emptiness and coldness of a one-night stand – "It's lust and loneliness but seldom love." Paul's lyrics tell a familiar story, "She takes a breath as he takes his key... he takes her hand and leads to the room."

Once the couple's intimate moment is over, "She slips away... now the need to get out, still carrying his seed which trickles down her leg and onto her shoe."

The Swingle Singers perform on 'The Story Of Someone's Shoe'. Ward Swingle had formed the outfit in Paris in 1962 and managed to keep his collection of singers together for several decades. They even recorded with the Modern Jazz Quartet in their earlier years. Paul said the song was influenced by the album that the Swingle Singers did with the MJQ, *Place De Vendome*. There's also a vibraphone part played by jazz musician Frank Ricotti. Like most of the *Confessions* album, this was unlike anything Paul had ever attempted to do before.

'Changing Of The Guard' begins with a piano followed by Paul's vocals which then merge with Dee C Lee's and they duet throughout much of the song, romantically and dreamily. White provides cymbals and uses brushes rather than sticks to create that jazzy atmosphere and the sweeping orchestral sounds add gravitas. It was one of the standout songs on the album and, incidentally, is a favourite of musician Robert Wyatt.

'The Little Boy In The Castle' and 'A Dove Flew Down', see more piano pieces from Talbot that guide the listener to the next track, 'The Gardener Of Eden (A Three Piece Suite) i. In The Beginning.

ii. The Gardener Of Eden iii. Mourning The Passing Of Time'. Rupert Parker plays harp, Camelle Hinds is on bass, Dee C Lee provides vocals and White sits in on drums pretty much picking up where he left off on 'Changing Of The Guard'. The whole piece is experimental with Paul pushing his own boundaries as much as that of the Style Council's. One does wonder what the Paul of 1977 would have made of the album.

Mick Talbot: "'The Gardener Of England' was really good but the part in the middle of the three-piece suite, the ornate orchestration, was much better when Paul had done a version with him singing and playing piano on it. I really got the emotion of it on that Paul version. It was pure. I had a cassette of that version but I've since lost it which is a pity because when we came to record it on *Confessions*, somehow, somewhere down the line, we lost something with that song. Part one and part three are everything they should have been, it's just that part two.

"I also think that some of the best parts of the *Confessions* album have elements of Brian Wilson. I can hear that and I can hear Marvin Gaye. Not that *Confessions* sounds like either Wilson or Gaye but there are influences in the way the songs all blend together. *Confessions* was a very complex album and it took a lot of work to make it. John Mealing, who worked on the string arrangements on *Our Favourite Shop*, played his part in helping to realise what Paul was trying to put across.

'Around the time of making the *Confessions*, Paul more than me was listening to Debussy. We also worked closely with John Mealing on that album. The great thing about John was that he wasn't snobby and up until working with him, both Paul and I had encountered difficulties getting string players to swing and groove, but John was able to get that. He was really good working with all sorts of musicians.

"The three-piece suite, 'The Garden Of Eden, In The Beginning, The Gardener Of Eden', leading up to 'Mourning The Passing Of

Time', included a quote from Debussy and around that time Paul certainly had a good knowledge of the composer. Those pieces of music were like soundtracks for a film that was in your head or a dream that you'd had.

"During the making of the *Confessions* album, Paul was writing a lot on the piano. That was how I heard those songs at first. We then worked from there. Some I interpreted and made my own and some I pretty much had to stick to what Paul had done because that was the best thing for the song.

"Paul would do something like play a half-bar in a place that you didn't expect, but it made sense in Paul's head. He knew where the song should be going, how it should feel, and I'd work with that. John Lennon would do a similar thing. It wasn't expected, but it would work. But there'd be times when I would try to talk Paul into playing the part himself. I know that sounds like I was talking myself out of a job, but our ethos, from *Café Bleu* onwards, was *put the song first*, not where's my bit or what do I sound like?

"I think if Paul had been a bit more confident back then he would have played some of those parts. I love that in his solo years he has done just that. Some of his strongest songs like 'You Do Something To Me' he leads on the piano.'

'Life At A Top People's Health Farm' is a track with a lot of very Eighties instrumentation. It's electronic from start to end. Paul shows that he's still angry at a great many things, still acting as a social commentator for the nation's youth. Trotsky and the Archers get a mention as does his old nemesis "And thanking Margaret Thatcher 'May you never come to harm'." 'Life At A Top Peoples Health Farm' b/w 'Sweet Loving Ways' was lifted from *Confessions* and hit the charts in May.

'Why I Went Missing' is another synthesizer-driven track. Paul takes the lead supported by Dee C Lee. In amongst all the synthesized sounds are reminders that both Paul and Talbot can still play 'proper' instruments and both deliver solos on organ and guitar respectively.

'How She Threw It All Away' appeared on the '1234 A Summer Quartet' EP along with 'In Love For The First Time', 'Long Hot Summer' and 'I Do Like To Be B-side The a-side'. A footnote credited the performances to The Mixed Companions. The EP was released on July 16, 1988.

Nick Brown played drums on 'How She Threw It All Away', Little Joo Ruocco played percussion and Sixties jazz musician Dick Morrissey played the flute.

'IWASADOLEDADSTOYBOY' is another synth-led tune with a heavy dance beat in a 'Big Boss Groove' vein, and a preview of what was to come in *Modernism – A New Decade*. The song is trance-like as it urges the listener to dance.

'Confessions 1, 2 & 3' revisits the gentler styles of the earlier part of the album. Camelle Hinds provides some smooth backing vocals and there's an interesting trombone solo played by Chris Lawrence while there are sounds of an audience applauding. By and large, 'Confessions 1, 2 & 3' meanders gracefully. If by now you hadn't gotten your head around the new Style Council it's unlikely you ever would.

A ten-minute song rounds off the album. 'Confessions Of A Pop Group' is a funky, electronic and poppy. After the lengthy intro, the lyrics begin – "Cheap and tacky bullshit land, told when to sit don't know when to stand." The mood gets even more edgier, "Bobbies on the beat again, beating blacks for blues again, it's one way to get involved in the community," he sarcastically writes. The line, "The great depression is organised crime," is just brilliant. On many levels, 'Confessions Of A Pop Group' is the perfect song to end The Style Council's fourth studio album.

"I listened to the *Confessions* album recently and I thought wow, there's so much in it musically," says Mick Talbot. "I think the album is too long and I think some songs go on too long. I think the album got more overlooked than it should have done and that was maybe because some people were still licking their wounds from the *Orange* album. 'It's A Very Deep Sea' and 'The Story Of Someone's Shoe' I think come off as really good songs."

TRACKLISTING

1. It's A Very Deep Sea
2. The Story Of Someone's Shoe
3. Changing Of The Guard
4. A. The Little Boy In The Castle
   B. Dove Flew Down From the Elephant
5. The Gardener Of Eden (A Three Piece Suite)
   i. In The Beginning
   ii. The Gardener Of Eden
   iii. Mourning The Passing Of Time
6. Life At A Top Peoples Health Farm
7. Why I Went Missing
8. How She Threw It All Away
9. IWASADOLEDADSTOYBOY
10. Confessions 1,2 & 3
11. Confessions Of A Pop Group

The Cost Of Loving

'Time here today is life tomorrow'

Keeping with the theme of participating in benefit concerts and helping to raise awareness for various causes, on April 25, 1986, the Style Council performed at a CND/Friends of the Earth rally and then on June 28 they performed at the Artist Against Apartheid (AAA) concert on Clapham Common. It was an impressive line-up that included Elvis Costello, Billy Bragg, Sade, Peter Gabriel, Sting, Boy George, Hugh Masekela and Gil Scott-Heron (with whom, over a decade later, Paul would record). Both the audiences were huge – something the Style Council were now familiar with.

Included in the 1986 film *Absolute Beginners*, 'Have You Ever Had It Blue' was released as a single in March. Having got a taste for the big screen industry, around £140,000 was raised to fund a film project that Paul wanted to do. Paolo Hewitt was drafted in to write the screenplay and filming began for *JerUSAlem* [sic]. Paul, Talbot, White and Dee C Lee were filmed having adventures through a surreal England.

The film was intended to be a sort of 'Magical Mystery Tour' but it lost something in translation for many viewers and met with mixed reviews. It begins, in black and white, with an image of a newspaper called the 'Daily Distraction' and the headline 'Style Council Out On Bail'. Charged with being "The best pop group ever," the four band members – Weller, Talbot, White and Lee – are seen running down a corridor and into a car while being surrounded by members of the pap. As they drive off, they pass a sign saying 'TSC The Band That Likes To Say No!'

Paul is then filmed seated on a throne dressed in eighteenth century garb and smoking a fag. Talbot sports a fake Edwardian 'tache and top hat, White is striking in a revolting shirt and shorts with a hanky on his head and Dee C Lee standing with a seagull on her shoulder, ushers in Angel. The band join her with their instruments (Paul plays a red and white Stratocaster) set up on a rock that looks out to sea.

There's a smattering of 'It Didn't Matter' before all four members ride out into the countryside on scooters TSC1, TSC2, TSC3 and TSC4 and filmed miming to a version of 'Heavens Above' up a windmill. They have an encounter with a bobby on a rocking horse and a firm of 'Let's all do the Conga' English football hooligans.

The end of the 30-minute film is in sight by this point (a sigh of relief for some) as Paul, Talbot, White and Dee C Lee stand trial in front of a judge accused of having style and inserting melodies into their songs. They are, of course, found GUILTY and then a bunch of revellers appear and a party begins and they all dance to 'Fairy Tales'.

In the mid-Eighties, Britain got its first taste of some new music that was coming out of Chicago. One of the earliest to hit the discos in the UK was 'Move Your Body' by Marshall Jefferson in 1986. In 1987 there was the equally influential 'Jack Your Body' from Steve 'Silk' Hurley.

Also making its presence felt was the Wag Club in Soho. It had opened in October 1982 on the premises of the legendary Sixties club the Whisky A Go Go. The Wag's Barrie Sharpe was one of the deejays driving the Rare Groove scene in London. Rare Groove was the name given to the type of funk and soul that was becoming popular along with Chicago's House music. And then, on top of the Rare Groove and House scene, the first tremors of Acid House were stirring. Naturally none of this went unnoticed by Paul.

In an interview in a 1988 edition of *The Face*, Paul was asked about House music "I much prefer council house music," he replied. However, in time he would backtrack on this comment and fully embrace the fresh new sound with its stomping beats and samples that were often lifted from some of America's greatest soul songs.

In 1987 the Torch Society ceased. "The Torch Society was really just a progression from The Jam fan club," says Nicky Weller. "One of the things we noticed that was different to The Jam fan club was there were more girls coming through. You could see this in the gigs that were attracting more girls and couples whereas with The Jam it was mostly lads. The Style Council fan club had more subscribers too than The Jam ever did.

"When fan clubs first started it was pretty basic stuff. We'd be scribbling most things down by hand on bits of paper. Then we got letterheaded paper and eventually a typewriter. Then we started to print stuff and do the little booklets that would were sent out every three months. Those booklets were filled with the stuff that fans would send in. There'd be photographs and pictures that fans had drawn and I was always doing competitions. *The Style Population* was a good thing to do and Paul would get very involved with that.

"At the time of running *The Torch Society*, I was also working in London and had developed other interests and at the time they were important. As a result, I sort of lost interest in the fan club side of things and so it eventually stopped. Mum continued with it, but it was a lot to do and over time it just sort of came to an end."

Ann Weller adds, "Another reason why *The Torch Society* finished was because people were getting older. Many of Paul's fans had been with him since the days of The Jam and they too were getting older. Things were generally just changing."

'It Didn't Matter/All Year Round', 'Waiting/Françoise' and 'Wanted/The Cost/The Cost Of Loving' were all released as singles in 1987. 'Waiting', a song that Paul felt had been influenced by Stevie Wonder, failed to even chart. There were also further releases for 'The Cost Of Loving' and 'Mick Talbot Is Agent 88'.

The Cost Of Loving was released in February 1987 on Polydor Records. It had to be played at 45rpm rather than 33rpm. Because of its album sleeve design, it quickly became known as the Orange Album. The Beatles had their so-called White Album and now Paul had his Orange one.

The Cost Of Loving was recorded at Solid Bond studios between

May and October 1986. "The actual musicianship on this LP is probably our best so far," were Paul's thoughts and the musicians he was referring to included Mick Talbot, Steve White, Dee C Lee, The Dynamic Three, Steve Sidelnyk, Camelle Hinds, Billy Chapman, Anne Stephenson, Guy Barker, Luke Tunnery, Pete Thams, Chris Lawrence, Roddy Lorimer, Ashley Slater and John Valentine.

'It Didn't Matter' begins with a delicious Eighties intro. Synth sounds, electronic drums and a funky bass (which Paul admitted was inspired by the bass line on 'Night After Night' by David Sea) are the foundations. Paul delivers his lyrics with support from Dee C Lee. She also takes the lead on the middle eight before Paul's funky guitar edges in. 'It Didn't Matter' worked as a single release and wasn't out of place at any club night.

'One Nation Under A Groove' gets dropped into 'Right To Go', the reference immediately apparent to any Funkadelic fan. 'Right To Go' is funky to boot and, with the addition of the Dynamic Three, a rap outfit from the Bronx, Paul had a song that would have alienated some of his fans but attracted newer ones. By 1987, Rap and hip-hop wasn't new, but it was still fresh and gaining in popularity. However, in an interview with Paolo Hewitt some years later, Paul said he thought the song was "fucking awful!"

Even the blues get a mention in the politically motivated lyrics – "No Tory's gonna tell you one in five... now once and for all the right must go, now once and for all, register to vote." The UK would be asking the same of its population some 30 years later.

Paul and Dee C Lee share the vocals on 'Heavens Above' and Steve Sidelnyk plays congas while Billy Chapman supplies some saxophone. Anne Stephenson's unexpected violin contribution works really well.

"Although I played with The Style Council on all their live stuff from 1984 onwards, *Home And Abroad* was the disc that I appeared on," says Steve Sidelnyk. "And then *The Cost Of Loving* album came along. I played percussion on 'Right To Go' and then congas on

'Heavens Above' and 'Fairy Tales'. From what I remember, I recorded all three tracks in one session.

"Working in the studio with Paul was a matter of, if he liked it, he'd keep it. The thing is, Paul can pretty much play anything, which means he kinda knows what he kinda wants. It's helpful and provides a sort of yardstick. Paul has a really good way of working with people too. He can be sympathetic and encourage you to try things this way or that way. Paul's songs were really a percussionists' and drummers' dream to play on.

Paul wrote more politically heavy lyrics for 'Heavens Above'; it was a trend throughout much of the album, although it would be Paul's last in this way. His message, plea even, is contained in the song, "Give it up before it's too late, give it up before you make the mistake, give it up while you still have the time, give it up, give us some peace of mind."

"The giant towers over all, but from close distance she don't seem that big at all," sang Paul on 'Fairy Tales'. Politics and the current government are never far away on this track.

Curtis Mayfield contributed to the mixing on 'Fairy Tales'. On July 3, 1988, Paul interviewed Mayfield at Ronnie Scott's Jazz Club. Paul wore a black and white striped roll-neck sweater with a neck chain and listened respectfully to the responses from the handful of questions he asked of a relaxed Curtis.

Paul's first question, "Did you draw inspiration from the whole blues connection to Chicago?" was met with a "Well not really," before Curtis went on to speak about growing up in a spiritual environment. Prompted by Paul, he then went on to talk about his early bands, choosing to play the kind of music that he wanted and inserting messages into his songs. He also talked of the importance the movie *Superfly* played in his career.

Paul also referred to Nixon, the Watergate scandal and whether Curtis ever got any flak from the establishment for his songs and political stances. Curtis said he hadn't.

"For history will prove in time that their laws today will be tomorrow's crimes." Credit where credit's due for this lyric as 'Fairy Tales' slides into an instrumental section. Paul intended *The Cost Of Loving* to be a reflection on modern soul. He achieved it.

'Angel' had originally been sung by Anita Baker and appeared on her debut album *The Songstress*. Paul had a copy of the record and decided to cover it. It's a beautiful ballad that works nicely on the album. The song is gentle and smooth and Paul and Dee C Lee's own loving relationship at that time shines through.

'Walking The Night' is another ballad that begins with a piano introduction. It's a song very reflective of the soul that was around at the time and oozing out of artists like Anita Baker or Jonathan Butler. The rootsy mix of jazz and soul was by now very familiar to Paul and something he could turn his hand to with ease. Guy Barker plays a neat flugelhorn solo.

'Waiting' is the third ballad on *The Cost Of Loving*. It's full of synths and electronic drums. The lines, "I don't mind what people say, they think the worst anyway" and, "I'm gonna love you anyway, I don't care what people say," are repeated several times as the song cruises along at a dreamy pace until the piano leads to fade. 'Waiting' isn't an outstanding song but it's a good fit for the Orange album.

'The Cost Of Loving' track is a timely funk pick-me-up. Paul takes the lead and the ever-present Dee and Steve White provide able support. Mick Talbot dishes up a splendid organ solo.

The album closes with 'A Woman's Song' with the opening line "Hush little baby don't you cry." We're all familiar with those words sung by mothers to their children for generations. The exact origin and author are unknown, but it's believed to have come from the USA because of the mockingbird reference as the creature is native to North America.

The song is about a struggling mother, "They've damned nearly taken away all I had," who needs the love of her child to keep her going, "All I have in the world is you." Dee C Lee sings the lead part on this song while Paul accompanies her on guitar. "All I have in the world is you, it's you and the future that sees me through." The message is understood.

TRACKLISTING

1. It Didn't Matter
2. Right To Go
3. Heavens Above
4. Fairy Tales
5. Angel
6. Walking The Night
7. Waiting
8. The Cost Of Loving
9. A Woman's Song

Our Favourite Shop

"I wonder – what will you do for me?"

The Style Council released four singles in 1983, their debut year, and their output showed no signs of abating when they put out a further four during 1984, 'My Ever Changing Moods/Mick's Company', 'Groovin: You're The Best Thing/The Big Boss Groove', 'Shout To The Top/Ghosts Of Dachau' and 'Soul Deep pt 1/Soul Deep pt 2'. All were top ten hits except 'Soul Deep' which only made it to 24 in the charts.

'Soul Deep' was a project driven by Paul to raise money for the group Woman Against Pit Closures. The B-side to the 12-inch release included a song called 'A Miner's Point'. 'Soul Deep' was released in December 1984 and raised £10,000 for the cause.

For the project, Paul and The Style Council recruited support from Motown legend Jimmy Ruffin, old friend and Respond artist Vaughn Toulouse, soul singer Junior Giscombe and Leonardo Chignoli of Animal Nightlife. Earlier in the year Paul sang backing vocals on Nightlife's song 'Mr Solitaire'.

In the same month as 'Soul Deep' was released, Paul also participated in Band Aid's 'Do They Know Its Christmas'. On November 25, 1984, Paul arrived at Sarm West Studios in Notting Hill to contribute some vocals on the fundraising song for the famine victims in Ethiopia. Over 30 artists including Sting, Bono, Boy George, Phil Collins and members of Bananarama and Duran Duran, gathered to record the song that had been written by Bob Geldof and Midge Ure. The single was released on December 3 and went straight in at No 1 where it stayed for five weeks selling over three million copies.

Around the time that 'Shout To The Top' was released, Paul had also become a vegetarian. This conversion had partly been brought about by his girlfriend Gill, who was already vegetarian, but Paul had also become increasingly interested in animal rights' campaigns,

especially relating to blood sports. On the picture sleeve of 'Shout
To The Top', Paul included, "Yes! To all involved In Animal Rights."
Many Weller fans also decided to turn their backs on meat as a result
and took an interest in animal rights groups and campaigns. Paul's
influence wasn't something to be underestimated.

In late 1984, Paul's record label Respond shut down. The label had
helped to provide a launch pad for artists like The Questions and
Tracie. A compilation album called *Respond: Love The Reason* was
released in 1983 and showcased The Questions, Tracie, A Craze and
Main T KO.

"In 1983 I answered an ad in *Smash Hits* for Respond Records, who
were looking for a drummer for one of their acts called A Craze,"
recalls Steve Sidelnyk. "I went for the audition but I didn't get offered
the job. However, about a week later Tracie Young contacted me
saying she was looking for a drummer for her band. I went along to
some studio near London Bridge and Tracie was there, along with Paul
and Kenny Wheeler. Paul's black Premier drums were also there and
because I'd grown up playing in punk bands and having no idea of a
volume level, I basically just went and destroyed Paul's drum kit. Paul
loved it and I got offered the job.

"Paul then invited me to go on the first Style Council European tour
and it was after that when I started recording for Tracie. Paul was
writing a lot of Tracie's songs and they were being recorded at Solid
Bond Studios. I sort of went through a period of playing drums with
Tracie and percussion with The Style Council.

"I also went on the Respond Package Tour. It included Tracie, The
Questions, A Craze and the Main T K O. I spent the tour sharing a hotel
room with Vaughn Toulouse. It was an amazing experience, the first
time I'd ever stayed in a hotel."

Paul was proactive in helping Tracie to get her one and only album,
Far From The Hurting Kind, released. He gave her the songs 'Souls
On Fire', 'Nothing Happens Here But You', 'Dr. Love' and 'Spring,
Summer, Autumn'.

Paul also played on the album and helped in the production. However, Paul and Tracie's relationship didn't always run smoothly.

During Respond's short life, Paul worked closely with many of the artists on the label. He even joined in with some members from the label's stable for a televised performance of 'Harvest For The World'. On that occasion, Paul played the congas whilst he sang.

By 1985, Paul was sporting polo shirts with neck chains worn on the outside and he had a wedge haircut (not quite Bowie, more football casual). Steve White's interest in casual-style clothing had clearly rubbed off on Paul. White would go and buy a Pringle jumper from a shop near to Solid Bond Studios and Paul would then go and buy several of them. The polo-shirt look made fashionable by designer sports brands like Lacoste and Kappa also became very popular within The Style Council camp.

The mid-Eighties were awash with vibrant pastel colours. Every other kid seemed to be wearing faded blue Lois jeans or jumbo cords, golfing jumpers made by Pringle and Lyle and Scott, kagools by Patrick and Adidas, trainers by Nike and Diadora, tracksuits from Fila and Sergio Tacchini and, to top it all off, a perm or a wedge haircut. And each Saturday the football terraces were full of Fila, firms and fighting. They were exciting, stylish and, sadly, violent times.

Paul observed the growth of the casuals and made some obvious connections to Mod. The casuals, like the Mods, were driven by many of the same things, especially where style and one-upmanship were concerned. The only thing the casuals didn't have was their own music. They had no genre they could latch onto. But many of them had grown up with The Jam so they were acceptable, as were The Style Council. The combination of football, fashion and music all worked in Paul's favour. He also took a keener interest in football as he got older and the club he found some affinity with was Chelsea. In more recent years he's been known to hang a Chelsea flag in Black Barn Studios.

The Style Council's Internationalist Tour kicked off on June 5, 1985, at the Brixton Academy. No support band toured with the band but Dizzy Hites was ever present to deejay. The tour took in Bournemouth, Portsmouth, Brighton, Birmingham, Sheffield, Nottingham, Manchester, Liverpool, Glasgow before Paul made his debut appearance at the legendary Glastonbury festival on June 22, 1985.

On July 13, Paul walked onto the Wembley Stadium stage to perform to another huge crowd and a worldwide audience at the Live Aid Concert. Boy George had suggested the idea of a charity concert to raise more money for the famine crisis in Ethiopia. Seventy-two thousand people packed into the stadium on that sweltering day.

The concert began with the Coldstream Guards Band performing 'God Save The Queen' (not the Pistols' version!) and they were followed by Status Quo. Next up was The Style Council. Paul, in red shirt and white trousers, told the crowd, "This shows what can happen if we all get together. This song is dedicated to that spirit, it's called 'Internationalist'." And then the band launched into a spirited version of the track. The second number they performed was 'Walls Come Tumbling Down' that saw Paul put down his guitar and dance.

Elton John, Paul McCartney, David Bowie, The Who, U2, Dire Straits and Queen also performed on that memorable day and over 40 million pounds was raised.

"Live Aid was just incredible," says Steve Sidelnyk. "I remember going to the sound check the day before. The weather was grey and miserable and we just expected the following day to be naff and a real disappointment. But then we all met at Solid Bond in the morning and the weather was just glorious.

"I have so many great memories from that day and just one is being in the toilet standing next to Francis Rossi. He turned to me and said 'Are you nervous?' I said I was. 'So am I,' he replied. The whole day was amazing and everybody was just brilliant."

In August, The Style Council flew out to Australia to promote their new LP *Our Favourite Shop*. This was a country that had eluded Paul up until now. It was while in Australia that Paul and Gill's relationship came to a head. There was a reported incident in the hotel where Paul was staying that apparently resulted in two grand's worth of damages. By the time Paul returned to the UK, his personal situation was looking very different.

Steve Sidelnyk: "Growing up I loved The Jam and all the punk bands. I loved bands like Joy Division and would go and see them often. And then there was the 2-Tone thing and reggae. Musically it was a really exciting time. When The Style Council came along and I heard those songs, it was just like wow! It was also such a massive departure from The Jam. Around that time politics was a huge part of the band and we ended up doing a lot of the Red Wedge concerts. We got to travel a lot and not just in the UK. It always amazed me how, when we went to other countries, they too identified with Paul."

In the autumn, Red Wedge got underway with Paul and Billy Bragg proudly flying the red flag. The concept was that a collective of musicians would attempt to engage young people in politics. Initially the idea had substance and, to some extent, it worked. It was an initiative that reflected the times, but it was never going to last.

However, Red Wedge did manage to gain huge popularity amongst Britain's young people. That period was one of the last when young people en masse actually took an interest in politics. In January 1986, the Red Wedge Tour kicked off. The Style Council appeared alongside Bragg, The Redskins and a bunch of comedians. It achieved what it set out to do which was to attract attention to the Labour Party.

Paul has since said his involvement with the movement was an error of judgement. "Our biggest mistake was to get hooked up with Red Wedge," he told an interviewer in 2006. "Meeting politicians reinforced what I'd always believed, they're all out for themselves."

The Style Council signed off a successful 1985 by playing three sell-out dates in Wembley Arena. Some Weller fans in the audience would've certainly been at the venue three years earlier when The Jam performed on their farewell tour..

Talking about The Style Council in 2006 Paul said, "I had a total belief in The Style Council. I was obsessed in the early years. I lived and breathed it all. I meant every word, and felt every action. *Our Favourite Shop* was its culmination."

In 1985, The Style Council released three singles – 'Walls Come Tumbling Down/The Whole Point 2/Blood Sports', 'Come To Milton Keynes/(When You) Call Me' and 'The Lodger's/You're The Best Thing/ The Big Boss Groove (Live)'.

Our Favourite Shop was released on May 9, 1985 on Polydor Records. It was recorded at Solid Bond Studios and produced by Paul Weller and Pete Wilson. In the US, the record was re-titled *Internationalists* and released on Geffen Records. Paul was enthused by what he'd created. "I've never believed so positively in any record as I do this one."

On June 8, *Our Favourite Shop* got toNo 1. In Mick Talbot's opinion, the album exactly reflected how things were in the Eighties.

The musicians that played on *Our Favourite Shop* included Steve White, Mick Talbot, Dee C Lee, Camelle Hinds, Stewart Prosser, David Defries, Mike Mower, Chris Lawrence, Gary Wallis, Clark Kent, Audrey Riley, Jocelyn Pook, Charlie Buchanan, Anne Stephenson, John Mealing, Tracie Young, Pete Wilson, Jeremy Wakefield, Patrick Grundry-White, Kevin Millar, Steve Dawson, Billy Chapman and Alison Limerick.

The sleeve design was credited to Simon Halfon and Paul Weller. It's without doubt one of the most interesting pop album covers of all time.

Oscar Wilde's *The Soul of Man Under Socialism*, Robert Tressell's *The Ragged Trousered Philanthropist* and George Orwell's *1984* and *Animal Farm* were all books that Paul enthused about. However, it was Richard Allen's *Suedehead* and *Skinhead* books and Nell Dunn's *Up The Junction* that made into the 'favourite shop'. There was also a Chelsea Football Club match day programme and copies of *The Prisoner* and *Shine On Harvey Moon* books.

The 'shop' itself was an Aladdin's cave of curiosities. There were various shots of Paul and Talbot taken by Olly Ball and Nick Knight. The meaning behind the inclusion of some items was blatantly obvious. But what did the white Rickenbacker, red military tunic with medals, a framed copy of *Rave* (the one with Steve Marriott and Ronnie Lane on it), a hat stand with a trilby like Mick wore and a wool skull cap like the one Paul wore on the front sleeve of 'My Ever Changing Moods', all mean?

Then there was the large poster for the film *Another Country*, images of George Best and John Lennon, a large *A Hard Day's Night* poster and a copy of *The Magical Mystery Tour*, a Curtis Mayfield LP, a pair of platform shoes, a cycling shirt, draws of pastel-coloured jumpers, a snooker cue and black and white photographs of Sherlock Holmes and Art Blakey and a white belt with Soul written on it (apparently Paul's favourite belonging).

Every item was selected by Paul and Talbot. Comparisons could easily be made to the *Sgt. Pepper* album cover but many a young Style Council fan had similar items on their shelves.

"We initially wanted the *Our Favourite Shop* album sleeve to be shot in a real shop," says Mick. "Paul had a shop in Woking that he wanted to use. It looked like an old gentleman's outfitters that hadn't changed for fifty years. It had worn wooden cabinets with brass fittings and so on. But it just didn't work and it wasn't practical. We had to abandon the idea and rethink it and so in the end we had to stage a set.

"Most of the items belonged to either Paul or me, but Simon Halfon also sourced some of the items. Paul and I literally went up into our lofts to find stuff and other items were just readily available on our bookshelves. There are things on the sleeve that can't really be seen but that tickles me and I know it's the same for Paul too. There's a miniature piano on the counter and on it is a little black and white card, a membership for a Mecca dancehall. For some reason, I'd kept it and to me it seemed so old-fashioned, like something out of the Ark. There's a pair of my brogues and inside them are some red towelling socks and that means something to me. I remember you'd get cheaper towelling socks at Marks & Spencer's but Brutus also made towelling socks for a while.

"There are some in-jokes too – a homo-erotic birthday card in there somewhere. A friend of mine had it made up for my birthday. It had Paul's head and my head grafted onto two bodies in a gay cartoon-type style.

"Certain people were represented that we didn't have anything for like the picture of Bridget Bardot. The Twiggy coat hanger I nicked off my brother. The George Best and John Lennon pictures belonged to Paul. The Otis Redding T-shirt was mine. I'd bought that in Amsterdam. The *Suedehead* book was mine, the *Skinhead* one was Paul's. There were all sorts of books that belonged to Paul and me.

"I wanted to include a picture of Peter Bonetti. He was the Chelsea goalkeeper nicknamed The Cat and I liked him. He seemed quite stylish and Adam Faith used Bonetti as rhyming slang for spaghetti, 'Come on Hazel you haven't even touched your Bonetti.' I grew up with a family that were Chelsea supporters. Nowadays, I have more of an affinity with the Seventies sides than what's happening now. There was also something about their look. The players seemed to reflect something that was happening on the terraces, to be in touch with what people were doing. I used to think that Osgood and Hudson looked like people in the crowd. Osgood almost looked like some of the Suedehead geezers in the terraces. There were a lot of Chelsea supporters going west out of London and into Surrey and Paul would have known that."

The Inner sleeve also included quotes from Tony Benn, Jimmy Reid, Lenny Bruce, Oscar Wilde and a Greenham Common Woman (April '82) and a photograph of Mick and Paul sitting almost back to back, Paul looking every bit the young model and sporting his wedge haircut.

A TV advert was made to promote the album. It begins with an image of a hat stand with two beige raincoats and a trilby hat hanging from it. Mick and Paul appear on the screen in slow motion and walk towards the hat stand. Paul bends down to pick up a copy of *Our*

Favourite Shop and as he and Mick look up to the camera, 'Walls Come Tumbling Down' begins to play. The voiceover was provided by British actor Rupert Everett, "Probably the best pop band in the world," a play on the Carlsberg lager catchphrase.

Our Favourite Shop begins with sounds from a train station and a tannoy announcement, evoking familiar scenes of cold, crowded train stations. But there's also a sense of anticipation, even excitement, for the journey ahead. Some of those journeys have been forced upon people and 'Homebreakers' is about a man leaving his family to seek employment in an unfamiliar place. "Good morning day, how do you do?" is an optimistic greeting to yet another day of adversity and struggle.

'Homebreakers' reflects Paul's disgust at politicians like Norman Tebbit and the detrimental impact they had on ordinary hard-working folk.

Dee C Lee's vocals and Talbot's smooth organ playing work fantastically with bassist Camelle Hinds. The song is atmospheric and a reminder of the harsh realities that faced numerous families in the mid-Eighties. Additionally, 'Homebreakers' introduces a brass section consisting of Mike Mower, David Delfries, Chris Lawrence and Stewart Prosser who stab their way through the song. Paul's guitar solo forms the outro as he repeats, "Father's in the kitchen counting out the coins," before the train station noises reappear. Welcome to *Our Favourite Shop.*

Next up is the Latin-based rhythm provided by Steve White and Gary Wallis for 'All Gone Away' with a jazzy flute delivered by Mike Mower. Lyrics like, "The grocers shop hangs up its sign, the sign says closed, it's a sign of the times," foretell the 2008 recession when High Streets suffered and established shops were pushed aside to make room for pound shops and cheap quality clothing outlets. Hubs of the community like the old-fashioned pubs closed weekly and the building industry collapsed. And once the shops and pubs close, they're closed for good, "There's nothing left, they're all gone away."

Paul had been travelling the length and breadth of the UK for years with The Jam and The Style Council. In the eight years between *In the City* and *Our Favourite Shop*, he had personally witnessed the effects of Thatcher's attack on hard-working British communities. 'All Gone Away' was a song about how Thatcher had purposefully dismantled so many of Britain's vital industries, leaving only depression and anger and a sense of hopelessness – "The town hall clock gives forth it's chime, for no one there to ask the time, like everything else they've all gone away."

'Come To Milton Keynes' was banned by several radio shows. When Paul penned the song, he hadn't been able to write from direct experience because he'd never been to Milton Keynes that had been designated a new town in 1967.

Paul's political message comes through loud and clear, "May I slash my wrists tonight on this fine Conservative night." The song, though forceful, is skilfully softened by drum flurries from White. The orchestration is by John Mealing. If you listen carefully, you'll hear a cricket commentator's voice, and a snippet of the *Sale Of The Century* theme music.

'Internationalists' makes a dramatic entrance and lifts the tempo of the album. The song is refreshingly new and vibrant, unlike anything else around at that time. Mick Talbot pumps out a brilliant keyboard solo. Our ears pricked up when we heard, "Rise up now and describe yourself – an internationalist." It rallied the troops!

"One minute the miners were the nation's heroes," wrote Paul at the time before highlighting the fact that in mid-Eighties Britain many people changed their opinion of them. Violent pitch-battles between striking miners and the police were televised daily. What Paul also observed was that the brutality inflicted on workers wasn't just localised to the UK, it was happening in other parts of the world too – "Chile, Poland, Johannesburg."

'A Stone's Throw Away' is a masterpiece. Paul is backed by Audrey Riley's cello, a viola played by Jocelyn Pook and violins by Ann

Stephenson and Charlie Buchanan. Quite simply, beautiful.

'The Stand Up Comic's Instructions' places the listener into a dark and seedy comedy club filled with fag smoke and reeking of stale beer and tells the story of a club owner instructing the new act what to say because he knows what the audience wants. There are references to queers, blacks, the Irish, Asians, white thugs and building site workers. For anyone growing up in the Sixties, Seventies and Eighties, the references are familiar. Comedian Lenny Henry delivers Paul's lines and in less than two minutes, the song is over.

Tracie Young returns to Paul Weller's inner circle to add some backing vocals on 'Boy Who Cried Wolf'. "And now the night falls down, upon my selfish soul, I sit alone and wonder, where did I go wrong?"

"I recorded a lot more vocals for 'Boy Who Cried Wolf' but they weren't all used," says Tracie. "My memories of the actual day are a bit hazy; it was a long time ago. I remember there was a lot of multi-tracking the harmony parts so the vocals were all done live. I don't even recall if Mick was in Solid Bond on the day. What I do remember is that when *Our Favourite Shop* came out, Paul and Mick sent me a copy which they'd signed. I actually gave it away to a charity many years ago.

"A few years back there was an EMI promo CD released with a version of 'Boy Who Cried Wolf' on it. The actual CD was a collection of Paul's songs but with a selection of other artists singing the songs. My version of 'Spring Summer Autumn' (B-side on the 12-inch version of 'My Ever Changing Moods') was on it as was Tracie Thorn's 'Paris Match'. And there was a version of 'Boy Who Cried Wolf' sung by Noel McCalla which included my backing vocals, the one's which weren't included on the album version."

Pete Wilson and Jeremy Wakefield provided the keyboard sequencing for this song and the addition of the electronic drums only adds to the essence of the song.

The sound of a church bells introduces 'A Man Of Great Promise'.

"I bought the paper yesterday and I saw the obituary," sings Paul's in tribute to his dear friend Dave Waller, former band member and Riot Stories collaborator. "He was a poet, a very talented one, but heroin put a stop to that," wrote Paul, expressing his love, respect, disappointment and anger. "But you were always chained and shackled by the dirt." Paul plays bass synth on the track, Dee C Lee is on backing vocals and there's a flugelhorn and trombone.

With its obvious French connection, 'Down in The Seine' could easily have appeared on *Cafe Bleu*. White abandons his drum sticks for this track, preferring instead to use brushes to achieve a jazzy flavour. Verses are also sung in French with translation by Paul Renee and Sarah Silvers.

Returning to political themes, 'The Lodger's' is about those taking up residency at 10 Downing Street. The track incorporates some fine organ work from Talbot, and White again demonstrates how talented a drummer he is. 'The Lodger's' is Eighties soul personified and Dee C Lee, significantly, is presented with a deserved leading role.

Paul is back behind the microphone for 'Luck' and the tempo is raised again. It's Paul, Mick, White and Dee, tight, united, The Style Council backbone.

White's in his element within the jazzy vibe of 'With Everything To Lose'. His use of ride cymbal and rimshots drives the song along at a spirited rate. Billy Chapman returns on sax and Mike Mower plays flute. The song is credited to both Steve White and Paul Weller and with lyrics written by White.

The title track is the album's only all-out instrumental. Since *The Gift*, Paul had been including at least one instrumental on his albums. The synth bass takes a prominent role here as does the percussion, but it's Mick's organ that keeps it all together. There's also a fantastic jazz trumpet solo from Steve Dawson. The track stands out amidst the Eighties electronic jazzy funk dross inhabiting the turntables and clubs of the day.

'Walls Come Tumbling Down' is the song that encapsulates what

Paul and his politically minded peers in the music biz were trying to do at the time. The lyric "You don't have to sit back and relax," was Paul having a swipe at Frankie Goes To Hollywood who had recently had a No 1 with 'Relax'.

The message is simple – "Unity is powerful." Helen Turner provides the piano part and, of course, Dee is ever present. And yes, "You don't have to take this crap," was chanted by a whole generation of Red Wedgers.

In 1990, Alison Limerick had a club anthem hit with 'Where Love Lies'. During her career she worked with Courtney Pine, George Michael and Frankie Knuckles, but in 1985 she was contributing vocals to 'Shout To The Top'.

'Shout To The Top' is equally as strong as 'Walls Come Tumbling Down'. It was an obvious choice to be released as a single and in October it reached No 7. "I played tambourine on 'Shout To The Top', but I wasn't credited on the album," says Steve Sidelnyk. "But the thing was back then, if you popped into Solid Bond there'd always be someone recording or doing something and you'd end up getting pulled in to help out. Sometimes it was as simple as that."

Paul's lyrics have a message to us all – "When you're on your back, and your life's a flop, and when you're down on the bottom, there's nothing else but to shout to the top!"

TRACKLISTING

1. Homebreakers
2. All Gone Away
3. Come To Milton Keynes
4. Internationalists
5. A Stone's Throw Away
6. The Stand Up Comic's Instructions
7. Boy Who Cried Wolf
8. A Man Of Great Promise
9. Down In The Seine
10. The Lodgers
11. Luck
12. With Everything To Lose
13. Our Favourite Shop
14. Walls Come Tumbling Down
15. Shout To The Top

Café Bleu

"The whole point of no return"

Describing in his autobiography *That's Entertainment* how he felt during those weeks following The Jam's last concert in Brighton, Rick Buckler said, "It felt like I was unemployed… Only then did it all really sink in and it felt like I was standing on the edge of a chasm." Bruce Foxton was also in a state of shock and wondering what he could possibly do next. Paul however, had already set the wheels in motion for The Style Council.

Paul had told his Jam bandmates and his family of his decision and intentions back in the summer of 1982. "Bruce and me were not at all happy with Paul's decision, not our fans, or his family, especially John (Weller)," Rick recalls. "We had all put a lot of work and energy and years into the band. We had also proven ourselves as a band and we had No 1 records."

By the time The Jam ended their final set with 'The Gift', everyone in the band had six months to prepare themselves for the end and look forward to any new beginnings. It had been almost six months since Paul had broken the news to his Dad that he was leaving The Jam and it had been almost six months since John had replied, "You're fuckin' joking ain't you."

Remembering The Jam's last Christmas party, a tradition the band had enjoyed for the previous three years and always held in a room above The Greyhound in Fulham, Rick wrote, "I felt very separate and disconnected. It was as if three different parties were being held in the same room."

But whatever the case, Paul was making preparations for his next musical venture.

The Style Council was chosen over The Torch Society for the name of Paul's new band. He also took over the old Phillips studios that he'd worked in with The Jam and renamed them Solid Bond Studios. They were located at Stanhope House near Marble Arch.

"The Jam did a photoshoot at the studios and when Polygram put it up for sale my Dad and Paul thought it would be a good idea to buy it," says Nicky Weller. "I was 21 and left a job I was doing in Woking and I started to work there as the receptionist. The studios had an old analogue desk that helped to produce that lovely warm sound that can be heard on the early Style Council records. And then there was a listening room. A guy called George lived and worked in there as the tape operator. There was also a guy called Arthur and he'd been working at the studios way back when it had been in the Polygram years."

Honorary Councillor, Hilary Robertson, also recalls Solid Bond with fondness "Being in Solid Bond and working with The Style Council was really exciting. There was also the aspect that it used to be owned by Philips and, during the Sixties, great artists like Dusty Springfield had recorded there. Also at the time the Wellers had their offices in Solid Bond, so there was also Nicky and John Weller being around every day. There'd be a lot of people poking their heads around doors and so on.

"Tracie was around a lot, as was Vaughn Toulouse. I met so many people at Solid Bond. And often after a recording session, a group of us would walk into the West End and go to some night club, bar or at times just some greasy spoon. But there were also a lot of parties going on in Solid Bond. After all, it was a great venue in a fantastic location. I don't recall if any of those parties was to launch *Café Bleu* though."

Paul's first post-Jam live performance was on January 5, 1983, at the ICA, London, at an Everything But The Girl concert. It had been less than a month since he'd played his last concert with The Jam in Brighton. Rehearsals for Paul and his new band mates were also being organised.

Paul would next perform with his new band at the May Day Show for Peace and Jobs at the Liverpool Empire organised by the CND. Back in 1980, Paul had written an article for the *Melody Maker* on the Campaign for Nuclear Disarmament (CND). CND was one of the first campaigns that Paul publicly supported. In 1981, The Jam played at a CND benefit concert at the Rainbow Theatre in London and in the same month performed at a CND rally held on the Embankment, London.

Next up for The Style Council was a European tour that took in Germany, France, Brussels, Holland and Switzerland. In Germany, Paul somehow managed to break his arm. In July, The Style Council also played a miner's fund raising show at Liverpool's Mountford Hall. During the show, they performed a Smokey Robinson number, 'It's Time To Stop Shoppin' Around', with Madness. The Nutty Boys were another of Britain's bands that had been showing their support for the miners.

What Paul realised, by the end of the first six months of his new band's life, was that he had something fresh and modern on his hands. He had a sound that blended his love of the Sixties with jazz and soul and he had a reason to smile again. He was going to enjoy The Style Council.

Mick Talbot was born September 11, 1958. He grew up on the streets of Wimbledon and played keyboards in the Merton Parkas, one of the Mod bands that sprung up during the so called 'revivalist' period. The band had one top 40 hit in 1979 called 'You Need Wheels'.

Paul had invited Talbot to play keyboards on The Jam's cover version of 'Heatwave', included on the *Setting Sons* album. "When I first met Paul I was in the Merton Parkas with my brother Danny," says Mick. "I had a day job in the City and he worked around the West End area and it was while Danny was buzzing around that he used to bump into Paul.

"Because of that, Paul found out about our band. There was even some talk about Paul producing something for us, but it didn't happen. The Merton Parkas did play upstairs at Ronnie Scott's and for some reason, Rick Buckler got up and played the drums for us when we performed 'In the Midnight Hour' for the encore. Because of those sort of things, Paul found out about me. He'd also been given a copy of our single, which he didn't particularly like, but he did like the piano solo which was on the B-side. That's why he rung me up one day and asked me if I would play on a Motown cover that The Jam were recording for *Setting Sons*.

"So my beginnings started with that piano on that B-side and over the years Paul and me would have deep and meaningful conversations about overlooked B-sides. I ended up going into Townhouse Studios and

QUIET PLEASE !

Above: an ad for what was at the time Paul's favourite iconic guitar manufacturer, Rickenbacker.
Opposite: Paul photographed for Flexipop magazine in 1983 at the Beehive Studio, Primrose
Hill. Photo: Neil Matthews

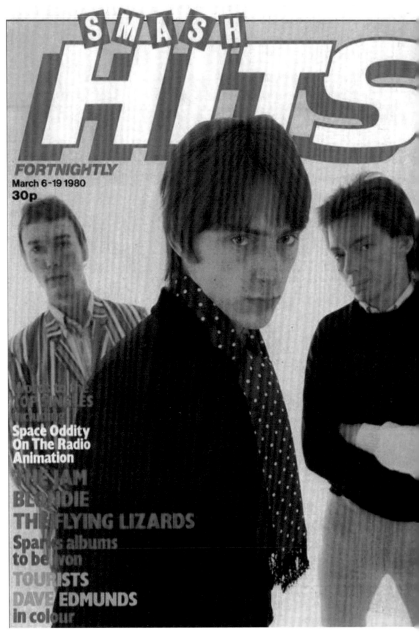

SMASH HITS

FORTNIGHTLY
March 6-19 1980
30p

Space Oddity
On The Radio
Animation

THE JAM
BLONDIE
THE FLYING LIZARDS
Sparks albums
to be won
TOURISTS
DAVE EDMUNDS
in colour

Dedicated followers of fashion: the Woking trio grace the cover of *Smash Hits* in
March 1980. Opposite Polydor promo poster (top) and a Jam business card (bottom)

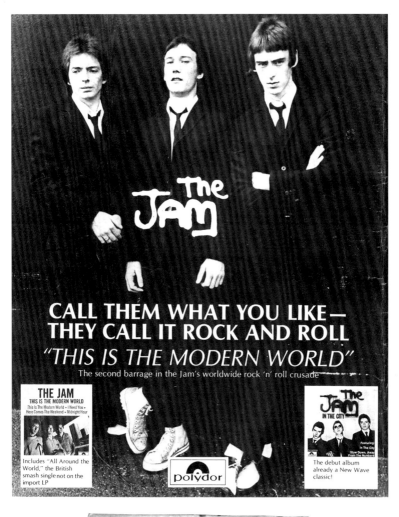

THE JAM

CALL THEM WHAT YOU LIKE — THEY CALL IT ROCK AND ROLL
"THIS IS THE MODERN WORLD"
The second barrage in the Jam's worldwide rock 'n' roll crusade

THE JAM
THIS IS THE MODERN WORLD
This Is The Modern World • I Need You •
Here Comes The Weekend • Midnight Hour

Includes "All Around the
World," the British
smash single not on the
import LP

polydor

IN THE CITY
Featuring:
In The City
Slow Down, Away
From The Numbers

The debut album
already a New Wave
classic!

The Jam   Woking 64717
ROCK & ROLL GROUP

Paul Weller Rhythm	**Steve Brooks** Lead Guitar
Bruce Foxton Bass Guitar	**Rick Buckler** Drums

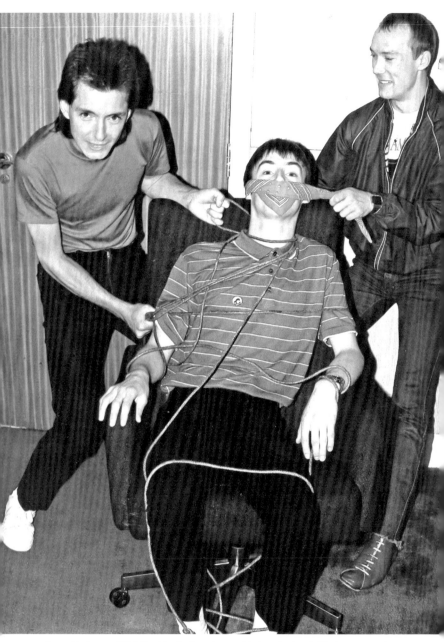

Bruce Foxton and Rick Buckler finally get a word in for a feature in Flexipop magazine – which certainly injected a bit of fun into a fairly maudlin world. Photo: Neil Matthews doing the track live with Paul, Rick and Bruce (and Rudi Thomson out of X-Ray Spex on sax) and 'Heatwave' was the first song that I recorded with Paul.

"I then did some live stuff with The Jam at the Rainbow, coming on with a piano for the encore. Then I didn't see Paul for about eighteen months. Out of the blue, he asked me to do some more live stuff and he wanted a Hammond played live on stage. There were some soul tunes The Jam were including in their set. This was near the last days of The Jam.'

After leaving the Merton Parkas, Talbot briefly did a stint in Dexys Midnight Runners before becoming a member of The Bureau which also included some ex-Dexys members. In 2012, Talbot teamed up with Kevin Rowland again during the *One Day I'm Gonna Soar* period

In Mick Talbot, Paul found a companion with whom he felt he could move forward. Talbot was an ally that could support his vision for The Style Council, a set up that would, as Paul described, be "More of a floating line-up." And the two young men seemed to see eye to eye. "We stand back to back, me facing East, he facing West and we still see the same things," Mick said at the time.

"I remember being in Nomis studios and Rick and Bruce wandered off to get something to eat," says Mick. "While they were gone, Paul, Dave Liddle and myself had a jam with some soul tunes. Paul alternated between some drums and then some bass. It was really good to do. I'm not saying that was when the seeds were sown for The Style Council, I really don't know. I just think that around that time I was on Paul's radar and it gave him something to think about. Also, when you spend time together like Paul and me did, you get to talk about things other than music, things that have shaped you like clothes and books. Paul and I had things we understood about each other."

Regarding the sort of music Paul and Mick wanted to make, Mick said at the time, "As far as we're concerned, our music is about feel." So they set about writing material together, much of which would appear on Style Council's debut album, *Café Bleu*.

Nicky Weller: "I liked the Parisian feel of *Café Bleu* and the whole feel of The Style Council at that time. It was so different from The Jam. At first Dad didn't know what to make of it. A lot of it was done so tongue-in-cheek and sometimes they were just taking the piss. But I also think *Café Bleu* was Paul just enjoying himself and trying something new. I mean he went from writing 100-mile-an-hour tunes in The Jam to some very melodic music that contributed to *Café Bleu*. With The Style Council, he also went from playing in a three-piece to playing with a much bigger collection of really good musicians."

Mick: "The first two to three years of The Style Council were full of excitement and exuberance. We had an attitude of wanting to try things even when people said don't do it or that's not you. We took a risk and it was worth it because it basically came off. Looking back, I admire that we had a go at certain things. And what we did attracted a different audience. I remember Paul telling me that he couldn't believe how many girls were in the audience. The Style Council had girls coming to the concerts in a way that The Jam hadn't. In the late Seventies and early Eighties there'd be quite a lot of violence at gigs. There was a football type crowd at concerts. But The Style Council concerts were different."

Once armed with some new songs and recordings, a mini-album called *Introducing The Style Council was* released. The album was initially only released in Australia, New Zealand, Japan, The Netherlands and North America, with copies being imported into the UK. Some Weller fans bought it just out of curiosity and whilst some instantly liked it, others took a while to come around, if they did at all.

The album had been recorded throughout June 1983 in La Studio Grande, Armee in Paris and included 'Long Hot Summer', 'Headstart For Happiness', 'Speak Like A Child', 'Long Hot Summer (club mix)', 'Paris Match', 'Mick's Up' and 'Money Go Round (Parts 1 & 2)'. Paul and Jam producer Pete Wilson co-produced the album. Paul sung a verse in French on 'Paris Match', a song he originally wrote the song for Suzanne Toblat. She recorded the song entirely in French but it was never released.

Throughout 1983, The Style Council released four singles – 'Speak Like A Child/Party Chambers', 'Money-Go-Round (Part 1)/ (Money-Go-Round (Part 2)', 'A Paris EP – Long Hot Summer/Party Chambers/The Paris Match/Le Depart' and 'A Solid Bond In Your Heart/It Just Came To Pieces In My Hand/A Solid Bond In Your Heart (Instrumental)'.

Paul's royalties from 'Money Go Round' were donated to the Youth Campaign For Nuclear Disarmament. 'It Just Came To Pieces In My Hand/Speak Like A Child' was also released as a fan club flexidisc in December 1984. Each song was very different but they did leave some of Paul's fans feeling somewhat confused, even alienated. On the one hand, there was the heavy Hammond led 'Speak Like A Child' (Paul had described Mick as "The finest young jazz-soul organist in the country") where Paul still looked like he did in The Jam. Then there was a song like 'Long Hot Summer' with its accompanying video that some people simply couldn't get their heads around or understand. Some asked what the fuck was he doing rolling around on the grass and lounging in a boat with Mick steering and looking like some French student in denim shorts and espadrilles (like soul boys and girls wore during that period).

'A Solid Bond In Your Heart' threw yet another spanner in the works with a video that began with Paul arriving at the grounds of Woking Football Club on a Lambretta, looking sharp in a mohair suit, crisp white shirt, tie and polished loafers and Mick also looking very Mod, like he was back playing in The Merton Parkas. Further into the video, and inside the club house, they are joined by a large group of Mods, who, along with Paul and Mick, all start dancing. Gary Crowley mans the decks and in the crowd is a young Eddie Piller who would go on to befriend Paul and form Acid Jazz Records. Mods and Jam fans could relate to that video. 'Speak Like A Child' and 'Long Hot Summer' left them a little perplexed.

'Speak Like A Child' included Tracie Young on backing vocals. She had appeared on The Jam's final single 'Beat Surrender' and also in the promotional video. Young, a cheerful-looking Paul dressed in a beige raincoat, dancing and prancing and Mick playing his Hammond were all filmed riding around in an open-top bus with a large banner on its side that said 'Really Free Aren't We'. It was all a bit of a piss take.

Incidentally, Nicky Weller was one of the females joining Paul as he pranced around the Malvern Hills. "The fact that The Style Council was a collaboration between a bunch of musicians worked," she says. "When Mick and Paul got together it would be hilarious. You can see the fun we had just from the videos."

Tracie: "I absolutely loved 'Speak Like A Child'. I loved my backing vocals on it, everything. I was thrilled to bits when Paul asked me to sing on it. It was such a great song and so different to everything that Paul had done before. The vocal arrangements that Paul and Pete Wilson came up with were amazing. I was so new to the industry at the time and being in the studio with Paul and Pete was so exciting and interesting.

"I learned to love studio work more than performing live. Working in the studio was creative and experimental. It was great. And then we did the video for 'Speak Like A Child' and that was so much fun. I can even remember which hotel we stayed in, The Cottage in the Woods. When we shot the video, it was very cold, it had been snowing. In between takes we would retreat to the coach to warm up. During one of these retreats, Paul was sat playing some air guitar and he was playing along to the bass intro on Kajagoogoo's 'Too Shy'. Then once the song got going he asked what the song was and I told him. 'Well it's fucking shit,' he said and stopped what he was doing. That was very Paul back then."

Mick: "I played the electric piano and Paul played electric guitar and then at a later stage the bass guitar too. By that point, the drums had already been recorded so Paul needed to play bass and it's not the easiest way to record, but he did it and it worked. He managed to get a sort of Chicago swing. For 'Money Go Round', Paul got someone in to lay down the bass but they didn't quite get the vibe that Paul had when he played it. People forget that Paul played bass in The Jam before he played guitar and I think he's quite underrated as a bass player.

"Paul's also a very good piano player and in the last couple of years in The Style Council I was constantly trying to encourage him to play the piano. I laugh now, because looking back it looks like I was talking myself out of a job, but I like to think that I care enough about recorded music where the aim is to try and get the best possible outcome for that song. It's capturing the essence that is important and you don't want to lose something that is pure and if that meant Paul should play the piano then so be it. I certainly enjoy a lot of the stuff that Paul has done in his solo years when he's been at the centre of a song playing a piano."

'Speak Like A Child' was billed as "A new record by new Europeans." The single was issued in a simple black sleeve. Ex-Polydor A&R man, Dennis Munday, has written about his admiration for the sleeve design – "I thought the sleeve was very clear and understated... but I had to proofread the bloody thing!"

"The producers of this record wish to thank this drum warrior (of only 18 summers) for his work and help in making this LP." Those were the words written in the *Cafe Blue* sleeve notes by Paul, about his new drummer, Steve White.

Steve was born on May 31, 1965, and hailed from Southwark, South London. He got his first drum kit at a very early age and it wasn't long before he was being tutored by Bobby Orr and Bill Bruford. There was a lot of soul and jazz-funk in South London in the Seventies and that naturally rubbed off on Steve.

At just 17, Steve was introduced to Paul via Dennis Munday. Paul was not only impressed by Steve's drumming but also by his keen interest and knowledge of jazz music. Steve played his first gig with Paul on May 25, 1983 – Paul's 25th birthday.

Steve wasn't a Mod. His fashion and style interests lay elsewhere and this was something Paul admired and welcomed. "The fact that I had never really connected with the Mod scene meant that when I first got to meet Paul, I wasn't intimidated by him," he says.

Alongside music, football was another of Steve's interests, Charlton Athletic being his club. With the holy trinity of fashion, football and music being priorities in his life, Steve was in his element when he joined Paul and Mick's new gang.

In the early Eighties the football casuals were a force to be reckoned with. Many Mods ditched their parkas, Fred Perry jumpers and bowling shoes favouring kagools, Pringle jumpers and Nike trainers instead and Steve took the casual thing seriously.

In more recent years, Steve can be found appearing at drum clinics. He has become recognised as one of Britain's greatest drumming talents and joining in with the clinics provides him with an opportunity to share his passion with an appreciative audience. Often during the clinics, Steve likes to fill the session with anecdotes of his time in the music industry and playing alongside Paul.

One story he likes to tell relates to the first day he was due to go on tour with The Style Council. Everyone, the band, crew, management, would meet up outside Earls Court. Steve arrived with his parents. As he was boarding the tour bus, The Jam's old tour manager and The Style Council's new, Kenny Wheeler, turned to Steve's parents and said, "If you're worried about the sex and drugs, don't be... I'll make sure he gets his fair share!'

"Working with Steve was amazing, says close friend Steve Sidelnyk. "When we started I was just 18 and he was only a year younger. At the time I thought I was quite a good drummer but then I met Steve and it was like 'fuckin' hell'. I learnt so much from Steve. I was a loud drummer and my technique was not great but Steve was so precise and so professional. He taught me about light and shade and he would spend time with me, showing me things and teaching me. Steve was a massive influence on me. By the time he was 18 he was already at a musical level that was far above most other people.

"Being around Steve was a hugely positive experience. He shaped me and enabled me to go on and do the other things I've done in my career. He pushed me a lot as well. I remember when we were doing a Red Wedge concert and The Blow Monkeys were billed too. Steve knew they were looking for a percussionist and he told me to go and ask them if they could use me and, they did and I ended playing with them.

"And if it hadn't been for Paul I wouldn't have done anything at all. Before meeting Paul and The Style Council, jazz wasn't on my radar at all. It was only after getting involved with them that I turned my attention to jazz music. The closest I had got was with bands like Santana and Weather Report – I loved *Heavy Weather*. Steve White was a huge jazz influence on The Style Council. He had that jazz technique. He also had that Buddy Rich showmanship thing too, which was great for the Council. When he joined for *Café Bleu* he completed the band."

Paul wanted The Style Council to be a vessel in which he could explore new waters. He'd been flirting with genres of music that were interesting him towards the end of The Jam, namely the jazziness of 'Shopping', 'Fever' and 'Pity Poor Alfie'. They were Jam songs but in other ways they weren't Jam songs at all. Whatever they were, at the time they certainly raised a few eyebrows and got people asking the question what was happening to *their* Jam. And now with Mick Talbot and Steve White by his side, Paul Weller could move forward with a clearer vision. And he was in a band again.

The Style Council's first official photoshoot took place in Boulogne, France. For their excursion, the members wore raincoats, turned-upped blue jeans and white socks with polished penny loafers. Pastel colours abounded, so all the jumpers and shirts were either pinks, blues, greens and yellows. It was all very continental, especially French.

"I actually have a French connection," says Mick. 'The correct pronunciation of my name is Talbo, the t at the end is silent. Apparently, it's something to do with a refined wine house. My brother looked into the family history and discovered it. It became part of The Style Council because around the start of the band, Paul and I were watching a lot of French new wave cinema. We were both enchanted by it. For some reason, around late 1982, Channel 4 had a season showing those sort of films and they all had interesting soundtracks, very French naturally, but also influenced by modern jazz. We had a big appreciation of that.

"We also saw how French folk musicians and composers like Debussy and Ravel broke the rules. It was a mixture of those things and the clothes the people wore in those films that influenced Paul and me at that time of starting up The Style Council. I would see Paul the day after he'd watched one of those films and he say something like, 'In that opening scene did you see that mac that bloke was wearing?'"

Paul wholeheartedly embraced the cafe culture. Photographs emerged of him wearing his wayfarers and a trench coat, sipping an espresso outside French cafes. The photos captured a feel that was fresh and exciting.

This French style life that Paul was now showing had been mostly lost on British kids, whose only experience of the continent were school day trips to Calais. Additionally, several photographs were taken of Paul and Mick sitting on walls with their jumpers hanging off their shoulders and the Eiffel Tower in the background. The Tower also featured on the sleeve covers of The Style Council's EP 'A Paris' and the majority of the sleeve notes was even written in French.

There were others before Paul that had been drawn towards the continent for style counselling as original Sixties Mod Gill Evans Catling recalled in the book about Mod girls called *Ready Steady Girls* (Snowball/Baxter/Brummell) "When I went out wearing the clothes that I'd made I would get odd looks from people; they genuinely thought I was quite strange because I wasn't wearing what everybody else was wearing. Gradually, some people started to get interested and they asked me what the look was all about. I told them it was the continental look and that I was a continentalist. This was the word I used before I started calling myself a Mod."

The Mods of the early Sixties had bought into the Italian and French styles as well as the US Ivy League look. Gill Evans Catling hadn't been alone in her quest for stylish continental clothing in the early Sixties any more than Paul was in 1983.

The continental look was The Style Council's 'birth of cool', and would inspire a whole new bunch of kids who had been aware of The Jam but not really into them. Some dyed in the wool Jam fans weren't able to stomach Paul's latest venture and join him on the next stage of his journey. But some, like Eddie Piller, adapted quite easily. "By '81 I'd fallen out of love a bit with The Jam's direction and I was glad when he set up The Style Council," he says.

There were three influential factors that The Style Council helped to introduce many young people to – style, jazz and politics. Following Paul's lead – and his Red Wedge comrades Billy Bragg and The Redskins – many young people delved into the values underpinning socialism, an education they didn't get in school. The nearest most Jam fans got to jazz was probably via their parents' record collections. And then there was style and Paul's new take on Modernism.

It took some people a while to get their heads around the fact that just because Paul had stopped being in The Jam he hadn't stopped being a Mod. One picture taken around 1983 shows Paul walking through a bunch of young Mods dressed in Parkas and wearing Jam shoes. They gaze in awe at Paul who is no longer looking like them. But Paul *was* still a Mod. He had simply moved forward.

Both Paolo Hewitt in his book *The Soul Stylist* and Phil Thornton in *Casuals*, make the connection between Mods and casuals. Paul's new look and that of The Style Council certainly combined elements of the two. "At the time of The Style Council forming I had an awareness of the casuals thing going on," says Mick. "I'm always loathe to label anything when it comes to clothes because as soon as you do, you get labelled as being part of that something and as soon as that happens someone throws a rule book at you and if you're not doing what's in their rule book, you're breaking the rules.

"For me at the time, I just really liked a lot of black music and I liked my clothes and there were plenty of others just like that. And that goes way back in English culture. Often, the next new cult that comes along doesn't always want to know about the history that went before it. I had an interest in the casual thing and I just cherry picked the bits that I liked. It was the same for Paul and then Steve (White) and we all fed off each other."

Arguably, there are no Mod clothes, there is no Mod music, there are no Mod attitudes, but there are clothes which Mods like, music that Mods can agree with and attitudes that Mods adopt. This way of thinking has been demonstrated by Paul Weller since the earliest days of The Jam and it's something some Weller fans have also been able to adopt.

Another important feature in the story of The Style Council was the 'Cappuccino Kid'. The Cappuccino Kid was a mysterious character who turned out to be Paolo Hewitt. In some ways, he provided the presence of another band member. Although he didn't play an instrument, he did still play an important role and his words thrilled many a Style Council fan.

In the booklet contained in the box set *The Complete Adventures Of The Style Council*, the Cappuccino Kid signed off his piece, "I am proud to say that I count my dear links The Style Council as a shining example." Paolo was there from the start and he was there at the end. He considered The Style Council's last gig at the Royal Albert Hall to be their greatest performance.

Café Bleu was released on March 16, 1984 by Polydor Records. It was recorded at Solid Bond Studios and produced by Paul Weller and Pete Wilson. The album reached No 2 in the UK charts, which wasn't a bad start for the new venture.

The musicians on *Café Blue* included Mick Talbot and Honorary Councillor's Steve White, Billy Chapman, Barbara Snow, Pete Wilson, Ben Watt, Tracey Thorn, Chris Bostock, Hilary Seabrook, Dee C Lee, Dizzy Hit and Bobby Valentino.

"The freedom of not having a set line-up, especially in the first year of The Style Council, meant that we could see each track as a little screenplay or a story and then we'd cast," says Mick about the Honorary Councillors. "Using that analogy, someone like Orson Wells would continually use the same actors and they became his company, but some of the actors don't appear in everything, he simply used the ones that were right for that part. That's how we did it with the Hon. Councillors. Over time, Paul and I got a company together that was tried and trusted and that meant we could do the songs live. But also there were times when, for the recorded version, we could do something unique with the song."

Hilary Robertson: "I don't know how Paul found me, maybe he'd seen me play or maybe someone had mentioned me to him. In 1983 I was doing lots of sessions and gigging all over London. It was on Wednesday September 28 (I know that for sure because it's written in my diary that I still have) when John Weller phoned me and asked if I could do an audition down at the Solid Bond Studios. I went down the following day and I remember arriving at the studios and being greeted by Paul who shook my hand and said, 'Hi my name's Paul Weller,' and I was thinking like, 'Yeah I know it is. My god it's Paul Weller.'

"I was introduced to Mick Talbot and we played for a bit. The only song I was familiar with was 'Long Hot Summer', which had been a big hit throughout the summer. I don't remember exactly what I played but whatever it was Paul and Mick must have liked it because the following week I found myself rehearsing with The Style Council for their forthcoming European tour. We played a full set on the tour that included songs like 'Speak Like A Child', 'It Just Came To Pieces In My Hand', 'Money Go Round', 'Here's One That Got Away', 'Mick's Up', a cover of 'Hanging On To A Memory' (Chairman of the Board) and 'Solid Bond In Your Heart'.

"It was only once we'd finished the tour and returned to the UK, and literally as we were getting off of the coach, that Paul came over to me and asked me if I would go into the studio the next week to record some songs. I wasn't going to say no.

"We had arrived back in the UK on the November 1 and on the tenth I was back in Solid Bond Studios. I went in a few times over the next couple of weeks but we also some did some TV and radio work too.

"On the tour I played alto sax, tenor sax and flute which I then used to play on certain tracks on *Café Bleu*. My name then was Hilary Seabrook. On the *Café Bleu* vinyl inner sleeve booklet that came with the album my name got spelt incorrectly on 'A Gospel'.

"When I went into Solid Bond to do the recording, Paul and Mick already knew what they wanted me to play and where I should play, but there was a strong element where they allowed me to do what was right for me. Because it was Paul's studio there wasn't the usual time constraints hanging over us, so Paul was happy for me to try things out. There was a great deal of musical freedom.

"It was clear that The Style Council was Paul and Mick's band and it did feel like it was an equal share between the two of them, it was just that Paul was the most well-known, and if Paul said the rehearsals started at 11am you had to be there for 11am. It felt good to be an Hon. Councillor and to have been part of The Style Council at that time. I feel really proud to have been part of *Café Bleu* and fortunate that Paul had found me. I'm grateful to him for that.'

Written in the evocative Blue Note mood *Café Bleu* sleeve notes was, "A smiling Paul Weller once said a couple of words on behalf of his generation, now a café catalyst who has put a cheerful step forward onto the doormats of our lives. He asks for nothing in return except sanctimonious smiles and a peace of mind." The point of "a couple of words on behalf of his generation" had certainly been true and many old Jam fans and new Style Council fans were still prepared to listen to what Paul had to say.

The sleeve notes continued with "For relaxation, he lists water polo and meeting deadlines as his main hobbies." The point of meeting deadlines echoes what Rick Buckler said in *That's Entertainment* – "So it seemed that Paul jumped off of one treadmill and straight onto another one," and was again finding himself under pressures and having to write songs to order. But by 1983 Paul was in a much wiser place and understood the music industry. He was finding ways in which he could stay in control and have a stronger voice.

The opening track on *Cafe Bleu* is a chirpy number called 'Mick's Blessings' written, funnily enough, by Mick Talbot. It's simple and pure with only a piano and tambourine, and it introduces The Style Council's debut album to the world in just one minute and 13 seconds.

Paul begins the second track, 'The Whole Point Of No Return', with just his voice and his new guitar, the Rickenbacker now being an instrument of his yesterdays. The song stops you in your tracks, demanding that you sit back and listen. It's like wandering into a Parisian cafe and finding Paul propped up on a stall in the corner, casually entertaining a small crowd

By the time the third track on the album begins, it's becoming clear that *Cafe Bleu* needs to be played while relaxing rather than cranking up the volume and crashing around the room like in the good ol' Jam days.

'Me Ship Came In' is the first all-in jazz number with White, who must have been in his element throughout the entire album, using the rimshot technique to capture that percussive feel that was so popular in the jazz clubs of the Fifties. White's sticks dance across his ride cymbal enhancing Mick's equally energetic piano work. Paul plays both bass and guitar and joining them is Barbara Snow on trumpet and Billy Chapman of Animal Nightlife on sax.

'Blue Café' begins with a jazzy guitar intro played skilfully by Paul. White joins in using the brushes technique to stroke his snare drum in between taking the occasional gentle swipe at his cymbals. The double bass and the string arrangement were provided by Pete Williams. 'Blue Café' is an atmospheric song that conjures up images of smoke filled basement jazz clubs in Soho in the days of absolute beginners.

It's unlikely that Paul knew of the origins of Mods when he first got interested in them as a teenager. Like many others of his generation, his first reference points would have been bands like The Who and the Small Faces and places like Carnaby Street and the Flamingo and Scene Clubs. The Modernists and the late Fifties jazz scene that sprung up in Soho was where it all began and in many ways *Cafe Bleu* acknowledges that.

"I had only really subliminally listened to jazz music," says Mick. "My Dad's a big modern jazz fan so that was always being played in the home. My Mum listened to the pirate radio stations and so there'd be Motown. It was a blend of both types of music that I heard growing up. As I got older, I understood jazz better and leaned towards the more gospel end of it and I saw how this connected to the roots of soul music.

"I listened to jazz and soul musicians but I just liked songs. I also really liked instrumentals. Growing up, my life was dominated by seven inch singles and a lot of what I got were instrumentals by people like Booker T. I also really liked the instrumental B-sides that bands like the Small Faces put out. Later I did a charity record with Kenney Jones and I told him about my love of those B-sides and he was really pleased."

Commenting on 'The Paris Match' in *Suburban 100*, Paul wrote, "I was going through my heavy French phase, so this was my attempt at a torch song, a Style Council chanson." The point is made simply.

'The Paris Match' is sung by Tracey Thorn of Everything But The Girl and she sings it beautifully, each moment capturing that blue mood of melancholy – "As I walk from cafe to bar." Thorn's vocals take the listener on a gentle stroll through city streets. The lyrics are moving, "I'm only sad in a natural way and I enjoy sometimes feeling this way." Many of us can relate to that.

Ben Watts, also of Everything But The Girl, plays guitar and Chris Bostock of JoBoxers plays double bass. "The early Eighties was so musically diverse," says Chris. "You could do anything and inspire people as long as you did it with full conviction. Styles were coming and going quickly. We were at the tail end of the Punk to New Wave to Ska to Rockabilly to New Romantic chain of events and I found myself part of Subway Sect's second coming with Vic Godard and the influences of Cole Porter and George Gershwin.

"We launched the new Subway Sect in 1981 under the banner of 'Cool Bop & Swing' at our newly-formed Thursday night 'Club Left' at the Whisky-a-Go-Go, later abbreviated to the WAG club. We were signed to Phonogram, released our *Songs For Sale* album and toured the UK with The Bureau – the original Dexys Midnight Runners line-up – and featuring none other than Mick Talbot on Hammond organ.

"We got on incredibly well with Mick and the group on that tour and between the tight performances also managed to have some hilariously high-spirited leisure periods. Mick took a keen interest in our set and later showed up at one of our recording sessions where I was laying down some tracks on double bass.

"Our group then became the JoBoxers when we were signed to RCA Records with our new singer Dig Wayne and our second big UK hit 'Just Got Lucky' – which I'd penned with Dig – was at No 7 in the chart. I got a message from RCA that Paul Weller had called up wanting me to do a session for him. I had been a massive Jam fan and loved the first Style Council single 'Speak Like a Child'. I could hear the Northern Soul/Motown leanings which were so close to our hearts in the JoBoxers, so I was very pleased indeed that he had called.

"I headed over to Paul's Solid Bond Studios that sunny afternoon not having a clue what to expect. It was a beautiful Regency building with a small lawn at the front and had a rich heritage as a recording studio that dated back to the Fifties. Outside I met Paul, who was taking a quick break and catching some rays and I noticed he had worked up quite a tan. Paul and I had an interesting chat and I remember explaining how 'Just Got Lucky' had been written and how we developed it as a JoBoxers track, before heading down into the studio to do some work.

'I quickly got down to recording the double bass part to 'The Paris Match'. No pickup was needed, just the bass and a single microphone in a small, close, partitioned area. The track included Tracey Thorn's gorgeously dreamy vocal as a guide, along with Mick's soulful piano and Ben Watt's heartfelt guitar and the brushed kit, so the bass track went down and that lazy haunting sound reverberated through the studio while the sun radiated relentlessly through the windows."

Dee C Lee also recorded an equally beautiful version of 'The Paris Match' and included it on the same disc as her hit record 'See The Day'. Another singer, Kristyna Myles, released a version in 2013. Steve White played drums on it, just like he had on Dee's version 30 years earlier and Damon Minchella, ex-Ocean Colour Scene bassist, played bass. Myles' version was very modern, but just like Thorn and Dee, she did the song justice.

Of 'My Ever Changing Moods', Paul pointed out in *Suburban 100* that

"On one level, this is about my own moods, which were probably even more dramatic at that time. I've slowed down in my old age."

The song is also about Paul's observations of society at that time and sharing his concerns. The threat of nuclear war was a very real possibility. Paul had sensed this threat since his Jam days and he helped bring organisations like CND to the attention of many young people. The imagery in the video of 'Going Underground' with the mushroom cloud rising high into the sky, was a frightening spectacle. Paul said that 'Going Underground' was his response to the political leaderships of Thatcher and Reagan "linking arms'", false nationalism and phoney patriotism. But for many back in 1980, what they really heard was just a great single, The Jam's first No 1. Thirty years later, 'Going Underground' was played at John Weller's funeral.

The version of 'My Ever Changing Moods' that appeared on *Cafe Bleu* was different to the one that was released as a single. Throughout The Style Council's career, Paul certainly favoured variety and enjoyed the freedom to record different versions of the same song. "Paul did a demo of 'My Ever Changing Moods' with him playing the piano and the album version is closer to the way he first heard it," says Mick. "I think you get more of a sense of the lyrical power of it too."

'Dropping Bombs On The Whitehouse' is another jazz number with the spotlight shining on White. Again Bill Chapman and Barbara Snow join the band and Paul plays bass.

This excerpt from the novel *Long Hot Summer* captures a mood shared by many young Style Council fans:

"Loz absorbed himself in the drawing and before long it was complete. As he laid the pad and pencil on the floor 'Dropping Bombs On The White House' burst into life. He snatched the pencil back and found another one so that he could drum along to the song. Steve White launched into his drum solo and Loz did his best to keep up with him, tapping the pencils furiously on his knees. The solo built and built until Loz's' favourite bit kicked in '1, 2, 1, 2, 3, 4,' cried Steve White inviting the rest of the band to re-join him. Even Loz was breathing heavily by this stage.

"Satisfied that he'd unleashed a brilliant drum solo of his own, Loz flung the pencils into the air and leapt up. The Style Council had set a mood and now they were about to inform his choice of clothing. Loz searched through his wardrobe for his blue polo shirt and blue jeans, that he always kept a one inch turn up on. Next he pulled on a clean pair of white flannel socks and pushed his feet into his favourite tasselled loafers. As he exited his bedroom he grabbed his three-quarter length beige raincoat, the one of a similar style to what Weller wore on the '*Café Bleu*' album cover."

The lead vocal, or rather rap, for 'A Gospel' is supplied by Dizzy Hite. 'A Gospel' is essentially a techno-funk song with Paul exploring new frontiers. The song uses electronic drum sounds, with drum programming provided by Pete Wilson.

Hilary Robertson: "Pete Wilson was also working with us in the studio. Pete was brilliant and I really loved working with him. Working with them all was really great. The thing with Paul especially is that he's always really, really professional."

'A Gospel' demonstrates Paul's ability and awareness to stay abreast of what was happening around him, to assimilate it all and re-craft it.

Track nine, 'Strength Of Your Nature' is another Paul composition, his sixth so far on the album. It's also another funky number complete with more drum programming provided again by Pete Wilson. It's also the first time that Dee C Lee makes an appearance.

Prior to joining The Style Council, the South London girl born on June 6, 1961, had sung backing vocals for Wham. Diane Katherine Seah (her real name) was a classic soul girl, one of the thousands that, in the late Seventies and early Eighties, helped make the East and South London soul and jazz funk music scene so fresh and thriving.

She then had a brief period as a solo artist before grabbing Paul's attention and being invited to sing on *Cafe Bleu*. Dee C Lee would remain an integral part of The Style Council story and indeed Paul's. Paul and Dee were married for ten years and they had two children together, Leah and Natt.

'You're The Best Thing' is quite simply wonderful. On the album version Pete Wilson provides the drum programming for the third time and Paul supplies both the bass and guitar synth sounds. There is nothing wet or gushy about this song. It all works, and Paul delivers a soft soulful vocal which would be heard time and again across the rest of Paul's career in and out of The Style Council. 'You're The Best Thing' was the second song on *Cafe Bleu* issued as a seven inch. It reached an impressive No 5.

'Here's One That Got Away' sees JoBoxer Chris Bostock back in the mix providing the bass part and there's a new Hon. Councillor in the shape of violinist Bobby Valentino.

Many Hon. Councillors came and went during The Style Council and they each contributed something that helped create the band's unique sound.

'Paul wanted a walking electric bassline with a Northern feel on 'Here's One That Got Away'," recalls Chris Bostock. "The backing track already had the drum track, Paul's guide vocal and acoustic guitar and Mick's organ, but no violin at that point. It has an infectious, swing feel which got us all clapping along. While recording this track, Paul played along on guitar and I became aware of his driving energy and determination, coupled with prolific song writing, continuing a recording tradition in the very space where the Walker Brothers and Dusty Springfield recorded a couple of decades before.

"It was most satisfying to finally hear both tracks on the *Café Bleu* album in their finished form when the album was released. *Café Bleu* was certainly a pivotal album for Paul that enabled him, with Mick, to break out when he had so much within. It's also one of those great albums that work from start to finish – plus it doesn't date. It will always be a favourite of mine and I'm delighted to have played a small part in its making."

Dee C Lee steps up to take a lead role in 'Headstart For Happiness' and her vocals are packed full of soul. There's also the addition of another Hon. Councillor – this time it's Hilary Robertson on saxophone. The whole track really swings and there's some great jazzy snare work from White.

The last song on *Cafe Bleu* is called 'Council Meetin', a Hammond led track with Paul feeding the song with the bass and a flute sound.

And that's the end of The Style Council's debut album, a record full of variety and dynamics that included a host of diverse musicians and sounds that would all feature heavily in the band's future. *Cafe Bleu* was only kept off of the No 1 position by Howard Jones' *Human Lib.*

"*Café Bleu* was mostly appreciated and by the time the album came out we had already had a few tracks released," says Mick. "We recorded a lot of songs in the first 18 months of The Style Council. Our debut album could have been a very different collection of songs.

"I'm proud of *Café Bleu.* I think it's got its moments. Some journalists tried to label the album and Paul and me with the jazz thing. We were not trying to be jazz musicians. Yes, there was a lot of jazz influences on *Café Bleu*, but for us, we were just aware that we were in a group and didn't want to be labelled as this sort of band or that sort of band. We didn't want The Style Council to be aligned with any particular cult. For us it was either good music or bad music. We knew what our influences had been and, what had led us to *Café Bleu.*"

TRACKLISTING

1. Mick's Blessings
2. The Whole Point Of No Return
3. Me Ship Came In!
4. Blue Café
5. The Paris Match
6. My Ever Changing Moods
7. Dropping Bombs on the Whitehouse
8. A Gospel
9. Strength Of Your Nature
10. You're The Best Thing
11. Here's One That Got Away
12. Headstart For Happiness
13. Council Meetin'

The Jam Years

"When I first met Paul, I was impressed by his 100 per cent belief in how he was going to make it as a musician and a songwriter. A day job was not on his agenda. Paul's writing was simply incredible – great songs with melody and meaningful lyrics. Playing those songs today has once again hit home how advanced and observant he was. My time with Paul was, and still is, one of pure excitement and love. Simply inspiring!"

Bruce Foxton

The Gift

"So keep on movin', movin' your feet"

I n 1981, Paul set up two record labels. One was called Jamming! which he asked Tony Fletcher, editor of a fanzine of the same name, to run. Tony went on to have a successful career in writing with the brilliant *Dear Boy: The Life Of Keith Moon* and *Boy About Town* that documented in detail his friendship with Paul. Paul's other record label, backed by Polydor, was called Respond.

'When I Was Dead' by Rudi, a band from Northern Ireland, was the debut release on Jamming! in September 1981. The first signings to Respond were Dolly Mixture and Scottish outfit The Questions.

Tracie Young was also signed to the label. But her relationship with Paul didn't always run smoothly. "In the early days of working with Paul he very much led the recording process in the studio," says Tracie. "When it came to recording my stuff he had a very clear idea of how he wanted those songs to sound. There were also budget restrictions with Respond so things had to be done a certain way. And I didn't always agree with Paul's way.

"One time we had a massive argument during the recording of 'Give It Some Emotion'. Some of my unhappiness had started back with 'The House That Jack Built'. There were things which Paul did to the track which I just didn't like. For example, the song had been sped up which altered my vocals. I asked if I could re-do my vocals but was told no. I just didn't like the way my voice had been pitched up and I didn't want people to think that's what my voice sounded like. Then there was a drum machine part in the middle eight which I hated. It was like somebody drilling.

"Most of the time spent working with Paul and the other artists on Respond was great. What Paul was trying to do with Respond was really interesting. He was trying to build something based on that Motown type blueprint.

"On the day of recording 'Give It Some Emotion', I walked into the studio and discovered that Paul had already recorded the backing track. We had previously done a demo which I loved, but the new version I absolutely hated. It bore no resemblance to the original demo and one of the things I really liked about the original demo was that it had a breezy pop feel to it with jangly guitars, but the new version was all drum machines and they were really heavy too. And then on top of that, there were the big synth sounds. It just wasn't what I'd envisaged at all. I was really upset and told Paul that I didn't like it. But Paul didn't like that I didn't like it and we started to argue.

"However, Paul put his foot down and said what he'd done was going to stay and so I stormed off. I went down to the toilet was so angry I slammed the cubicle door shut but as I did the handle fell off and I got locked in! By this point I was absolutely steaming and just sat on the floor fuming. Because I was locked in, I stayed there quite a long while. Eventually, Paul sent a guy called Arthur, who was the caretaker at Solid Bond, to find me. He tapped on the door 'Trace, you alright? Paul was wondering where you are? Are you in there?'

'Yep', I replied. And then Paul showed up too, 'Are you coming out Trace?' 'Well that depends' I answered, 'On what?' Paul asked. 'Well, on whether someone opens this bloody door!' I screamed.

"It was very humiliating. Anyway, Paul still wouldn't climb down or change his mind about the track. I never liked 'Give It Some Emotion', ever! However, in 2009 I did a show in Shepherds Bush and performed the song acoustically, just me and guitar and saxophone and it was played how I had envisaged the song should have been and it was so nice.

"Paul and I had another big row during the making of *Far From The Hurting Kind*. Again, Paul had some set ideas which I didn't like and I wanted 'Far From The Hurting Kind' to be released as my next single. I thought it was very me but Paul wanted to go with 'Nothing Happens Here But You'. He said if 'Far From The Hurting Kind' was issued as a single I would get labelled as a little soul girl, and I was like, 'Well what's wrong with that?' In the end 'Soul's On Fire' was released as the single."

While Paul was busy with the record labels, The Jam started 1981 by playing some low-key gigs. The first was on Valentine's Day at The Cricketers pub in Woking. Two days later, the band played at the Woking YMCA followed by another gig at Sheerwater Youth Club with support from Respond's The Questions and Dolly Mixture. That show was filmed for *Something Else* presented by Woking boy and Sheerwater student, Steve Carver.

Throughout the year, The Jam did extensive tours in the UK, Japan and Europe armed with some new material. They also had their latest single, 'That's Entertainment/Down In The Tube Station At Midnight' to promote. The record had been issued as a German Import.

In May, they released their twelfth UK single 'Funeral Pyre/ Disguises'. The Jam's third single of the year, 'Absolute Beginners/ Tales From The Riverbank' was released in October 1981. The video showed Paul, Foxton and Buckler sprinting around the streets that surrounded Nomis Studios.

At Christmas, the fan club issued a flexidisc of 'Tales From The Riverbank' and the band gave their final live performance of 1981 on December 19 at the Hippodrome, Golders Green, followed by their traditional Christmas party at the Greyhound in Fulham.

In February 1982, The Jam had their third No 1 record with 'Town Called Malice/Precious'. It had gone straight in at No 1, achieving something only The Beatles and Slade had done previously. In March their sixth and final studio album, *The Gift*, was released and became The Jam's only No 1 album.

In June, 'Just Who Is The Five O' Clock Hero/The Great Depression' was released as a Dutch import. It appeared that the band were going from strength to strength. But by the time 'The Bitterest Pill/ Alfie/The Fever' was released in September, the band knew their lives were about to change (and who noticed or really cared that the guitar intro to 'The Bitterest Pill' sounded the same as the *Bagpuss* theme?).

In the summer of '82, Paul announced he was splitting up the band. Although Rick, Bruce and John Weller hoped that Paul might change his mind, he didn't and 1982 was the final year of The Jam. Their story and legacy, however, would go on.

Looking back to the meeting at Red Bus Studios, called by Paul on return from his holiday, Rick remembers that, "Everyone tried to dissuade Paul – me, Bruce, John, the record company, everyone. But it was too late."

Rick remembers that Paul's explanation was, "He felt he was on some kind of a treadmill that was dictated by the band's contractual obligations with Polydor and he felt that he was just going around and around. Basically, Paul told us he was leaving The Jam."

Nicky Weller: "When The Jam split up, I wasn't really that bothered. I was twenty years old and had other interests. My Dad was absolutely gutted, as were Rick and Bruce. But when The Style Council happened I really liked that and got really involved with that too. What was great was that unlike The Jam, all of a sudden women would be at Style Council concerts and everything had a different feel about it. And The Style Council was a fun time!"

Ann Weller: "Looking back, I think Paul had already planned to split up The Jam. It was just a matter of doing it at the time he thought was right."

Nicky: "I had a conversation with Paul just the other day and he told me that he couldn't be a 57-year-old man and still doing songs like a 17 year- old."

Having digested the news that Paul was effectively breaking up The Jam, everyone concerned started to plan for the months ahead. Bruce took it especially hard, even at one stage refusing to commit to the final tour. It was only after Glen Matlock's name was thrown in as a possible replacement that Bruce reconsidered and agreed to play. There were also new single releases to promote and they would eventually be joined by an album, plus the fans had to be told.

On a windswept December day in 1982, Paul was interviewed by BBC's *Nationwide*. Dressed in a beige raincoat and scarf, he already looked like a member of The Style Council.

The presenter said, "At 24, Paul Weller has become somewhat of a spokesman for the new beat generation. He has pronounced on politics, life and music to enthusiastic fans who receive his message. They've come from America and Japan to hear him"

The scene then shifts to Paul and the presenter standing on a promenade beside a choppy sea.

Presenter: "The band is amazingly successful – why stop now?"

Paul: "I feel we have achieved enough. I think we've done all we can do as the three of us and I think it's a good time to finish it. I don't want it to be going on for the next 24 years and become nothing. I want this to count for something. I want the past five or six years to count for something."

Paul then shares his feelings of dissatisfaction about the social system. "I'd like to see the power and wealth distributed properly."

Presenter: "Is music going to help with this?"

Paul: "I don't think music can overthrow it directly, but it can help communicate (the issues) to different people. Music is the only real culture that young people have got."

Presenter: "You've done very well for yourself, aren't you being a bit self-righteous?'

Paul: "I think you've got to try and work out what you're best at, so that's what I intend to do."

Presenter: "Your future appears to be mapped out."

Paul: "The Jam is a group regardless of me being portrayed as the front man. I think a lot of our fans think of it as being a group... as three of us."

Presenter: "What do the other two think? Some people might say you're dumping them."

Paul: "Well that's a load of crap aint it! The Jam is a group and it's not my responsibility."

Presenter: "Are they happy about the break-up?"

Paul: "I wouldn't say they are happy, but it's just something I felt inside me, and I have to go by my instinct. And I felt it's the right thing to do. I thought about it, it wasn't like I just made up my mind overnight. What's nice about it is it's the first time for years that I haven't had any definite plans. I don't know what is going to happen, which I'm quite enjoying at the moment. Whatever I do I want to be successful or else there's no point in doing it."

For many Jam fans, this was how they got hear about The Jam splitting up, even though rumours had been circulating for weeks before The Jam's Fan Club's official announcement on October 30.

However, before Paul's announcement at that Red Bus Studio meeting, The Jam had started to promote *The Gift*. Most of March and April was spent touring the UK and Europe and for a large chunk of May the band toured the US and Canada. In June, the band returned to Japan and in September, October and November they were back touring the UK. Planned European dates were cancelled and they played their final concerts in December.

December 1-5 they played at Wembley Arena, on the 6th the Royal Spa, Bridlington, the seventh the Apollo, Manchester, the 8th Bingley Hall, Stafford, ninth Civic Hall, Guildford and the very last Jam concert was on December 11 at the Brighton Conference Centre. "There was certainly no after-party," says Rick. "It really felt like me, Bruce and Paul simply walked away from The Jam."

The set list from that final Brighton concert: 'Start', 'It's Too Bad', 'Beat Surrender', 'Away From The Numbers', 'Ghosts', 'In The Crowd', 'Boy About Town', 'Get Yourself Together', 'All Mod Cons', 'To Be Someone (Didn't We Have A Nice Time)', 'Smithers-Jones', 'Tales From The Riverbank', 'Precious', 'Move On Up', 'Circus', 'Down In The Tube Station At Midnight', 'David Watts', 'Mr Clean', 'Going Underground', 'In The City', 'Town Called Malice', 'Butterfly Collector', 'Pretty Green', 'The Gift'.

The infamous Eton Rifles Dance Troupe (ERDT) also put in an appearance at that final show. "At one of Paul's recent gigs I met one of the girls who was in the Eton Rifles Dance Troupe," says Nicky Weller, an honorary ERDT member. "I hadn't seen her for years.

"That whole thing only came about from a guy called Pete Barrett. I think Paul suggested to him to come up with an idea that would be completely mad. We had a laugh but it didn't go down well and we got booed off stage. The audience just didn't get it at all. But then we were dancing like hippy dippy hippies – just taking the piss really. We even dressed up in hippy costumes, beads hanging around our necks, wigs and we put flowers in our hair. The troupe was me, a couple of girls, Gary Crowley, Carl Badger and Pete Barrett."

The Jam's final single, 'Beat Surrender/Shopping/Move On Up/ Stoned Out Of My Mind/War' released on November 26, had been in the charts for two weeks by the time of the last show. It reached No 1 and stayed there for two weeks. The upbeat 'Beat Surrender' had been a perfect choice to end The Jam's run of singles but it almost didn't happen because another song, 'Solid Bond In Your Heart' had also been a contender.

Tracie Young, only 17 years-old at the time, was invited to sing backing vocals on the track.

Tracie had come to Paul's attention after she had replied to an ad she'd seen in *Smash Hits*. "Paul Weller is looking for a female singer for his Respond label, aged between 18-22." Tracie posted Paul a cassette of her singing a Betty Wright song called 'Shoo-Rah! Shoo Rah!'. She later discovered it was that choice of song that interested Paul.

Gill Price contacted Tracie and invited her to come to the Solid Bond Studios and meet Paul. On the day of the audition, Pete Wilson played Freda Payne's 'Band Of Gold' and the Four Tops 'Reach Out, I'll Be There' on the piano and Tracie sang along with Paul.

"I ended up performing 'Beat Surrender' with The Jam on *Top of the Pops*," says Tracie. "Paul can be very funny at times. When we knew we were doing *Top of the Pops* he decided it would be a good idea for me to wear a ski-jumper. I was okay with that and went out and got the boots and some ski-pants to go with it. At the time Paul was really into the ski-jumper look. But then Paul turned up with some ski goggles and he wanted me to wear them, saying it would be very cool and very funny. But I said no way. I mean it was going to be my debut *Top of the Pops* appearance. Funny for others but not funny for me.

"I was still only 18 years-old and was about to appear on the nation's biggest music TV programme. So I put my foot down on that one and I didn't wear the goggles."

Air Studios in London's Oxford Street was chosen as the studio to record *The Gift*. The Jam began recording in October and by the end of the year had five songs in the bag. The other six tracks were recorded throughout January 1982. Air Studios had been constructed in 1969 by legendary producer George Martin. Paul McCartney even popped his head round the door one day when The Jam were using the studios. Paul Weller would go on to have further encounters with McCartney.

The album's front cover photograph of Buckler, Foxton and Paul (the order of line-up had changed by this point) was taken by Twink on the Air Studios roof. The idea of photographing the band literally running on the spot was an obvious connection to the song 'Running On The Spot'. The album sleeve was designed by Alwyn Clayden.

The production on *The Gift* was credited to Pete Wilson and, for the first time, The Jam. All songs were composed by Paul except 'Circus' which was credited to Foxton.

Musicians who played on *The Gift* included Steve Nichol on trumpet, Keith Thomas on saxophone and Russ Henderson on Hammond and steel drums. *The Gift* was released on March 12, 1982, and it hit the top spot!

'Happy Together' is introduced by somebody saying, "For all those watching in black and white, this one's in Technicolor." Paul is letting everyone know there's absolutely nothing outdated about The Jam's new album – which he knew would be their last. And it's true, all the songs are vibrant, alive and colourful. Paul then screams Babeeeeeeeeeeeeeeeeee!" and that's followed by bass and hi-hats.

'Happy Together' is punchy and Buckler's uplifting punky Tamla four-four does the song credit. Throughout *The Gift*, Buckler returns to the same snappy-drum pattern several times, more so than on any other Jam album. It's essentially a soul beat made famous and mastered by Motown's 'snake-pit' drummers and Funk Brother members, Benny 'Papa Zita' Benjamin and Richard 'Pistol' Allen. Rick put his own twist on it.

"I was trying to call out to my generation, a rallying call in the name of inspiration and fulfilment," Paul wrote of 'Ghosts' in *Suburban 100*. Paul has always supported like-minded people and encouraged, even empowered them, where possible. He spots a grafter and respects that. Paul's early output was frequently underpinned by the notion of 'escape' and doing something that will the sense of fulfilment. Paul grasped what life was at an early age and set his mind on living it to the best of his ability. It's what he wanted for his generation too.

'Ghosts' is the first song on the album to feature a brass section.

Nicky Wire of the Manic Street Preachers told *Uncut* magazine that he always listened to 'Ghosts' when he drove into London. The song does exactly what it says on the tin – "Keep on shuffling to this ghost dance beat." The arrangement is simple, as is Buckler's drumming, mostly just hi-hat and rimshot. Coming in at just two minutes long, it's a haunting song that doesn't outstay its welcome.

By his own admission, 'Precious' is Rick's least favourite Jam song. He once took a tape of it, before it was officially released, to a disco and asked the DJ to play it. People happily danced, unaware it was a Jam song and thinking it was just another run-of-the-mill disco number. The fact that the bass line was similar to Pigbag's 'Papa's Got A Brand New Pigbag' didn't go unnoticed either.

Nothing The Jam had done previously compared to 'Precious'. It may have been a brave thing for the band to include on the album. But Paul was on the move and he wanted Jam fans to move on up with him. He refused to shackle himself to any genre of music, desiring to experience new sounds that his more ardent Mod fans wouldn't have expected from him. For example, Paul loved Michael Jackson's *Off The Wall* and Bob Marley's *Legend*.

Paul uses a wah-wah peddle skilfully and that, mixed with Bruce's funky bass, Buckler's soul-disco beat and the brass section, creates a powerful vibe.

'Just Who Is The Five O' Clock Hero' is Paul writing about his Dad but also reacting to something that Prince Phillip had said about the ordinary man needing to pull his socks up and make a bit more effort that obviously got beneath Paul's skin.

Rick produces an unusual sounding, awkward drum pattern for 'Just Who Is The Five O' Clock Hero?' and that, coupled with the way the bass and guitars prod the brass section, shouldn't work at all. But it does. Totally. The public thought so too because when it was released as a single it got to No 8.

Paul introduces 'Trans-Global Express' with an extended hiss. And then the song punches its way through the verse. It's the snappiest song on *The Gift* with some cultured brass. Paul once said of Rick, "He was absolutely the right drummer for The Jam."

The instrumentation on 'Trans-Global Express' was inspired from the funky-soul track 'So Is The Sun' by World Column. On the album sleeve there was a scene from a Northern Soul all-nighter and the four to floor stomper 'Trans-Global Express' wouldn't have been out of place caressing a sweat-soaked Wigan Casino floor.

'Running On The Spot' reflects the sense of disappointment that Paul felt at the time. The high hopes he had for the generation he was a part of were being kicked in the bollocks. Paul's inherent Modernist way of thinking and living resonates with every note – life offers great opportunities and when things don't happen, you become stale. Paul will battle the stale until the end

'Running On The Spot' begins with Paul's "1234" count in and it's another full-throttle surge. The band sound tight and sharp, Rick impressing with some sassy snare, reminiscent of 'Funeral Pyre'. Twenty-five years later 'Running On The Spot' became a regular feature in Paul's live sets.

'Circus' is the quirkiest track on this diverse album. It's a Bruce composition which explains the prominent bass part. It's a two-minute instrumental, a mixing pot of noises that clash but connect.

The words of 'The Planner's Dream Goes Wrong' are just as relevant today. The sponsors of The Space Between sculpture of The Jam in Woking by Richard Heys, were Barratt Homes who have contributed to the changing face of the British landscape.

In the decades that followed 'The Planner's Dream Goes Wrong', Paul's predictions proved to be pretty accurate. "They were going to build communities" but the results have often produced anything but positive results. As Paul once pointed out, the planners never need to live in their own creations.

The bass, drums, brass and steel drums add texture to Paul's voice and demand that you listen to the lyrics.

In 1999, Simon Halfon compiled the album *Fire And Skill – The*

Songs Of The Jam that featured various artists covering Jam songs. 'To Be Someone' was recorded by Noel Gallagher, 'English Rose' by Everything But The Girl and 'A Town Called Malice' by Gene. 'Going Underground' by Bill Janovitz was released as a single with 'Carnation' by Liam Gallagher, Steve Cradock, Damon Minchella, Steve White and even Paul playing the keyboard.

Throughout Paul's career, collaboration has been a byword. He's performed with such diverse artists as the Purple Hearts, Peter Gabriel ('And Through The Wire'), the Cockney Rejects ('England I Miss You Now').

'Carnation' is a pop art poem, "If you give me a fresh carnation, I would only crush its tender petals."

When Paul wrote 'A Town Called Malice' in 1981, Margaret Thatcher had been Prime Minister for two years. People threw parties when she died in 2013, "Hey-ho the witch is dead…"

Paul too was passionately vocal in his opposition to Thatcherism throughout his career. Before she died Paul said, "I hope she rots in her own hell." He firmly believed Thatcher and her cronies tried to destroy traditional working class communities and he channelled his anger into music.

Paul's lyrics succeeded in deconstructing the shit, pumping out messages free of intellectualism. Ordinary kids in council towers could identify with that deconstructed shit because it told tales of lives similar to their own.

It's no surprise that 'A Town Called Malice' became a No 1 hit. It's a foot-tapping, lipsmacking, fingerclicking homage to the Detroit dream machine of Motown and Rick gets down and dirty with it.

"In Town Called Malice" I did a drum roll which was my way of trying to recreate the sound of a train rattling along the track," says Rick. "There were times when Paul's lyrics would inspire my drumming. Another example was the drum roll on 'Down In The Tube Station At Midnight'. There's the part where the drums come back in, sounding like a train echoing down the track."

The track also contains one of Bruce's finest bass lines along with some of Paul's most recognisable lyrics, "Struggle after struggle, year after year."

'A Town Called Malice' has since been used in movies like *Billy Elliot* and John King's *Football Factory*. It's also a favourite of Ray Davies who said he especially liked the sound of the snare drum and the Tamla Motown style riff.

The Gift is not only The Jam's farewell song on the album, it was also the last song they performed together as a band on stage at the Brighton Conference Centre. For that fact alone, the song holds an endearing place in the hearts of Jam fans.

'The Gift' is the most aggressive track on the album. It's forceful with swirling Hammond sounds that complement Paul's angry guitar and no-nonsense vocals. "Move, move, I've got the gift of life."

In 2005. Rick Buckler formed a band called The Gift. His reason was simple – he simply wanted to play Jam songs again. Within a couple of years, Bruce joined Rick and The Gift morphed into From The Jam. For many Jam fans, it was an opportunity to hear The Jam's back catalogue all over again live. After Rick left From The Jam in 2009, Bruce continued to grow the band into the hugely popular outfit they are today.

TRACKLISTING

1. Happy Together
2. Ghosts
3. Precious
4. Just Who Is The Five O' Clock Hero?
5. Trans-Global Express
6. Running On The Spot
7. Circus
8. The Planner's Dream Goes Wrong
9. Carnation
10. Town Called Malice
11. The Gift

Sound Affects

"No matter where I roam..."

The Jam decided to cut short their tour of the States and return to the UK. The reason was simple – they wanted to celebrate 'Going Underground' reaching No 1.

Having a No 1 record meant an automatic invite on *Top of the Pops* and when they appeared Paul wore an apron with the Heinz beans logo on it. But he had to wear it inside out because of the advertising laws.

Riot Stories was established in January 1980. The project was a joint venture between Paul and his schooldays pal Dave Waller and their first publication was Dave's *Notes From Hostile Street*. Other publications included a collection of poems from different poets called *Mixed Up, Shook Up*, the fanzine *December Child, Beat Concerto* and *Internationalists* in 1985. *Riot Stories* effectively ended after Dave Waller's tragic death from a heroin overdose. Paul's song 'Man Of Great Promise' was a fitting tribute to his friend.

In April 1980, Paul met with Pete Townshend at the Trinifold offices in Old Compton Street, Soho. By all accounts, the meeting of two of the greatest Mod minds wasn't as fruitful as hoped. They discovered they didn't have very much in common – at least then. Years later their paths would cross again with a very different outcome.

The Jam visited Japan and played their first concert on July 3, 1980, at the Mainichi Hall, Osaka. They performed five concerts in total, three of which were in Tokyo. This was to be the beginning of a long love affair with the country. The Jam returned for more gigs in May 1981 before heading off to play a handful of concerts in Canada, another place with which Paul has forged a long-lasting relationship.

October and November were mostly spent gigging around the

UK with a few dates in Europe. The band concluded their most successful year to date with a show at the Coliseum, St Austell.

Sound Affects was the last album that Vic Smith worked on. It was recorded in Townhouse Studios, London and released on November 28, 1980.

The album sleeve was designed by Bill Smith. "Paul came up with the idea of wanting to produce an album sleeve that looked like one of the BBC sound effects albums," says Bill. "There was a whole library of such albums at the BBC and Paul had come across some of them lying around in the studio. It was also Paul's idea to change sound effects to sound affects, a clever play on words. Every one of the BBC sound effects albums was numbered so I called it Sound Affects No.80 because the album was released in 1980.

"With Paul's idea in mind, I then set about pulling in the various images for the album sleeve. I took and sourced some of the shots and the photographer Martyn Goddard took the others. And with every image I tried to relate to lyrics from the songs on the album. The pound sign, for example, related to 'Pretty Green'. I'd get my ideas for album sleeves after having heard the songs. My ideas for any album sleeve I ever did were always fed by the music. For instance, when The Jam were recording in the Polydor studios at Stratford Place, I would sit in and have a listen. I was working in the building at the time as Polydor's Art Director.

"The telephone box was in a street in Gravesend town centre. I took the photograph when I lived there. The pylon was in the countryside just outside Gravesend. I took the photograph of the crowd on the terraces at Charlton's ground because I used to go and watch Charlton play. I took the photo of the people waiting at the bus stop and the Dansette was mine. The picture of the skyscraper with the thunderbolts was done by an artist that I worked with on other projects. The girl's face I found in a fashion magazine and pulled it out to use. The dog was my girlfriend's parents dog whose name was Max. I did the handwriting piece of 'from the cradle to the grave'. I took the photo of the screwed up wrappings on the tiled floor. They were food wrappers for fish fingers and garden peas.

"Martyn took the photo of the baby who was one of his relatives. He also took the shot of the hearse and recently the funeral directors who owned the vehicle contacted him asking for a copy of the original photo after seeing it at The Jam exhibition in Somerset House. The jukebox was also one of Martyn's photos because he owned it! The picture of the police car was one of his and I think he also took the shot of the roof tops from *Coronation Street* on TV."

The sleeve also included a poem by Shelley, 'Masque of Anarchy', and several photographs taken by different rock photographers – the aforementioned Martyn Goddard, Pennie Smith, Andrew Douglas and Andrew Rosen.

"It's every bit an album of this decade, a point which won't need labouring after the release day," wrote Paul Du Noyer in the *NME* November 15, 1980. Du Noyer also noted that while the songs on the album were "extremely melodic… the old attack was still there."

Sound Affects begins with 'Pretty Green' and Bruce playing five bass notes, which he repeats three times. The notes are captivating. Then a single strike of a snare drum and the hi-hat kicks in. The production is full of reverb – you already know this won't be anything like their previous album, *Setting Sons*

Paul then strikes in with, "I've got a pocket full of pretty green." He's singing about money; back then one pound notes were green and white. Money was just starting to roll into The Jam's coffers by the time of *Sound Affects* and by 1980 Paul was earning a decent wage from his songwriting.

The verse sits back a little but the rock chorus presses forward with Paul reminding us that, "You can't do nothing unless it's in your pocket – oh no." 'Pretty Green' is the perfect album opener. At one stage, it looked like the song would be released as a single instead of 'Start'.

Paul revealed that he pinched the name 'Pretty Green' from an

American TV game show host who would say, "Here's a big barrel of pretty green for you, folks!". Paul would often find time to watch US TV when the band were touring. The difference between British and American TV then was vast, especially when it came to game shows. In Britain contestants were happy to walk away with a new toaster or cuddly toy but in America they were awarded large cash prizes and extravagant items, like, as Paul joked, "submarines and Cadillacs."

In 2009, Liam Gallagher launched his own clothing label and called it *Pretty Green* after the song. The label's statement said it all, "Since the birth of rock 'n' roll in the late-Fifties, British street culture has been influencing fashion and music worldwide. *Pretty Green* has an authenticity born of a deep understanding of that culture and the things that make it relevant today."

In August 2010, *Pretty Green* opened its flagship store in Carnaby Street. A year later the label collaborated with Paul on an autumn and winter range. The venture was something that pleased him. "I enjoyed designing my first capsule collection for *Pretty Green* and wanted to continue the collaboration by designing a larger range," he said. "I've taken my inspiration from the Sixties and Seventies and have reflected my own style in the collection." The range included coats, shoes and knitwear.

Monday is the most romantic day of the week, according to Paul. 'Monday' is a song about the first stages of love, the period when lovers can do nothing but think about each other all the time. 'Monday' was the sort of love song that Jam fans could relate to.

Next to 'English Rose', 'Monday' is Paul's second most moving ballad from The Jam years. "I will never be embarrassed about love again," were just the sort of words teenagers wanted to hear as they experienced the joy of new love and the agony over its loss.

'But I'm Different Now' opens with a blistering guitar riff, the kind of attack that Paul Du Noyer was referring to in his *NME* review. Despite its Who-imbued ferocity, it's essentially another love song –

"But I'm different now and I'm glad that you're my girl."

'Set The House Ablaze' is about the neo-Nazi groups that were springing up around the UK in the late Seventies. It was commonplace to have extreme right wing pamphlets shoved into your hands at football grounds and rock concerts. Skinheads often aligned themselves to such groups, a far cry from what the purer, original skinhead spirit of '68 had been all about "The black boots butch, but oh what a bastard to get off."

'Set The House Ablaze' opens with one of The Jam's most memorable guitar intros. It's a pulsating riff that blossoms with the introduction of drums and bass and Paul whistles the tune throughout the track.

Revisiting the imagery of 'black boots', the track ends with Rick playing a marching-style rhythm on his snare as Paul pounds out a plethora of "na na na nas."

It's no surprise that 'Start' was The Jam's second No 1. It's so original, despite the critic's fixation with the bass line sounding like 'Taxman' by The Beatles.

'Start' was recorded in Townhouse on June 19, one of the earliest from the *Sound Affects* sessions. "Loves with a passion called hate" is up there with some of Paul's most memorable lyrics. He cuts the song dead with another wonderful line, "And what you give is what you get."

Paul wrote the lyrics for 'That's Entertainment' in ten minutes on returning home from the pub one night; the tune came the next day. He'd been inspired by a poem called 'Entertainment' by Paul Drew from *Mixed Up, Shook Up*:

> "*A dead body on the hour, one, six nine or ten – that's entertainment.*
> *A rape before the Horlicks, a simulated orgasm before the Bovril –*
> *NOTHING IS FUNNY ANYMORE*
> *That's entertainment*
> *Murder with a point or without a point while offspring throw toys at each other*

Poison in the air you laugh with the comedians know they are watching
Elite defeat your thought – CRYPTIC CRYPTIC
Tea or coffee, gonorrhoea, cream bun, Cambodia, doughnut, syphilis,
The Daily Express, the British Movement, Marks and Spencer's,
Harrisburg,
Degree in geography, cancer, ELO, UDA
It's all the same isn't it
Murphy's War and the Vietnam war, it's all the same
That's entertainment."

Paul's song 'That's Entertainment' is a masterstroke. It's the first time he put down his Rickenbacker and recorded with an acoustic as the lead instrument, although there is one part where some psychedelic sounding guitar passes through. Rick contributes with the occasional rimshot and tambourine and Bruce plays sparingly. The song doesn't speed up or slow down, 'That's Entertainment' is designed to promote the words.

The references are familiar to working class Brits – "A police car and a screamin' siren, pneumatic drill and ripped up concrete, a baby wailing, a stray dog howling, the screech of brakes and lamplight blinking. That's entertainment…"

Ray Davies would've been proud of such lyrics.

Paul is enjoying 'paranoia' in 'Dreamtime'. The music and vocals swirl around as Paul describes a sense of helplessness, "My feet were glued and my tongue was tied," and while in that dreamlike state he's alone – "I'm so scared." The song is left hanging with Paul's final words, "My love comes in frozen packs," and the guitar fades away, ushering in another dreamtime…

On a June day in 1980, a young Martin Gainsford spent a day at Stratford Place interviewing Paul for his South-London Mod fanzine, *On Target*. Gary Crowley and Vaughn Toulouse were also hanging around the studio and all three were invited to sing backing vocals on a demo of 'Dreamtime'. It was an experience that Martin would never forget.

'Man In The Corner Shop' is another story of everyday British life. Corner shops were a very British thing, essential to local communities. They served as meeting places and abounded with local gossip. Paul uses that grand tradition to point out that all men are not created equal and that society is full of divisions. He drew on his own experience of growing up in Woking where he saw both rich and poor alike.

The song is also about the grass is always greener mentality, "He is sick of working in the factory, says it must be nice to be your own boss really."

All of the songs on *Sound Affects* were credited to Paul as the writer apart from *Music For The Last Couple* that was credited to all three members of The Jam. It's an instrumental apart from a couple of lines. The song includes sounds of a cowbell, shakers, a plastic cup being squashed and a fly buzzing around. Everything was captured live in Townhouse.

"See me walking around, I'm the boy about town that you heard of," sings Paul on the albums jolliest track. 'Boy About Town' is an infectious joy of a song. The brass adds a dynamic dimension, and after a mere one minute 55 seconds, it ends on a Daltrey-like "Ooh ooh."

For the album's last track, 'Scrape Away', Bruce provides a bass line that takes your hand and leads you through the song. Paul sings of being dried up and drives the point home by repeating across one section, "You're scraping away, you're just scraping away." Someone speaks in French, an interesting twist and something that would reappear in The Style Council, which at this point was still three years away. Maybe The Beatles' 'Michelle' had something to do with it?

Sound Affects was experimental on many levels, but then the same could apply to all The Jam's albums. Every album was an attempt to push back the boundaries that surrounded them at that time.

Paul was also taking notice of pioneering bands like Joy Division and Wire, "Those sort of bands were a definite influence on *Sound Affects*, " he said.

TRACKLISTING

1. Pretty Green
2. Monday
3. But I'm Different Now
4. Set The House Ablaze
5. Start!
6. That's Entertainment
7. Dream Time
8. Man In The Corner Shop
9. Music For The Last Couple
10. Boy About Town
11. Scrape Away

Setting Sons

Stick together for all time

One night in November 1979, The Jam played at London's Marquee Club under the alias of John's Boys. They also played another gig using the name The Eton Rifles.

Recorded at RAK Studios on January 9, 'Strange Town/The Butterfly Collector' was released on March 17, 1979. The single's cover, designed by Bill Smith, included a soft-focus image of a man standing at a crossroads in a strange town. The location was actually in Norfolk and the man was Martyn Goddard who had been photographing The Jam since 1977. In August 2015, Martyn and Bill Smith did a Q&A at The Jam exhibition in Somerset House, recounting their memories of those creative Jam years.

In September, 'When You're Young/Smithers-Jones' reached No 17 in the singles' chart. Neither 'Strange Town' nor 'When You're Young' found their way onto any of The Jam's studio albums. The band gained a favourable reputation for not exploiting their fans by not packing out albums with singles.

Setting Sons was released on November 27, 1979 and reached No 4. Paul was writing a lot of poetry during the making of the album and was also reading poets like Adrian Henri, Roger McGough and Brian Patten, who had produced the magnificent poetry anthology *The Mersey Sound*. On November 30, 1980, Paul was involved with a poetry event at the Vic Theatre in London, alongside McGough.

Now a permanent fixture, Bill Smith was drafted in to design another sleeve. "Paul's intention for *Setting Sons* was to produce a concept album about three friends that also included references to a Britain that he'd grown up in and knew about," says Bill. "The inclusion of the soldier element, like in 'Little Boy Soldiers' kind of stuck with me and that fed where I went with it.

"At the time I was working with a photographer called Andrew

Douglas and I sent him down to the Imperial War Museum to take a few shots. One was of a little bronze statue I'd found there called *The St John's Ambulance Bearers* by Benjamin Clemens. I felt the statue summed up so much that reflected the content of the songs on *Setting Sons*.

"The image of the statue provided a great presence on the album and on the early pressings the image was embossed which gave a sense of the figures standing out from the rest of the background.

"The shot on the back of the sleeve of the bulldog and the Union Jack was done by someone Paul knew called Andrew Rosen. He liked it and wanted to use it and it fitted in with the album sleeve design too. Out of all the members of The Jam, Paul was the one who got most involved with the album and single sleeve designs."

Paul says this era was his "literary years." On the one hand *Setting Sons* is about the formative lives of the three characters featured in the album who are not yet bogged down by responsibilities. On the other hand, it's also about their mature years when they must deal with the harsher pressures of everyday existence. Jam fans these days are mainly in their 40s and 50s but the band entered their lives when they were much younger. Now they are able to relate to the older concept of *Setting Sons* in a more tangible way. It all makes sense. Some of those fans are still friends with the people that discovered *Setting Sons* with them, the sort of friends that stick together through thick and thin. That's a real privilege to have in this life.

In the interview for *On Target*, Martin Gainsford asked Paul where did the idea of *Setting Sons* being a 'concept album' came from?

"It wasn't meant to be like a *Tommy* or *Quadrophenia* type thing," said Paul. "It was meant to be more like a reflection of my own school days or of loads of blokes like me. I was really close mates with two other blokes and all three of us have grown up and gone our different ways and that was the main basis of it really.

"Originally that was what it was meant to be about. We don't really want to do anything like The Who did because that's sort of a step backwards I think. Those sort of albums are ten years old maybe. Most of them are boring and a bit self-indulgent too. I suppose it was right for that time with them touring and performing the entire album and probably daring and different, but to do anything like that now is a step backwards in the Eighties."

'Girl On The Phone' starts with the Townhouse Studio receptionist's phone ringing, then crash, in come the band. Wilko Johnson would surely have been proud of a song like this. Recorded in October, it was one of the last from the *Setting Sons* sessions.

'Girl On The Phone' isn't about a stalker bothering Paul. He did have his own experiences of being bothered and had to install metal bars on the windows of the flat that he and Gill shared in London. But this song isn't about that.

The title was taken from a Roy Lichtenstein pop art painting from 1964, the one with a blonde-haired girl speaking into a white telephone saying, "Oh Jeff...I love you, Too...but..."

The female voice on the track was provided by the actual receptionist at Townhouse.

'Thick As Thieves' begins with Rick's memorable and totally infectious tom-toms. The production behind *Setting Sons* really starts to warm up now – the sound is full and strong.

Paul told *NME* that *Setting Sons* was about those three close mates who ultimately all head off in different directions. In 2007, Paul revealed that the three characters were inspired by the original group of Steve Brookes, Dave Waller and himself. "People change and friendships dissipate," he said, whimsically.

For the true fan, 'Thick As Thieves' is one of the most endearing of all The Jam's songs. It's about them, their friends, their exploits. It was a no-brainer for the authors (Stuart Deabill and myself) of The Jam fan-based book *Thick As Thieves* to use that title. The song said so much about youthful relationships, tight bonds and the sense of adventure.

'Private Hell' is about a stereotypical bored housewife who

wishes she had something else in her life. The woman in question is a victim of her own misery, stuck in a daily routine of "catalogues and numerous cups of coffee." She is a shadow of her former self, a nameless host to a nameless ghost. Paul actually based the character on the mother of one of his friends. He also said he wrote the lyrics with the idea of a dysfunctional family in mind who all live together in a house with no love.

Bruce's bass introduces 'Private Hell' and the pace picks up at this point in the album. The song, like all on *Setting Sons*, sounds impeccably well-rehearsed, partially due to the fact Rick and Bruce spent hours practicing the songs long after Paul had gone home to catch episodes of *Coronation Street*.

The dark atmosphere of the song is perfectly captured as "private hell" is repeated until the song fades away. This was one of the songs, along with 'Girl On The Phone' that Paul wrote in Nomis Studios while under pressure to come up with more tracks for the album.

'Little Boy Soldiers' could be The Jam's mini-opera, their own *A Quick One (While He's Away)*. It has all the ingredients, wrapped up in three minutes and 34 seconds.

The song jogs along at a comfortable pace as it passes through its various sections. There are sounds of exploding bombs, Rick's military style snare work, a mock lullaby part, all building to the crescendo with Paul announcing "We won!" and a piano chord rings out. Hollywood star and Jam fan, Ray Winstone, said he played 'Little Boy Soldiers' when getting into the character of a part he was playing in a play about a tank crew in World War One.

A flute is included in 'Wasteland', an unusual addition even for The Jam. It's the most melodic tune on *Setting Sons* and the lyrics describing wastelands of old tyres and bric-a-brac are captivating. The song acts as a mirror to our own lives, moments that we all share, "tumbling and falling, exactly like our lives." Paul was no different from his fans.

'Burning Sky' is a letter beginning with dear and ending with yours. This song is about one of the three characters in the *Setting Sons* story who becomes a businessman and the most successful out of the three. It's he who writes the letter – "How are things in your little world? I hope they're going well and you are too.'

The song is again about growing up and the weakening bonds between friends as life's pressures and values change. Paul was experiencing this when he wrote the songs on *Setting Sons*.

'Smithers-Jones' is Bruce's reaction to events he'd witnessed in his own life. He knew how it felt when his father was made redundant. This is arguably the best song that Bruce wrote for The Jam and he sings it over a backing of woodwind instruments. Although other versions were available, the album version was the one with strings that were arranged by Pete Solley.

'Smithers-Jones' is a wake-up call, a reminder that life can throw all sorts of things at us as we journey "from the cradle to the grave."

Beginning and ending with "la, la, las", 'Saturday's Kids' is a song of celebration about teenagers having a good time and "Not giving a fuck." But Paul saw some of his school friends heading into a life of dead-end jobs and pushing prams around at ridiculously young ages. He reminds us, and himself, that there's more on offer.

Paul wrote 'Saturday's Kids' in a caravan in Selsey Bill while it pissed down outside. He wrote 'The Eton Rifles' on the same day.

"As a family we would go on holiday every year," says Ann Weller. "We would get the train there. This was around 1962/'63. Paul always liked to wear a hat and we have photographs of him wearing cowboy ones. He looked like Woody from *Toy Story*."

The sentiment behind 'Saturday's Kids' is warm and welcoming and nostalgic. There are images of young kids building go-karts out of rubbish salvaged from dumps; the next age group up are whizzing about on battered hand-me-down bikes, making goal posts out of their jumpers and breaking into allotment sheds with the locals girls for another session of "if you show me yours I'll show you mine", and then there's the older kids who go to watch football, try to master dance moves at their local disco and attempt to get served down the boozer. Most of us have been Saturday's kids.

The inspiration for 'The Eton Rifles' was a march by the unemployed that had set off from Liverpool and took in Eton College en route. Flush-faced Etonians jeered, "Hello, hooray" as the marchers passed by and they, in turn, reacted strongly. What Paul saw was a class war being played out before him.

Paul's lyrics reflect the class differences. On the one hand, he writes of people who sup up their beer, collect their fags and are up for a row down near Slough and he also writes of those who represent the establishment, backed up by their ties and their crests. Rugby players also get a mention, maybe a reference to the Leeds event and his run-in with players from the Australian rugby team?

Talking to Martin Gainsford in 1980, Paul said, "The Eton Rifles was just a title I had in my head for a long time. But then it suddenly came together and I wrote it in about fifteen minutes. It's like a piss-take on this class war thing and all these sort of 'Urban Revolutionaries'. It was mainly written around a character who is one of my mates. He's a real leftist revolutionary but in the end, after he's spouted off about stuff, he's just permanently drunk so he's never gonna do anything.

"I just don't believe in revolutions anyway. I don't think it ever achieves anything. It's all bullshit. I think I've got a more reformist attitude."

'The Eton Rifles' was the only track lifted from *Setting Sons* to be used as a single and got to No 3.

The Jam had been including Sixties soul songs in their sets since they first started out – Wilson Pickett's 'In The Midnight Hour' had already appeared on their second album, 'This Is The Modern World'. So 'Heatwave' was a natural inclusion. The Motown song, written by Holland-Dozier-Holland in 1963, was first recorded by Martha and the Vandellas and later covered by The Supremes, Dusty Springfield and The Who. The Jam's version is the meatiest of them all, a fresh take on the great song. Mick Talbot provided the piano part.

TRACKLISTING

1. Girl On The Phone
2. Thick As Thieves
3. Private Hell
4. Little Boy Soldiers
5. Wasteland
6. Burning Sky
7. Smithers-Jones
8. Saturday's Kid's
9. The Eton Rifles
10. Heatwave

All Mod Cons

"Didn't we have a nice time"

On February 24, 1978 'News Of The World/Aunties And Uncles/Innocent Man' was released. 'News Of The World' was a Bruce Foxton composition. The promotional video showed The Jam playing their instruments beneath the giant towers of Battersea Power Station on a sunny day. Three decades later, the song would be used as the theme music to a BBC 2 programme *Mock The Week*.

In 1978 the Mod revival was becoming an important influence. Paul was supportive of bands like The Chords and Purple Hearts. He even played piano on the Purple Hearts track 'Concrete Mix', that only saw the light of day some years later thanks to Eddie Piller at Acid Jazz.

In 1980, Martin Gainsford quizzed Paul about Mod. "Most of the kids back in '77 and '78 were just Jam fans who tried to dress like us and that created a sort of Mod look," said Paul. "They didn't call themselves Mods. People seem too quick to put labels on themselves or on other people and felt it easier to say 'These kids are Mods' rather than 'These kids are Jam fans.' Do you know what I mean? It hasn't hurt us at all. Most of the kids are still with us whether they consider themselves Mods or not.

"It's like this whole badge and Carnaby Street tee shirt thing with targets and Union Jacks with THE JAM written across it. It gets on me tits. It's other people labelling us who are nothing to do with the band or the record label or anything and they're putting stuff out that pigeonholes the band and we have no control over it. None of the things we put out officially tie us into the Mod thing.

"Your badge, (Paul points at a Polydor official *All Mod Cons* badge I am wearing) is a couple of years old and that album did have a lot of that stuff of course, but that was back in '78 not like all the crap you see about now. Yeah, that does piss us off.

"I reckon there are a few good bands that came out of the Mod thing, The Chords especially. They'll be around for a long time, way after the revival is gone. Chris Pope, he's a good writer. I guess it's the same as punk. So many bands fell by the wayside and others stepped in who were inspired by the early ones and that's a good thing. I reckon if only three or four bands come out of the Mod thing and are still playing and releasing records in a few years, it's worthwhile.

"It was only a bit later when we were touring with *All Mod Cons* that we'd see kids coming up in parkas and some were telling me they'd bought scooters or were forming bands. *All Mod Cons* was never meant to be the catalyst of some Mod masterplan, it just all sort of came together at the same time really.

"It's the same pigeonhole thing where magazines say, 'The Jam started a new Mod revival.' To me it's always been kids themselves who started things on the street or in youth clubs or pubs or wherever. The Northern lot though always seemed to have been into it with the scooters and stuff and clocked us as being sort of similar very early on. Then there was the East End lot from London too. Sometimes a band can be a focal point and from that it grows but I remember seeing the Sex Pistols in 1976 and there were just 30 or 40 what you would call 'Punks' in the audience but I doubt they called themselves that at the time. It's the whole tag and label thing again. It's just how you want to dress.

"I wear what I wear coz I like it. I've got a parka and all that too, even now, but when things get on a nationwide level with thousands of kids out there doing it, it makes it all a bit silly, like little kids dressing up. It sort of cheapens it a bit too.

"This style of dress is what I like and I've dressed like this for about the last five or six years and probably always will, but I don't label myself as a Mod. I can't ever see me or the band changing direction either musically or style wise to something totally different. I am into the Sixties thing, simple as that, and I think I always will be.

Bruce and Rick love all that, maybe not as much as me, but we are all into similar stuff. We never come out and say, 'We are a Mod band and we dress like this all the time.' even though I do but that doesn't really matter. It's the music that is important and what we say in those songs.

"I wonder if Mods would like us if we wore bondage trousers?"

The Jam spent much of 1978 on the road. A short trip to France and Brussels in February was followed by gigs at the Marquee and 100 Club. And then in March they flew out to the States where they supported Blue Oyster Cult in Cleveland. The concert didn't go in their favour, the Cult fans just didn't 'get' The Jam at all.

Back in the UK in June, the band toured and in July they started recording *All Mod Cons*. In October they played two gigs in Ireland, Dublin and Galway, and then most of November was spent touring the UK promoting their new album. On November 29, 1978, they were invited to perform at the Wembley Great British Music Festival along with Slade and Generation X.

The Jam army have been fuelling rumours of a lost third album for three decades. They refer to a period when the band were demoing songs, but the material was considered not good enough to be committed to vinyl. In more recent years, demos of the songs that were ditched have found their way into the hands of some fans. One such song is 'Simon' that never got properly finished. When Rick was writing his autobiography, he was played the song. He couldn't even remember making a demo of it. Rick said The Jam recorded lots of demos and many just didn't leave the confines of whatever studio they happened to be rehearsing in at that time.

Paul had his own thoughts on the songs from that period. Talking to John Reed in 1992, he said , "I had no ideas, I'd dried up. We went into the studio to do some demos but they were fucking dreadful really'. It was the kick up the arse that Paul needed to come up with better material and those songs would form the basis of *All Mod Cons*.

Bill Smith was responsible for the sleeve design. It was packed full of Mod references including a Creation record, a *Sounds Like Ska* record, a packet of Rothmans (The Jam smoked like troopers), the image of the Battersea Power Station – an instantly recognisable reference to The Who's *Quadrophenia* album, some 100 Club matches, a diagram of a Scooter that was taken from a Haynes manual and three Union Jacks. It was like and A to Z of Mod.

"With the sleeves for *In The City* and *This Is The Modern World* it was very much three people in a situation and I wanted to keep that going and hold on to the imagery of three guys," says Bill Smith. But by *All Mod Cons*, everybody knew that Paul, Rick and Bruce were three musicians in a band, so I didn't want a sleeve that showed them playing their instruments. On the back of *This Is The Modern World* for example there was the picture of The Jam on stage. I liked sleeves that had the band as people on one side of the sleeve and the band as musicians on the other side.

"The sleeve for *All Mod Cons* was meant to be like a narrative – a little story. It was meant to say, here is an empty room and what do these guys do? We used a photography studio just off Wardour Street for the shoot and the idea was to capture the three band members at some point in the story of the album sleeve. It was like trying to capture a moment or a single frame in a film. The front cover of *All Mod Cons* is meant to show three guys who have walked into a room and decided to sit down for a minute and then they get up and go and do something else.

"For the back cover of *All Mod Cons*, we hanged Paul's and Bruce's guitars up by wire. This was also the first time that the new style of lettering got used. The idea came from Paul. He liked the lettering on the Small Faces record label Immediate and it was his nod to the Small Faces. I then had to recreate the lettering by hand. There was no other way to get all the other letters needed so it had to be hand-drawn."

The images of Paul, Rick and Bruce on the album's sleeve were equally of interest, especially the monkey boots worn by Paul and

Converse ones that Rick wore. And who didn't own a pair of pale blue Sta-Prest trousers between 1978 and 1982?

Talking about the *All Mod Cons* cover in the *Thick As Thieves* book, Bill explained that he, "wanted to find an enclosed space with an urban-type feel to it. The instruments and tape recorder featured on the back cover were meant to represent each band member and, the music they played."

"*All Mod Cons* musically was very advanced for us," says Paul. "We didn't look back after that." Paul also accepted that after *All Mod Cons* he started to take his song-writing more seriously, beginning to view it as a proper art form that needed to be worked at.

In many ways, *All Mod Cons* was the album that served as a turning point for the band. It was their 'A bomb' and Paul was fully aware of that fact. "*All Mod Cons* was when we really started to take off."

The album was recorded at RAK and Eden Studios through July and August 1978 with production credits awarded to Vic Coppersmith-Heaven and Chris Parry. It was released on November 3, 1978.

"The Jam are the ones you have to beat," wrote Charles Shaar Murray in the *NME*. Their fan base was growing at an incredible speed and they were producing fantastic songs. *All Mod Cons* was a hit with many music journalists. Garry Bushell writing for *Sounds* at the time enthused "They just blast away 12 years of blind-alley 'progression' and take up the mantle of Townshend/Lennon-McCartney for the modern world." It appeared that The Jam had come of age in the eyes of the press. In 2013, the *NME* ranked *All Mod Cons* at No 219 in the 500 Greatest Albums of All Time.

A count of four from Paul and 'All Mod Cons' bursts into life. It's a punchy, jerky number barely more than a minute's worth of Weller feedback guitar, raw drums and bass. "Artistic freedom – do what you want." Welcome to *All Mod Cons*.

'To Be Someone (Didn't We Have A Nice Time)' isn't about Paul at all. He said he was too young to be writing about himself, he was still just 20.

It's a song full of melody and dynamics. One moment Paul sounds angry, the next he's softened. "But didn't we have a nice time," is repeated before grinding to a halt and Paul ends by singing, "To be someone must be a wonderful thing."

'Mr Clean' is a response to Paul's observations of the commuters waiting on the platform at Woking station and heading into the city. It has a bleak feel – Pete Townshend admitted to *Uncut* magazine that the song gave him the "willies." There's also something else behind the lyrics…

In a hotel bar one night during a tour, Paul's girlfriend Gill slipped over. A seemingly helpful man rushed to Gill's aid and helped her to her feet. However, in the process of doing so he groped her breast and Paul witnessed this. Paul directed his anger at this man through his lyrics on 'Mr Clean'.

Having started with a bass line, the track quickly builds. The lyrics are captivating, even the threatening "And if I get the chance I'll fuck up your life." In another lifetime, Ray Davies might have written 'Mr Clean'.

'David Watts' was on *Something Else By The Kinks* in 1967. The Jam's cover of the song was released as a double A side with 'A Bomb In Wardour Street'. 'David Watts' is about someone who had a crush on one of the members of The Kinks. When Ray first met Paul, at a festival in 1978, Paul was wearing a pin badge that said, "Who the fuck is David Watts?"

The Jam's version definitely has more drive and momentum than The Kinks original, there's some snazzy piano work too.

Paul wrote 'English Rose' when he was touring the States and missing Gill and his beloved England. The title wasn't included on the album cover or the lyric sheet that came with the album, but it's one of Paul's most loved songs.

It begins with the sound of waves lapping against the shore, there's also a fog horn which further helps to set the mood. You can visualise a foggy grey British morning, a ship returning home and the white cliffs of Dover just coming into sight as the fog lifts. The waves are still kissing the pebble beach as Paul's acoustic guitar begins to introduce the song. The sound of the fret buzz contributes to the atmosphere.

'In The Crowd' is a catchy song with intelligent lyrics. The track heads towards an extended psychedelic section with swirling fed back guitars, backward guitars and Paul repeating, "Away from the numbers," before fading away.

Incidentally, to coincide with the release of Rick's autobiography *That's Entertainment*, he embarked on a series of Q&A events that he called *In The Crowd*. Rick would show a 20-minute film of himself visiting Jam related locations in the West End of London including Soho Market, 100 Club and Bond Street tube station.

"Billy Hunt, Billy Hunt, Billy, Billy, Billy" has become a Jam Army chant. It's rough and ready and full of brash energy, a brilliant pop song in every way. 'Billy Hunt' was also mooted as a possible single to be used instead of 'David Watts'.

'It's Too Bad' has that casual, jolly 'Boy About Town' vibe. It's a clear reminder of just how good a songwriter Paul is and how perfect Rick and Bruce were for his songs.

'It's Too Bad' is another song about relationships and their volatile nature. Paul sings about the challenges and difficulties that can occur, noting the reality of "It's too bad that we had to break up," although when he sings it, he doesn't sound too cut up about it!

Paul dusts off his acoustic for 'Fly' another haunting song. The fret buzz is retained which, like 'English Rose', only adds to the overall feel of the song. Rick and Bruce only contribute at certain parts. It's all 'Fly' needs.

'The Place I Love' picks up the tempo again. "The place I love is a million miles away," sings Paul, almost longingly. The simplicity of the song's structure is typical of *All Mod Cons*.

Then it's 'A Bomb In Wardour Street'. Rick still owns the cowbell that makes a distinctive contribution to the song. *All Mod Cons* reflected Paul's departure from the punk scene that had given him a leg up only a year before. The Roxy club in Wardour Street gets a mention, representing something that Paul didn't really feel part of – "I don't know what I'm doing here. This is not my scene at all."

'A Bomb In Wardour Street' proceeds with fire and skill. It deserved to be released as a single and should have got higher than 25.

Paul wrote the lyrics to 'Down In The Tube Station At Midnight' as a long poem and not all the words he wrote made it onto the song. In fact, Paul had even tossed the lyrics into the bin and it was only because Vic Coppersmith- Heaven retrieved them and encouraged Paul and the band to persevere with it that the song even saw the light of day.

"In the studio, The Jam were always discovering new ways to go about recording songs," says Rick. "It helped that Vic Smith's production skills were brilliant. 'Tube Station' just wouldn't have been recorded at all if it wasn't for Vic. For some reason Paul had doubts about the song and was hesitant about it being included on the album. In the studio he got so frustrated with it that he wanted to abandon it. Thankfully, Vic thought the song was really good and encouraged Paul to continue and we eventually recorded it."

For the song, Paul draws on his own experiences of paranoia and many of us who grew up in the Seventies and Eighties can relate to that. Back then, if you walked down the street and heard behind you the klick klack of a Blakey (a metal plate in the sole of a shoe), you were never quite sure if they were friend or foe. Skinheads, Mods, rude boys, they all wore Blakeys in the soles of their loafers.

The song begins with Rick's rapid hi-hat work meant to represent the sound of a train rattling down the tracks. Vic Coppersmith-Heaven had recorded the sound of a train down in St John's Wood tube station. Later in the song, Rick gets the opportunity to pound the tom-toms.

When The Jam performed the song live, Rick's solo would provide the opportunity for Paul to slip away for a few minutes and have a quick fag. Rick remembers how he would often find himself trying to gain Paul's attention with a look saying, "C'mon Paul, I can't keep this going for much longer, finish your fag and get back on stage."

Paul yobbishly roars, "Have you got any money?" It's so intense, a reminder that what's unfolding in the story could happen to any one of us. Paul considers 'Down In The Tube Station At Midnight' to have been the first song when people started to take The Jam seriously.

'Down In The Tube Station At Midnight/So Sad About Us' was released as a single on October 6, 1978. A photograph of Keith Moon was included on the rear cover. Moon had died the month before the song's release. Covering The 'Who's So Sad About Us' was The Jam's tribute to one of rock's greatest drummer's and characters. Many years later, Paul would duet with Pete Townshend at Albert Matalonja Ventura to perform an acoustic version of the song, a very special moment indeed. And what was a plum? London tube tickets in the Seventies were plum coloured...

TRACKLISTING

1. To Be Someone (Didn't We Have A Nice Time)
2. Mr Clean
3. David Watts
4. English Rose
5. In The Crowd
6. Billy Hunt
7. It's Too Bad
8. Fly
9. The Place I Love
10. A Bomb In Wardour Street
11. Down In The Tube Station At Midnight

This Is The Modern World

"I don't give two fucks about
your reviews"

On top of having recorded and released *In The City*, The Jam continued to spend 1977 gigging relentlessly. They also needed to find time to get back into the studio because Polydor wanted them to record a second album, and quickly.

They worked harder at building up a strong following by playing venues around London like the Red Cow, Rochester Castle and any college, university or polytechnic that would have them.

On August 8, The Jam were due to play in France at the punk rock festival in Mont de Marson. But in the end, they didn't appear. In the meantime, Paul managed to get arrested.

In a Leeds hotel bar, Paul was involved in a disagreement with Australian national rugby team. A fracas ensued, involving several members of the team whose captain, Jim Caldwell, was hit with a glass. Paul was arrested after the incident and was hauled up before the court the following morning but was discharged. Outside the court, Jam fans wore tee shirts proclaiming 'Paul Weller Is Innocent'.

Bruce later said it had been a frightening experience and Paul in the hotel bar "finished up being treated like a rugby ball."

The band's rigorous touring schedule included their first visit to the USA. In October they played two nights at the legendary Whisky-A-Go-Go in Los Angeles before heading to the East Coast to play Boston's Rat Keller and the famed CBGBs in New York, launch pad for such bands as The Ramones and Blondie.

Backstage at CBGBs, The Jam met Joey Ramone and Patti Smith. Their conversation with Joey was cut short because he sat on a scalding hot radiator. "A few moments after he sat down, Joey realised he was virtually on fire. He leapt up, screamed and legged it out of the dressing room!"

By mid-November the band were back touring the UK and promoting their second album, *This Is The Modern World*.

After a gig in Dunstable, Paul meet Gill Price. They became romantically involved and within a few months they were living together at a flat in Baker Street. It was the first time Paul had left the family home.

In the dying months of punk's explosion, new bands were grabbing media attention. Punk was on its way out and new wave was on its way in. The Jam were no longer considered a punk band, they were 'new wave'. The sobriquet meant nothing to Paul who continued to write the songs he wanted.

'All Around The World/Carnaby Street' was released in July and made it to No 13. The single's sleeve design included all three members of The Jam dressed in their black and white outfits, complete with Jam Gibson shoes. The back showed them eschewing stage clothes and wearing colourful button-down shirts with Paul holding a tightly patterned dog-tooth jacket and Rick in dark glasses and a pale blue jacket. Beneath each member was one word – Paul 'Direction', Rick 'Reaction' and Bruce 'Creation'. Rick was in the centre and Paul and Bruce positioned either side, just like they were on the *In The City* and *This Is The Modern World* album sleeves.

"For the *This Is The Modern World* album cover I worked with the photographer Gered Mankowitz," recalls Bill Smith. "He'd worked with the Rolling Stones and Jimi Hendrix. I wanted to try and give the sleeve a postmodern feel. I felt that the songs on the album sounded very modern and urban. I wanted to create a strong graphic too.

"I chose a location under part of the Westway in London that helped capture the imagery of the concrete and the black shadows with all the angles. Although the shoot was taken during the day, we also used flashlights and this helped to give those very hard looking black shadows with the band sort of coming out of them. It provided an abstract type background. And I thought having the flats in the picture worked too.

"The Jam were always heavily into their look and I remember on the day they turned up for the shoot Paul was wearing a white jumper. He started telling me about a picture he's seen of Pete Townshend where he was wearing something that had arrows on it. It was very pop art. So, we found some gaffer tape and stuck the two black arrows onto Paul's jumper."

The illustrations on the inner sleeve of the album were drawn by Conny Jude. Bill had told her some of the song titles and lyrics and Conny used them for inspiration

This Is The Modern World was released on November 4, 1977, on Polydor Records just five months after the release of their debut album. Some critics slated the album, saying it felt rushed and wasn't in the same league as *In The City.*

However, *This Is The Modern World* reached 22 in the charts, just two places lower than *In The City's* highest position. A majority of Jam fans were happy. Speaking in 2011, Eddie Piller said Paul once told him that he was the only one of his mates who said *This Is The Modern World* was his favourite album. Paul's own thoughts in 2015 were typically honest and blunt, "It wasn't great by any standards."

The Jam did find solid support from a few music journalists. *Record Mirror's* Barry Cain noted a "definite progression", suggesting "Weller is making an obvious attempt at creating a Jam sound." It was positive stuff and Barry's words would ultimately ring true. Barry was also pleased because he got a credit on the album's sleeve, 'Mr B. Cain (Teenage Blue)'. This was because Paul had read one of Barry's descriptions of the moods at a Jam concert which he likened to the three colours of the Union Jack, "Red hot expanding into white heat and contracting into teenage blue." Paul especially liked the phrase 'teenage blue' and it found its way into 'Life From A Window'.

Plus, Paul didn't give two fucks about reviews anyway…

This Is The Modern World was the last album that Chris Parry was involved with, apart from two songs that appeared on *All Mod Cons* – 'It's Too Bad' and 'To Be Someone'. Due to some internal issues and differences, Chris and the band parted company.

There does sound like something is missing, lacking even, on the album's production. *In The City* captured an energy and brightness that seemed to elude *This Is The Modern World*. And some of the songs weren't quite up to scratch. They were under-rehearsed and the limited studio time had detrimental consequences. That said, although *This Is The Modern World* probably isn't the first album that fans reach for when they need a Jam fix, it's still an album with patches of brilliance.

'The Modern World' was the only single lifted from *This Is The Modern World*. It was released on October 15, 1977, backed with live versions of 'Sweet Soul Music' and 'Back In My Arms Again'. Steve Diggle of The Buzzcocks loved the song and said it was up there with 'White Riot' that had been recorded on September 22, 1977, the same day as 'The Modern World'.

"This is the modern world," sings Paul and Bruce joins him for the second line. The song continues at a tempo similar to 'Pretty Vacant', not rushed or urgent and far from punk brutal.

Paul's guitar work is redolent of a young Pete Townsend and it's easy to imagine Paul giving it the windmill arms during the recording.

"Even at school I felt quite sure," suggests an awareness of something tangible outside of the mainstream. Twenty years later, Liam Gallagher sang, "We'll see things they'll never see." It's a comparison that resonates with the sussed.

Paul never really clicked with school. The line, "The teachers said I'd be nothing," is him taking a swipe at them and their system. Paul had discovered punk and what punk offered to young people like himself was a way out, a permission to do so much more than wallow in staid education. Punk empowered Paul.

Bruce Foxton wrote and sang 'London Traffic'. It's punchy and rough and that's its charm. The lyrics are not the deepest but it doesn't matter because the harmonies shape the song. It's one and a half minutes of pure punk, like a car tearing off at speed.

In the mid-Sixties, Britain's youth, especially those connected to the Mod scene, had their own music TV show that went out at 6.30 on Friday nights. *Ready Steady Go!* included all the best music with regular appearances by The Who and Small Faces. Mods could check out the latest fashions and dances and it was essential viewing. Paul borrowed the show's slogan, "The weekend starts here," and used it in 'Standards'.

The track has a Who-type riff similar to 'Substitute'. Paul's vocals stab like a blunt knife and lyrics like, "We make the standards and we make the rules," pick up from where 'The Modern World' left off. It was 1977 and punk was ushering in the modern world and Paul was making his contribution.

'Life From A Window' is one of Rick's favourite Jam songs. There are some studio noises before Paul counts in his two bandmates. The song is instantly accessible, wrapped up in a warm and welcoming melody. 'Life From A Window' was certainly one of Paul's best songs up until then and it gives the Post Office Tower in London a new identity.

"When you're in a crowd, you see things as they really are," sings Paul on 'The Combine'. He wants to breakaway "but the ties are too strong." It's a notion shared by the young Mod Jimmy Cooper in *Quadrophenia*, a film that hadn't been made at that point. The desire to be an individual is thwarted, "Life is very different when you're in a crowd."

Bruce also wrote the interestingly titled 'Don't Tell Them You're Sane'. It begins with one of The Jam's most creative intros and again, the harmonies spice up what may have been a less enjoyable song otherwise. Full credit to Bruce for managing to get two songs onto the album.

'In The Street, Today' is credited to both Paul and old friend and former Jam guitarist, Dave Waller. The track begins with a punky intro, Rick banging his trusty floor-tom and the guitars ripping open the box and unleashing the song inside.

'London Girl' sees Paul asking girls if they know what they're looking for in a city where the streets are not paved with gold. He's begging them to seek a better life, to not surrender themselves to the 50-year long work treadmill.

'I Need You (For Someone)' exposes the softer side of Paul, reflected in his guitar as well as his lyrics. Paul and Bruce double up on vocals and that helps to highlight the sentiments behind the words, "I need you to turn me off, when you think I've said enough." By the time Paul wrote this song, his relationship with Gill was growing stronger every day.

"OK, alright, here it comes," ushers in 'Here Comes The Weekend', a song that any hard working person will identify with – "From Monday morning to Friday night…"

Paul borrowed the title of 'Tonight At Noon' from poet Adrian Henri, who in turn had taken it from the 1965 Charles Mingus album *Tonight At Noon*.

Henri was born April 10, 1932, in Birkenhead, Cheshire, and had been one of the founding members of the Liverpool Scene who released four albums before disbanding in 1970. Adrian also painted and in the late-Fifties had even played washboard in a local skiffle band. Paul said he really admired Adrian's poetry and used another of his poem's titles, 'I Want To Paint' for a song that to date has never been officially released.

Adrian wrote about, "Children from happy families will be sent to live in a home, white Americans will demonstrate for equal rights," and, "Girls in bikinis are moonbathing." Paul wrote the equally poetical, "When we meet in the midnight hour I will bring you night flowers (coloured) like your eyes. Tonight at noon I'll touch your hand, held for a moment amongst strangers, amongst the dripping trees."

Paul's words were hardly those of a puking punk spitting venom about riots and anarchy. And yet the year was 1977, arguably the year of punk. 'Tonight At Noon' demonstrated a softer side to The

Jam. Paul had conviction in his own ability to write lyrics that had substance, depth. There was nothing rushed about 'Tonight At Noon'.

At the end of Adrian's poem, he writes, "and you will tell me you love me, tonight at noon," and it's only then the reader realises that Henri's poem, like Paul's song, is simply about love.

Odd noises and effects are dropped in between some tracks on the album. Before 'Tonight At Noon' for example, someone is heard blowing a raspberry. The idea had been employed by The Beatles on their albums and what was good enough for them was good enough for The Jam.

Wilson Pickett's Sixties' soul classic, 'In The Midnight Hour' completes the album. Like every other cover The Jam attempted, it's brash and raw and they make it their own. Whether the band included the track because of lack of material or whether they wanted to, doesn't really matter. It's a perfect finale, just like an encore.

TRACKLISTING

1. The Modern World
2. London Traffic
3. Standards
4. Life From A Window
5. The Combine
6. Don't Tell Them You're Sane
7. In The Street, Today
8. London Girl
9. I Need You (For Someone)
10. Here Comes The Weekend
11. Tonight At Noon
12. In The Midnight Hour

In The City

"I know I come from Woking and you'll say I'm a fraud"

A t a packed Paul Weller show at Subterranea, London, in April 1991, one fan was overheard saying to his companion: "I would prefer to go into the ring with Mike Tyson rather than John Weller,". I bet that fan didn't know that John Weller, the undisputed champion of Paul Weller's career, had been a featherweight boxer during his early life in Lewisham, South London.

Not that boxing was to everyone's liking in John's life. "John had been boxing since he was 12 and then he continued when he was with the RAF," says Paul's Mum Ann. "I only ever saw him box a couple of times and that was just before he packed up. Well I didn't actually see him because I kept my eyes closed throughout the entire fights."

John Weller undeniably contributed to the success of The Jam, The Style Council and his son's solo career. Fans have only positive things to say about him with countless tales of how John allowed them into a sound check or invited them backstage so that they could meet Paul and the band. On one occasion, John spotted a Jam fan with a broken leg in the crowd and went off to get a chair and made space for the fan to sit and enjoy the gig in comfort.

Nobody has ever accused John of being a hard, ruthless manager like Don Arden or Peter Grant. Yes, John was old school, yes, he was tough and yes, he didn't suffer fools gladly. But he loved his son, his family, The Jam and The Style Council dearly and supported whatever his son chose to do without question, even though he didn't always agree with him. John was as gutted as everyone else when The Jam split up, but he accepted Paul's decision.

But John was no fool and he could be tough when required. That Weller fan was right – you'd probably not want to have got into a ring with John Weller when he was a young man in the Fifties or when he was the manager of Paul's solo career in the Nineties.

John Weller was born November 28, 1931, in Brighton. "I was 16 when I met John and he was a good six years older than me," says Ann. "I used to work in an office as a junior at a place called the Lion Works in Woking. At the time, John was working for a local firm called Morrison Roads who did tarmacking and he came into the Lion Works to lay some tarmac.

"Every afternoon I had to take a load of stuff from my office over to the main office and John used to chat me up. We started going out together and within a year we were married. I was 17 and when I was 18 we had Paul."

Ann gave birth to Paul on May 25, 1958. 'Who's Sorry Now' by Connie Francis was at No 1. Francis had shared the first half of 1958 with the likes of Elvis Presley and Jerry Lee Lewis. Even by the spring of 1958, rock and roll still had a sense of being new, fresh and exciting and Bill Haley's 'Rock Around The Clock' had turned heads two years earlier. They decided to name their new son John William Weller but changed their minds a few days later and settled on Paul instead.

"The first place we lived in was in Walton Road in Woking," says Ann. "We were only there for about seven months because we found a cheaper place to rent, and that was 8 Stanley Road. The rent was one pound five shillings. John was earning ten pounds a week working as a hod carrier. When Paul and Steve (Brookes) were older, he used to take them to work with him. Steve was a good worker but Paul was just lazy and they even found him asleep in the wheel-barrow on one occasion!"

Stanley Road was built in the 1890s. At the time, Woking was a thriving town. When John and Ann moved there, much of it was being redeveloped and the population was expanding rapidly with Irish, Italian and Pakistani families all contributing to its facelift.

"8 Stanley Road had three bedrooms, an outside loo, no bathroom and no hot water," says Ann. We had to boil the kettle and then wash with that. I used to pop over to my mother-in-law's once a week so I could have a bath. Well it was the Fifties!"

Woking offered plenty for young families with easy access to London. The train time to Waterloo is just 24 minutes.

The town was mentioned in the Domesday Book and one of its claims to fame was the writer H G Wells writing *The War Of The Worlds* between 1895 and 1897 when he was a Woking resident. The town was also the site of the first mosque to be built in the UK in 1889. The Brookwood Cemetery, also known as the London Necropolis, was, for many years, the world's largest cemetery and even today it retains the title as the UK's largest.

Long after the Wellers had left their Stanley Road home and moved to 44 Balmoral Drive, the Stanley Road sign was still being stolen by light fingered fans due to the success of Paul's *Stanley Road* album in 1995. Nowadays, the sign is glued on rather than bolted and the original homes in the road were demolished.

Nicky Weller: "We were always playing music around our home in Stanley Road. We had a record player that could stack up to six records at any one time. Mum was always playing records by Chuck Berry, Elvis or the various artists on the Tamla Motown label. She was always singing along with them. Dad liked music too. We had a piano which was kept under the stairs and he could play absolutely anything on the black keys – but not a thing on the whites. You could hum him a tune and within moments he could play it on the blacks. But it was Mum who was really into her records and different sorts of music and I think that's what helped to inspire Paul to discover various genres of music."

Ann: "Paul had a chest of draws in his bedroom and where most boys would keep their clothes in there, Paul would keep all this stuff about The Beatles instead. He had records and bits of memorabilia but all his clothes would be left on the floor."

Because of Paul, and to be fair Rick and Bruce, fans have made pilgrimages to Woking. In the days of The Jam, it wasn't unusual for John or Ann to face yet another fan on their doorstep in Balmoral

Drive asking if Paul was home. A lucky few would even be allowed in and handed a cuppa.

The importance of Paul's fans over the years hasn't been lost on the Wellers. "Paul has been so lucky with his fans," says Ann. "They've been there with him all the way through his life."

Nicky: "There was a grassy area outside our home in Balmoral Drive and fans would actually camp there. Mum would make them bacon sandwiches and cups of tea. When The Jam split, a load of fans showed up and hung around for days.

"Unlike most rock bands, The Jam were an approachable band. They were on the same level as the fans and Paul wrote songs that they could relate to. Paul has always written about what he sees. He wrote 'Town Called Malice' for example about Woking and the fans could relate a song like that to their own lives and towns."

It was at Balmoral Drive that The Jam's fan club was formed. "Mum and me started to run the fan club from home," says Nicky. "In the beginning, we would hand write everything, then we got a typewriter. Dad was still going to Polydor's offices for meetings and he would take me with him so I could use their photocopier. There were times when the fan club business got really busy and we ended up asking neighbours to help with writing addresses onto envelopes and the worst job of all, licking those envelopes!

"Luckily, we got friendly with the postman and one day when he came down to collect a few sacks he told us that if we took the sacks ourselves to the post office we could frank the envelopes there. That was really helpful.

"When we moved to Balmoral Drive, Dad converted the coal bunker into the offices of The Jam Fan Club. The location of the club was the worst kept secret. I used to advertise in *Sounds* and the *NME* and I put our actual address in it, which was our home. We had all sorts of people turn up. In Jonathan Ross's book, he wrote that he even turned up. We never turned anyone away."

Ann: "There was some young man who showed up and he was

from Iowa. He ended up sleeping on the settee for three days. We had three Japanese girls too. They knocked on the door and we tried to have a chat, even though their English wasn't very good. I don't know why, but I phoned John and said, 'You need to come home because there are three Japanese girls standing on the doorstep.' John replied, 'Well what do you want me to do? I've only been to Japan, I can't bloody speak it!' Then I added, 'Oh by the way, they've just had your dinner!'"

The bond The Jam had with their fans was unique and stories abound of Jam sound checks. "Fans getting into sound checks was quite a big thing," remembers Nicky. "Dad was always letting them in. The thing was, a lot of the kids were probably too young to be there. They probably couldn't afford the price of tickets either."

Ann: "It was quite funny in the early days because school uniforms looked a bit like the clothes The Jam wore, so you couldn't always tell if the kids should have been at school or whether they had bunked off to get to a sound check'.

Nicky: "It was Kenny's (Wheeler) job to then go and try to get them out after the sound check and they would hide in all sorts of strange places hoping they wouldn't be found. Then they could creep into the gig that night. It happened all the time."

Ann: "To value the fans was very much a philosophy of The Jam. Without them the band knew they had nothing."

In 2012, the authors of *Thick As Thieves* had a book signing in the Woking branch of Waterstones and Rick Buckler joined them. That evening the Wake Up Woking fundraising campaign held an event that included live bands. Between the book signing and the evening event, two old Jam fans, and even older friends of Paul's – Steve Carver (Steve appeared in the 'Art School' promotional video along with a young Nicky Weller) and Sam Molner – ferried Jam fans around Woking in a hired mini-bus, pointing out Jam-related sights and en route they bumped into Ann who gave the Jam tourists a warm welcome.

In 2012, Woking also recognised the importance of three of its own and erected a seven and half ton oak sculpture called *The Space Between*. The sculpture isn't everybody's cup of tea, but it does serve its purpose as a piece of art that celebrates The Jam and their connection to Woking.

A young Paul grew up in an everchanging Woking. His formative years were spent doing what a typical kid did in the Sixties – including getting himself a job. "When Paul was a bit older he got himself a couple of paper rounds," says Ann. "However, he didn't always turn up and I would end up having to do it for him. It was often the evening round he didn't want to do because he wanted to go to a disco instead. But sometimes I would also do the morning one too and this was because he'd been playing a gig the night before. I even used to do the rounds on his bike. I think some people actually thought I was him. When it came to the tips, he still wanted them though!"

Talking about those days, Paul says, "Financially something was missing, but love compensated for that."

When Paul was 12, John got him his first acoustic guitar. He didn't take to it with all guns blazing and within a few months it had been shoved under his bed. But Paul was starting to develop a real interest in music and discovered The Beatles. Their influence helped him retrieve that guitar and learn to play it. When he saw them play on TV he was, "Hooked from there onwards."

He learnt a few chords and Beatles songs from his copy of *The Beatles Song Book* and by then had befriended Steve Brookes at Sheerwater Comprehensive.

Steve was 13 and a half, one day younger than Paul, and he and Paul made an instant connection and forged a close and special friendship that has endured to this day. Brookes had got an acoustic guitar for Christmas and, like Paul, had been learning to play it. As their friendship developed, so did their skill on those guitars.

Ann: "Paul and Steve and then their friends would come to Stanley

Road after school (if they'd actually been) and play their instruments in Paul's bedroom. I counted 14 of them up there one day. I had to leave the tray of tea outside Paul's bedroom door because I couldn't get it into the room. I didn't mind them coming round, but they had a cut-off point and that was 9pm. It had to be that time really because Stanley Road started to quieten down by then, the buses would be less frequent. We had really good neighbours and they were very understanding."

Steve Brookes went to live at the Weller's for a time and shared Paul's bedroom. Between neglecting their homework, sleeping and playing records, they worked harder at learning to play songs from *The Beatles Songbook.*

"Paul's fanatical obsession with The Beatles, and particularly Paul McCartney, cannot be overstated," Steve wrote in his own book *Keeping The Flame.*

Steve also developed a special relationship with John. "John was like a surrogate Dad to me. He was great, the perfect sort of guy that you'd want around you. In many ways, Paul and I got on with him more like a mate, rather than a father and son sort of thing. But he still used to dish out the odd bollocking when we needed it."

Ann: "Steve came to live with us at Stanley Road and was due to stay for a few weeks but ended up staying for a year. It was during this time that they learnt to play their guitars and write songs, rather than doing their school work. Sometimes it would be like listening to an Apache war dance. Two of the first songs that Paul learnt to play were 'Elusive Butterfly' by Bob Lind and 'A Groovy Kind Of Love' by The Mindbenders."

Nicky: "It was when Steve was living with us that Paul started writing more poetry and lyrics for songs. When I was putting bits together for The Jam exhibition I found some of Paul's old books and they are full of poetry and mad rantings. Even at that age, Paul was writing down some quite radical stuff."

Other Sheerwater pupils and friends of Paul and Steve's included

Dave Waller, Neil 'Bomber' Harris and Roger Pilling. During lunchtime, they chose to hang around the music room listening to music and trying to improve their playing. They formed a sort of gang called The Clan. It was during of those sessions that Paul met Rick Buckler.

Rick was older than Paul having been born on December 6, 1955, but he played drums and because of that Paul welcomed him to the lunchtime sessions and their friendship developed.

By the time Paul and Rick met, Paul and Steve had already played a few gigs as a duo. Their first public performance had been in the Woking Working Men's Club on Walton Road in late 1972. Woking Working Men's Club was only a stone's throw from 8 Stanley Road. Paul was still only 14 years-old.

Ann: "We went to every gig in the early days. When Paul and Steve played their first ever gig together of course we were there. There was only a handful of people in the audience but we got up and danced for the boys. In the early days, they were a brilliant rock and roll band. They built up quite a following too. When we lived at Stanley Road we even had a group of Teddy Boys hanging around outside when the boys were rehearsing up in Paul's bedroom."

Woking Working Men's Club would also serve as a crucial venue for The Jam. Sadly, the building was demolished in 2014.

Ann: "We all used to socialise in the Woking Working Men's Club. Another family that also used the club was the Parfitts and they had a son called Rick. He went onto become a founder member of Status Quo. When Rick was home he'd be around the club with us too. I remember I used to drive a small car with just an 1100 engine and I would take Nicky and her friends to a disco, but it was a squeeze. One day Rick turned up with his Jag and offered to help. So, Nicky and all her friends jumped into his car and he took them instead."

Nicky: "We'd spend most Friday and Saturday nights in the Woking Working Men's Club and when my Dad first started getting gigs for Paul and Steve there, he'd encourage me and Mum to get up and dance. So, there we were, trying to dance along as Paul and Brookesy played Everly Brothers songs. They were nice times.

"Once The Jam started getting gigs in London, my Dad would let me go with the band to London. I was just 14. Mum would write a letter to school giving some reason for my absence. I would go around the audience selling badges and black and white photos for ten pence each. It was a really exciting time."

Paul and Steve's duo evolved into a band with Dave Waller and Bomber Harris. The four-piece became the earliest version of The Jam.

The band learnt Beatles and Chuck Berry songs, amongst others, that were relatively easy to play and they'd started to gig at venues mostly sourced by John who had been taking a keen interest in them.

Nicky: "Dad had real foresight when it came to The Jam and he pushed them. When he was contacting record labels to try and get the band a deal, he truly believed in them."

John strived to move The Jam forward in any way he could, and sometimes it had its risks.

Ann: "In the early days of The Jam playing in London, John, Paul, Rick and Bruce used to drive there to put posters up. Returning from one of those nights, John was in the car with Rick and Paul was following them in Bruce's car. They ran into some roadworks and the car that John and Rick were in hit a railway sleeper and lost control. When the car eventually came to a halt, both John and Rick got out, shocked and stunned. They also felt all this wetness on their heads and thought their brains were coming out. It turned out it was just the wallpaper paste that they'd been using to stick the posters up! It must have been horrible for Paul to watch the car spinning out of control but neither John or Rick were hurt at all'.

John Weller would in time also find himself introducing The Jam at every gig and his words became a legendary part of the event. "Before each gig, Dad used to go on stage and introduce The Jam with 'The best fucking band in the world!'" says Nicky.

Rick eventually took over drumming duties from Bomber Harris.

Dave Waller also quit the band but not before he helped introduce Paul to poetry.

The only two subjects Paul did well in at Sheerwater were English and Art, getting a CSE in each one in 1974. But Paul wrote lots of poems and one, 'Room 101', even got special praise from his tutor. It was a poem inspired by George Orwell's book *1984* which Paul had made a connection with. On the album cover of The Style Council's *Our Favourite Shop*, a copy of 1984 can be seen hidden amongst other items from Paul's past.

With Rick now in The Jam and Waller having departed, the dynamics shifted. Paul had also tried his hand at playing bass which left Steve as the sole guitarist, but something wasn't working. It was decided that an addition was needed. Several people were auditioned in the spring of 1974 and in the end another older Sheerwater boy was recruited.

Bruce Foxton was born on September 1, 1955. Although he knew how to play guitar, he ended up on bass. Not agreeing with the direction the band was heading in, Steve Brookes eventually left.

With Steve now gone, The Jam became Paul Weller, Rick Buckler and Bruce Foxton. And they had John Weller as their 'make things happen' manager.

Once The Jam had settled into a three-piece line-up, Paul knew what he wanted to do with his life. Commenting on Steve's Brookes *Keeping The Flame*, Paul said, "It's a great picture of a young group determined to escape and make it big." Whether this attitude was adopted by Paul's bandmates is questionable, but it does tell us what Paul was thinking at the time. He was going to give "escaping" his best shot.

The Jam worked hard in those years. They were playing weekly, frequenting such places as Michael's Club in Woking and a host of other clubs and pubs in and around Woking. By 1976, Paul knew the band needed to be playing in London. The city had fascinated him since he was young and it has continued to excite his sensibilities.

The London music scene was changing big time at this stage. The pub rock bands had caught Paul's imagination with Dr Feelgood and their guitarist Wilko Johnson especially inspirational. He liked their brash and aggressive sound and they seemed to be the only band around that made any sense to him.

"I liked Dr Feelgood," says Ann. "I took Paul with me to see them at the Guildford Civic Hall. He was really affected by the way Wilko Johnson played guitar and moved around the stage. After that gig something in Paul changed. Then there was the Sex Pistols concert that Paul saw and that was that! Somewhere around that time, Brookesy left. He could see Paul going in a direction that he didn't want to go in."

Paul, along with Steve, Rick and others from Woking, would venture into London to see bands and it was on one July night in 1976 after they saw the Sex Pistols at the Lyceum that, as Rick wrote in his autobiography, "The Jam changed."

Punk literally was the explosion that it has since been called. It was brief but effective and it was just what the music industry needed to shake it up. Out went long hair, flares and bowing and scraping to the bare-chested rock gods of the Seventies, and in came anarchy, anti-fashion and a DIY approach to playing an instrument, writing a song, forming a band and even creating your own clothes.

While some punks preferred to purchase clothes from SEX in the Kings Road, Paul, Bruce and Rick stuck to wearing their Hepworth's suits. It wasn't always the most pleasant of experiences either because they only had one suit each. Rick remembers during their first tour of the States they had to wear the same suit night after night. "They never properly got to dry out, which meant that after a few dates our suits stunk to high heaven!"

Ann: "Paul loved his clothes from an early age. He got into the Mod thing when he was about ten years-old. He even swapped his bike once for a Ben Sherman shirt. One night the police came to the door and said they'd stopped some lad with a bike and had been told it had been swapped for a shirt. They didn't believe it so came to check out the story. I had to tell them it was true!"

Nicky: "Mum used to take Paul to Petticoat Lane because that's where he could get the clothes he wanted in sizes that fitted him; his Crombies and Sta-Prest. He used to save up his paper round money for those trips."

Ann: "In the early Jam days, they had a look where they'd wear black suits, with white shirts and black ties. Their white socks would poke out from their shortened trousers. There was a reason for that. Paul, Bruce and Rick would be soaking wet when they came off stage. The suits would have to dry out and as time went by they started to shrink, which meant the trousers went up and then their socks would be on display."

Rick: "We went to the shop next door to SEX called Johnsons because they sold striped boating jackets. The stuff they sold in SEX was not for us, it was way too extreme. All that bondage and fetish gear wasn't for The Jam and even most of the punks never wore it anyway."

With the onset of punk, bands were springing up everywhere. The Jam responded in their own way. The brought in a guy called Bob Grey to play keyboards. However, the four-piece arrangement didn't work and Bob left. But he did play with The Jam when they supported the Sex Pistols at the Queensway Hall, Dunstable on October 21, 1976.

Five days before that gig, The Jam tried to attract the attention of the music papers. They realised how essential those publications were in shaping the careers of up and coming bands. "We thought by doing the Soho thing it would achieve either one of two things – we'd get mentioned in the music press or we'd get arrested," says Rick.

On October 16, the band set up their equipment in Soho Market. At around 12.30pm, they played a few songs to passers-by, tourists and shop workers. Even some firemen leaned out of the widow of the nearby fire station and watched. Also witnessing the scene were members of The Clash, punk champion and journalist Caroline Coon and Mark Perry, the editor of the fanzine *Sniffin' Glue*. Music journalist John Ingham was also present and in his review pointed out that, "Guitarist Paul Weller must be the quietest guitarist in rock, quite Wilko Johnson influenced, but capable of providing some real excitement."

In *The Changing Man*, Paolo Hewitt noted that, "Witnessing punk's birth was just the shot Paul needed."

Now that Paul was interested in punk, The Jam discarded some of the songs from the set that they'd been dragging around for a couple of years and surged forward armed with new, edgier, rawer material. Paul set about writing tougher, angrier tunes, but retained the familiar structure of verse chorus verse chorus, middle eight and spread over three and a half minutes.

But he also wanted to infuse his songs with melody and not just write fast, aggressive tracks to appease an amphetamine drenched audience. Paul simply wasn't prepared to compromise or ignore what he knew he was good at – writing songs that set The Jam apart from everyone else. This attitude has never changed in 40 years.

Included in that Soho Market set was a song called 'In The City' which Jonh Ingham also made reference to in his article. "There are some good things in there, especially 'In The City I've A Thousand Things I Want To Say To You'."

Now that The Jam were getting regular gigs at popular London venues like the Red Cow, The Hope and Anchor, The Marquee, The Greyhound and the 100 Club, they were all too aware of A&R men from the various record labels sniffing around trying to sign the next Clash or Sex Pistols.

"One such A&R man was Chris Parry from Polydor Records. He saw The Jam, liked what he heard and organised for them to record some demos. Chiswick Records were also interested in them but in the end The Jam, with guidance from John, signed to Polydor on February 15, 1977, securing an advance of £6000. Because John didn't have a bank account, they had to be paid in cash.

Polydor were nervous about keeping John on as a manager, questioning his ability to manage as the band moved forward. But no one in The Jam agreed. "We had absolutely no intention of signing a deal with Polydor or any other label that would result in John getting side-lined," says Rick. "I think Polydor suspected that our reaction would be to defend John and they agreed to allow us to continue using him as our manager. But they did say he'll have to take advice from the professionals in the industry such as the booking agents, solicitors, publishers and accountants. After we signed we went back to the Princess pub in Maybury to celebrate."

Within weeks of signing, The Jam went into Polydor's recording studios in Stratford Place. Vic Smith worked alongside Chris Parry as the producers and in less than two weeks The Jam had recorded their debut album, *In The City*.

In time John Weller also made Stratford Place his second home. "My Dad managed to blag an office for The Jam in the building where Polydor Records was located," says Nicky. "It came about because Dad got friendly with the two security guys in the reception. They found him a room that he could use and for a year my Dad ran Jam affairs from that room until he got found out."

Although The Jam's first songs had been played over and over again to enthusiastic audiences and were well rehearsed, Parry and Smith still had their work cut out with regards to recording the album. The band had been playing live. They considered themselves a live band and they worked hard at it. But studio work had mostly eluded them. They had a few rough demos from previously self-funded sessions, but working with professional producers like Parry and Smith was a whole new ball game.

"It took Vic and me ages to get the excitement and energy into the mix for *In The City*," says Chris Parry. "Once I got Rick to simplify his drumming and understand that the first rule in the studio is timekeeping, things went well. They all learnt quickly and were rightly excited."

One single was lifted from the album and 'In The City' was released on April 29, 1977.

Rick: "'In the City' was identified as the song that should be our debut single and 'Takin' My Love' was to be the flip side. We were happy with the decision too. It was one of our newer songs and we felt it showed who we were and what we were intending."

'In The City' was a song hard not to instantly like and recognise the influence of another of Paul's inspirations, Pete Townshend. The same can be said for the rest of the album with its trademark Sixties feel spiced up with a punk twist. In 2015, Paul revealed that 'My Generation' was his favourite Who song and his song writing on *In The City* was heavily influenced by mid-Sixties Townshend.

Paul does come across as an angry young man on the album. An example of that anger can be found in the lyrics of the title song, "In the city there's a thousand men in uniform, and I now hear they have the right to kill a man." This is a direct reference to an incident that outraged many members of the public. On the night of January 16, 1976, 39-year-old Liddle Towers was arrested outside a club in Birtley, County Durham. Six police officers bundled him into a van and took him to Gateshead police station.

Early in the morning, Towers was taken to a local hospital complaining of injuries he said were sustained at the hands of officers. He was discharged from the hospital and later told a friend of his ordeal in the police cells – "They gave us a bloody good kicking outside the Key Club, but that was naught what I got when I got inside." Towers died a few days later on February 9, 1976. On October 8, 1976, an inquest returned a verdict of justifiable homicide.

Paul was fully aware of the Towers case, enough to have included the lyrics in a song that also celebrates the vibrancy of city life, his own fascination with the streets of London and what was happening with the punk scene, "I wanna say, I wanna tell you, about the young idea."

Addressing the resistance to The Jam by some of the media and the hardcore punk fraternity, Paul sang, "In the city there's a thousand things I want to say to you, but whenever I approach you, you make me look a fool.' He also did other, more demonstrative acts such as publicly burning a copy of *Sniffin' Glue* on stage and draping his amplifiers in Union Jack flags. It was hardly subscribing to the idea of anarchy in the UK.

In The City was released on May 6, 1977. The album sleeve was designed by Bill Smith, a former London College of Printing art student who had been employed at Polydor as their art director since 1976. "*In The City* felt like it should be black and white," says Bill. "My idea for the album was to depict three guys that are in a band. They've just done a gig and are on their way home and have popped into an underground toilet. Then someone shows up and says 'Oh, aren't you The Jam?' to which the band members reply, 'We are' and then they spray paint the band's name onto the wall.

"To recreate this story, Martyn Goddard and myself hired a studio and built a wall upon which we put the white tiles. The band turned up, we worked to get the positioning right and then they got out of the way and I went up to the wall and sprayed the words 'The Jam' onto it and then we got the shot of the band against the wall with the words behind them.

"Martyn only took about 36 shots in total and from those we chose the ones we ended up using on the album sleeve. I loved Paul's expression and I loved how Rick's head is tilted back and how the light is reflected in his glasses. One of the other shots that didn't get used had Rick resting his head on Bruce's shoulder and there were others of the three of them laughing. They were all exhibited in The Jam exhibition at Somerset House. The idea for keeping the album sleeve in black and white was meant to capture the sense of a professional press shot."

Maybe some of Smith's inspiration came from having seen The Jam wearing their black and white stage outfits at a Hope and

Anchor gig that he'd attended. The front cover of the album showed Paul, Rick and Bruce from the waist up in black suit jackets, black ties and white shirts. Behind them was a white tiled wall with 'The Jam' painted onto it in black and then the album title below it written in a light blue.

There have been different versions of how that particular Jam logo came about "The band literally got marched out of Polydor's offices, we found a brick wall nearby and Bill Smith spray painted the words 'The Jam'," says Rick. "It just turned out that way, it was liked and it was kept and it became The Jam's first logo."

The album begins with 'Art School'. The band were actually filmed for a promotional video for this one and half minute no messing track. The three band members played their instruments on a large stage while the Carver brothers from Woking and Nicky Weller splashed paint onto three long white paper backdrops. Paul wore a black jumper with arrows taped across it and white Sta-Prest trousers and played his red and white Rickenbacker guitar. It all ended with the sound of feedback – all very Pete Townshend.

'Art School' opens with Paul strumming four chords, A G D E, before counting in the rest of the band with a Ramones-style "1234." The band launch into the song with Rick and Bruce driving it along while Paul's spiky guitar pokes through the verse.

"Say what you want coz this is the new art school." Paul was aware of the part art schools had played in the formative lives of some of his musical heroes like Townshend.

In its own way, 'I've Changed My Address' is another song that celebrates being young. It's about not settling down and becoming chained to debt to when there's still so much to be done and experienced, "I've got to be free."

'Slow Down' is the first of two songs that appear on *In The City* that Paul didn't write. It was written by Lawrence Eugene Williams, better known as Larry Williams, an American rocker. In the late Fifties he also released such songs as 'Bad Boy' and 'Dizzy Miss Lizzy' that The

Beatles covered. Williams died at his home from a gunshot wound to his head on January 7, 1980, in a suspected suicide.

Although 'Slow Down' is from a completely different era it works perfectly. It's tight and sounds well-rehearsed and retains the tension and energy that The Jam gave to the song when they performed it live.

'I Got By In Time' is another full-on rocker with that unique abrasive sound that The Jam were able to capture around this period. As the years passed, they refined that sound but never let it go. Paul's guitar work is imaginative and he sings with such haste that there hardly seems time to suck in air. 'I Got By In Time' is a fast song but it's not rushed. The first verse is about one of Paul's earliest girlfriends whose name was Sharon Boxall, the second verse is about Steve Brookes and the third about relationships. It's hard to know how Paul feels about the lyrics on this song or, indeed, any of the songs from *In The City*. When his book *Suburban 100* was published in 2007, not a single song from *In The City* got a mention, which beggars belief. Why?

Track five on the album, 'Away From The Numbers', is still a firm favourite with Jam fans. Maybe it's because of the obvious Who sound; the "ooh oohs" in the backing vocals are so reminiscent of The Who. The guitar parts, drums and bass also create that Sixties Who feel.

Mod gave Paul a base from which he could write. When Paul wrote 'Away From The Numbers', the first real book about Sixties Mods, simply called *Mods* by Richard Barnes, hadn't even been published. Mods who were part of the second wave during the late Seventies, now referred to as the Mod Revival, often consider that book to be the bible on the topic. In *Mods*, Barnes educates the reader with regards to the various names associated with Mod:

"The hierarchy contains the following ranks: Modernists, Mods, Faces, Stylists, Individualists, Numbers, Tickets, Mids, Mockers, Seven and Sixes, States, Moddy Boys and Scooter Boys'.

Mod was becoming increasingly important to Paul as he learned more about it. But who were the numbers that he wrote about in the song, what did he mean when he sang, "Away from the numbers, is where I'm gonna be, where I am free"?

Neal Hefti was a jazz musician born in Nebraska and was commissioned to score the theme tune for the television series *Batman*. The superhero had been appearing in DC Comics since 1939 but the television series didn't begin until 1966. In total, 120 episodes starring Adam West as Batman were shown over a two-year period. Paul would have been just the right age to enjoy scoffing his tea as he watched another episode of the show with Batman and Robin chasing the Riddler, Penguin and Joker around Gotham City. Paul even had a Batman poster on his bedroom wall. That poster now belongs to a Jam memorabilia collector.

"The 'Batman Theme' had also been recorded by The Who and The Kinks," says Rick. "The Jam's version is certainly a unique take that's full of punk energy. The song was a fun thing to do. We just played around with it one day in the studio – we certainly sped it up."

'Sounds From The Street' is another obvious nod to The Who, especially the style of backing vocals. And again, Paul isn't ashamed to draw on his experience of the streets where he grew up. Maybe he did feel frustrated with the responses from some quarters with lyrics like, "You say I'm from Woking and you say I'm a fraud, but my heart's in the city, where it belongs'. The Who, The Small Faces and The Kinks had all come from London, The Jam didn't. Mind you, neither did The Beatles and they didn't do too badly.

Paul took the opportunity to use the song to celebrate being British. "The USA's got the sea, but the British kids got the streets. I don't mind, the city's right, sounds from the streets, sounds just fine." Paul had grown up surrounded by youth cultures like the Mods, skinheads and suedeheads and these sub-groups were a British phenomenon. Their clothes and their music thrilled Paul. What he didn't know at the time was that within months he would be spearheading a whole new Mod movement and people would be looking to him for inspiration, direction and answers.

At that time, no other 'new' bands came from backgrounds like Paul, Rick and Bruce who cut their teeth on soul and R&B standards. Paul had never been to the Wigan Casino or Blackpool Mecca, but he knew what Northern Soul was and loved the style of music that Motown, Atlantic and Stax produced. He also frequented Northern Soul nights at Bisley Pavilion. The Bisley Nightshift Club still operates Northern Soul nights at the venue four times a year.

'Non-Stop Dancing' pays respect to that soul scene. In 2005, a demo was unearthed of a song Paul wrote in 1976. It was called 'Left Right And Centre' and had all the ingredients of classic Northern Soul. For whatever reason, the song never appeared on any Jam records – they recorded shitloads of demos that never went any further. But in 2006, Lord Large featuring Dean Parrish recorded a version of 'Left Right And Centre' and it was released on Acid Jazz Records.

'Time For Truth' sees Paul don his political hat once again with an attack on James Callaghan, Prime Minister between 1976 and 1979 who had even visited Woking. "And the truth is you've lost uncle Jimmy, admit your failure and decline with honour while you can." And the police make an appearance – "You're trying for a Police State, so you can rule our bodies and minds... while killers roam the streets in numbers dressed in blue." Paul revisits the Liddle Towers topic again – "Bring forward those six pigs, we wanna see them swing sod high."

'Takin' My Love' was the song selected to be used as the B-side to 'In The City'. It's another straightforward rock and roll tune with caricature rock and roll lyrics. "Your shakin' all over and feeling alright now." The track harks back to the Steve Brookes days of The Jam.

The last song on the album, 'Bricks and Mortar', sees Paul taking a well-aimed swipe at authority and lays into politicians and their destructive decisions. When Paul was growing up in Woking he would have noticed the old town getting the once over from the, "Yellow bulldozers, the donkey jackets and JCBs," and as he toured the UK he would have witnessed so many other towns affected by the blight of development. "While hundreds are homeless, they're constructing parking spaces."

"Knock 'em down!"

In The City was the album where Paul got to share with us his hopes, his loathing, his dreams, his depressions, his fears, his joys, his infinite capacity for love. We understand and sympathise with his angst. What he feels we feel. He's one of us. Being able to relate to Paul Weller is what has got us, and him, through these 40 unimaginable years.

NME writer Phil McNeil was spot on when he wrote in his review of *In The City* that Paul's songs "capture that entire teen frustration." Equally Barry Cain, writing for *Record Mirror* in 1977, was pretty accurate when he said that The Jam were, "Armed and extremely dangerous," adding, "If you don't like them, hard luck, they're gonna be around for a long time."

Truer words had never been spoken.

TRACKLISTING

1.	Art School	7.	In The City
2.	I've Changed My Address	8.	Sounds From The Street
3.	Slow Down	9.	Non-Stop Dancing
4.	I Got By In Time	10.	Time For Truth
5.	Away From The Numbers	11.	Takin' My Love
6.	Batman Theme	12.	Bricks And Mortar

"I can't imagine my life without music – it's my religion."

Paul Weller

Index

A

B

C

the beatles

Ever wished you'd seen The Beatles live?

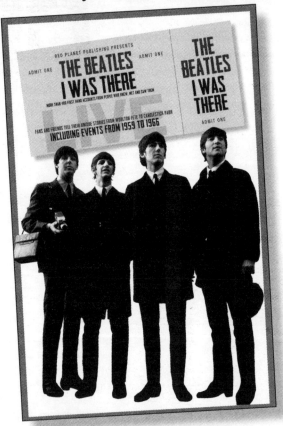

This book provides a fan's-eye account of the Fab Four as they conquered the world. From their skiffle days as The Quarrymen, their thrilling early gigs at the Cavern Club in Liverpool through to the Beatlemania of the Shea Stadium concerts in the USA.

Share in the excitement of over 400 first-hand encounters with The Beatles: the teenagers, kids, twentysomethings, promoters and support bands who can all proudly say 'I was there!'

Featuring anecdotes, stories, photographs and memorabilia that have never been published before, this book is a portrait of an amazing era. It's like being at your very own Beatles gig

ISBN: 9781905959945 Editor: Richard Houghton 400 pages Illustrated

From Me to You

This fascinating book looks at the songs The Beatles wrote for other artists – many of which they never released on record themselves. Author Brian Southall, a long-standing former EMI executive, delivers a unique insight into what The Beatles played live and which of those songs made their way into the studio sessions. The book takes a look at some of the more no-teable cover versions of The Beatles songbook – versions The Beatles loved...and hated!

ISBN: 978190595923 Author: Brian Southall
160 pages Illustrated

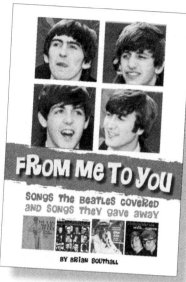

Dead Straight Guide to The Beatles

The Beatles are the most important pop group of all time. It's impossible to imagine modern music without them. This book tells the band's whole story, from their teenage skiffle-group beginnings, through Beatle-mania, to global megastardom.

With detailed reviews of all the Beatles albums, solo albums, cover versions, movies and TV appearances, plus in-depth analysis of the greatest 50 Beatles songs and a wealth of Fab 4 trivia, rumours and legends, here is all the Beatles you will ever need.

ISBN: 9781905959600 Author: Chris Ingham
400 pages Illustrated

Available from ***www.redplanetzone.com***
www.redplanetzone.com, Amazon, HMV and all good bookshops

ROCK ATLAS
UK AND IRELAND SECOND EDITION

800 great music locations and the
fascinating stories behind them

Rock Atlas is more than just a guide to over 800 music locations. You can visit many of the places or simply enjoy reading this extraordinary fact-packed book's fascinating stories. Some are iconic, others are just plain weird or unusual, such as Bob Dylan turning up unannounced on a public tour of John Lennon's childhood home or the musical park bench commemorating Ian Dury's life that plays recordings of his hits and his appearance on Desert Island Discs.

Providing insights into many performers' lives, Rock Atlas includes artists as diverse as The Beatles, Sex Pistols, Lady Gaga and Lonnie Donegan. Presented in an easy-to-read, region-by-region format, every entry provides detailed instructions on how to find each location together with extensive lists of the pop and rock stars born in each county.

Illustrated with hundreds of rare, unseen and iconic colour and black and white photographs, Rock Atlas is a must for anyone with an emotional tie to contemporary music and the important places associated with it.

On sale now
For information on Red Planet books visit www.redplanetzone.com

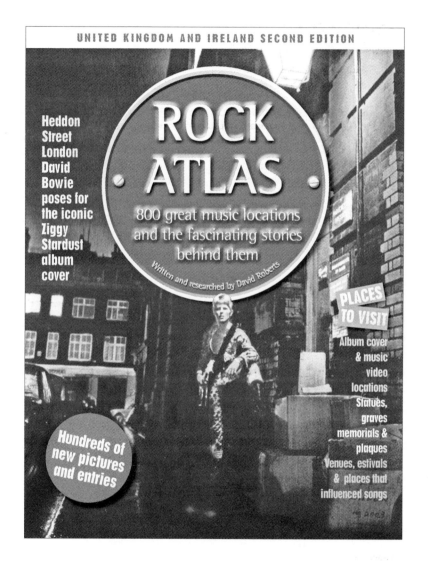

UNITED KINGDOM AND IRELAND SECOND EDITION

Heddon Street London David Bowie poses for the iconic Ziggy Stardust album cover

ROCK ATLAS

800 great music locations and the fascinating stories behind them

Written and researched by David Roberts

PLACES TO VISIT

Album cover & music video locations Statues, graves memorials & plaques Venues, estivals & places that influenced songs

Hundreds of new pictures and entries

www.redplanetzone.com

Discover musical history and facts
for 366* days of the year

www.thisdayinmusic.com

*including February 29

Sign up now
for the
**Red Planet
Newsletter**
and receive
news about
our new
books and
special
offers
(its free, it'll
save you money,
and we promise
not to mail you
too often or sell
your details)

sign up right now at
www.redplanetzone.com

77 SULPHATE STRIP

AN EYEWITNESS ACCOUNT OF THE YEAR THAT CHANGED EVERYTHING

FEATURING:
SEX PISTOLS
THE STRANGLERS
THE CLASH
THE DAMNED
THE RAMONES
THE VIBRATORS
THE TUBES
THE JAM
BLONDIE
X-RAY SPEX
SHAM 69

THE BOYS
THE DRONES TELEVISION
GENERATION X
THE HEARTBREAKERS
ALTERNATIVE TV
IAN DURY
RADIATORS FROM SPACE
AND MANY MORE

BARRY CAIN

The acknowledged seminal work on punk: a fast-paced trip through an extraordinary year. This book includes major new interviews with Paul Weller, Johnny Rotten, Strangler Hugh Cornwell and Rat Scabies of The Damned.

www.redplanetzone.com